SICK!

*Diseases and
Disorders,
Injuries and
Infections*

SICK!

Diseases and Disorders, Injuries and Infections

volume

1

A to **C**

**David Newton,
Donna Olendorf,
Christine Jeryan,
Karen Boyden,
Editors**

AN IMPRINT OF THE GALE GROUP

DETROIT · SAN FRANCISCO · LONDON
BOSTON · WOODBRIDGE, CT

Sick!
Diseases and Disorders, Injuries and Infections

David Newton, Donna Olendorf, Christine Jeryan, Karen Boyden, Editors

STAFF

Christine Slovey, *U•X•L Editor*
Carol DeKane Nagel, *U•X•L Managing Editor*
Meggin Condino, *Senior Analyst, New Product Development*
Thomas L. Romig, *U•X•L Publisher*

Shalice Shah-Caldwell, *Permissions Specialist (Pictures)*

Rita Wimberley, *Senior Buyer*
Evi Seoud, *Assistant Production Manager*
Dorothy Maki, *Manufacturing Manager*
Mary Beth Trimper, *Production Director*

Robert Duncan, *Imaging Specialist*
Michelle Di Mercurio, *Senior Art Director*

GGS Information Services, Inc., *Typesetting*
Michelle Cadoree, *Indexer*
Cover illustration by Kevin Ewing Illustrations.

Library of Congress Cataloging-in-Publication Data

Sick! diseases and disorders, injuries and infections/ David E. Newton...[et al.].
   p. cm.
Includes bibliographical references and indexes.
Summary: Presents articles describing the causes and symptoms, diagnosis, treatment (both traditional and alternative), prognosis, and prevention of various diseases, disorders, injuries, and infections.
   ISBN 0-7876-3922-2 (set)
   1. Diseases—Encyclopedias, Juvenile. [1. Health—Encyclopedias. 2.Diseases—Encyclopedias.] I.Newton, David E.
R130.5 .S53 1999
616'.003–dc21
                                                     99-044739

ISBN 0-7876-3922-2 (set)
ISBN 0-7876-3923-0 (vol. 1)
ISBN 0-7876-3924-9 (vol. 2)
ISBN 0-7876-3925-7 (vol. 3)
ISBN 0-7876-3926-5 (vol. 4)

Printed in United States of America
10 9 8 7 6 5 4 3

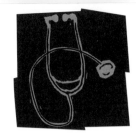

Contents

VOLUME 2: D–H

VOLUME 3: I–P

VOLUME 4: R–Z

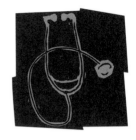

Reader's Guide

Sick! Diseases and Disorders, Injuries and Infections presents the latest information on 140 wide-ranging illnesses, disorders, and injuries. Included are entries on familiar medical problems readers might encounter in daily life, such as acne, asthma, chickenpox, cancer, and learning disorders. Some rare and fascinating illnesses are covered as well, such as smallpox, hantaviruses, and Creutzfeld Jakob disease (also known as mad cow disease).

Entries are arranged alphabetically across the four-volume set and generally range from three to eight pages in length. Each entry provides the details students need for reports and other health-related assignments under the following standard subheads: definition, description, causes, symptoms, diagnosis, treatment, prognosis, and prevention.

A "Words to Know" box included at the beginning of each entry provides definitions of words and terms used in that entry. Sidebars highlight interesting facts and individuals associated with the medical condition discussed. At the end of each entry, under the heading "For More Information," appears a list of sources for further information about the disease. The set has approximately 240 black-and-white photos. More than 80 images appear in color in an insert in each volume.

Each volume of *Sick!* begins with a comprehensive glossary collected from all the "Words to Know" boxes in the entries and a selection of research and activity ideas. Each volume ends with a general bibliography section listing comprehensive sources for studying medical conditions and a cumulative index providing access to all major terms and topics covered throughout *Sick!*

Related Reference Sources

Sick! is only one component of the three-part U•X•L Complete Health Resource. Other titles in this library include:

- *Body by Design:* This two-volume set presents the anatomy (structure) and physiology (function) of the human body in twelve chapters spread over two volumes. Each chapter is devoted to one of the eleven organ systems that make up the body. The last chapter focuses on the special senses, which allow humans to connect with the real world. Sidebar boxes present historical discoveries, recent medical advances, short biographies of scientists, and other interesting facts. More than 100 photos, many of them in color, illustrate the text.
- *Healthy Living:* This three-volume set examines fitness, nutrition, and other lifestyle issues across fifteen subject chapters. Topics covered include hygiene, mental health, preventive care, alternative medicine, and careers in health care. Sidebar boxes within entries provide information on related issues, while over 150 black-and-white illustrations help illuminate the text.

Acknowledgments

A note of appreciation is extended to U•X•L's Complete Health Resource advisors, who provided invaluable suggestions when this work was in its formative stages:

Carole Branson
Seminar Science Teacher
Wilson Middle School
San Diego, California

Bonnie L. Raasch
Media Specialist
Vernon Middle School
Marion, Iowa

Doris J. Ranke
Science Teacher
West Bloomfield High School
West Bloomfield, Michigan

Comments and Suggestions

We welcome your comments on *Sick! Diseases and Disorders, Injuries and Infections.* Please write: Editors, *Sick!,* U•X•L, 27500 Drake Rd., Farmington Hills, Michigan 48331–3535; call toll free: 1–800–877–4253; fax: 248–414–5043; or send e-mail via http://www.galegroup.com.

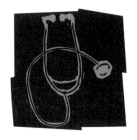

Please Read: Important Information

Sick! Diseases and Disorders, Injuries and Infections is a medical reference product designed to inform and educate readers about medical conditions. U•X•L believes this product to be comprehensive, but not necessarily definitive. While U•X•L has made substantial efforts to provide information that is accurate and up to date, U•X•L makes no representations or warranties of any kind, including without limitation, warranties of merchantability or fitness for a particular purpose, nor does it guarantee the accuracy, comprehensiveness, or timeliness of the information contained in this product.

Readers should be aware that the universe of medical knowledge is constantly growing and changing, and that differences of medical opinion exist among authorities. They are also advised to seek professional diagnosis and treatment for any medical condition, and to discuss information obtained from this book with their health care provider.

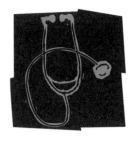

Words to Know

Diseases that are featured as main entries in *Sick!* are not covered in Words to Know.

A

Abortive: Describes an action that cuts something short or stops it.

Abscess: A pocket of infection within tissue.

Accommodation: The ability of the lens of the eye to change its shape in order to focus light waves from distant or near objects.

Acetylsalicylic acid: The chemical name for the primary compound from which aspirin is made. Shorthand terms for acetylsalicylic acid include acetylsalicylate, salicylic acid, and salicylate.

Acute: A disorder that comes on suddenly and usually does not last very long.

Acute retroviral syndrome: A group of symptoms resembling mononucleosis that are the first sign of HIV infection in 50 to 70 percent of all patients and in 45 to 90 percent of women.

Adenoid: A mass of lymph tissue located near the pharynx.

Adenoviruses: A group of viruses that usually cause infections of the lungs and ears.

African endemic Kaposi's sarcoma: A form of Kaposi's sarcoma that affects boys and men, has symptoms like those of classic Kaposi's sarcoma, and can spread rapidly and cause death.

Agoraphobia: A fear of open spaces.

AIDS dementia complex: A type of brain dysfunction caused by HIV infection that causes confusion, difficulty thinking, and loss of muscular coordination.

AIDS-related Kaposi's sarcoma: A form of Kaposi's sarcoma that occurs primarily in gay and bisexual men; it is much more dangerous than classic Kaposi's sarcoma.

Allergen: A substance that provokes an allergic response.

Allergic reaction: A series of events initiated by the immune system against substances that are normally harmless to the body.

Alveoli: Small air sacs at the ends of bronchioles through which oxygen passes from the lungs into blood.

Amalgam: A mixture of mercury, silver, and other metals used to make fillings for dental cavities.

Amenorrhea: Absence of menstrual periods.

Amnesia: Loss of memory sometimes caused by a brain injury, such as a concussion.

Amniocentesis: A medical procedure in which a sample of the fluid surrounding the fetus in a woman's womb is withdrawn and examined.

Amputation: A surgical procedure in which an arm, leg, hand, or foot is removed.

Anaphylaxis: An increased sensitivity to an allergen causing dilation (expansion) of blood vessels and tightening of muscles. Anaphylaxis can result in sharp drops in blood pressure, difficulty in breathing, and death if left untreated.

Androgen: A male sex hormone found in both males and females.

Anemia: A medical condition caused by a reduced number of red blood cells and characterized by general weakness, pale skin color, irregular heartbeat, shortness of breath, and fatigue.

Aneurysm: A weak spot in a blood vessel that may break open and lead to a stroke.

Angiography: A method for studying the structure of blood vessels by inserting a catheter into a vein or artery, injecting a dye in the blood vessel, and taking X-ray photographs of the structure.

Anti-androgen: A drug that slows down the production of androgens.

Antibiotic: A substance derived from bacteria or other organisms that fights the growth of other bacteria or organisms.

Antibody: Specific protein produced by the immune system to destroy specific invading organisms.

Anticoagulant: Describes a substance that prevents the blood from clotting.

Anticonvulsant medication: A drug used to prevent convulsions or seizures that is sometimes also effective in the treatment of bipolar disorder.

Antidepressant: A drug used to prevent or relieve depression.

Antigen: Any substance that stimulates the body to produce antibodies.

Antioxidant: A substance that prevents oxidation from taking place. Oxidation is a chemical reaction that can create heat, pain, and inflammation in the body.

Anxiety: Feeling troubled, uneasy, or worried.

Anxiety disorder: An experience of prolonged, excessive worry about the circumstances of one's life.

Aplastic: Having incomplete or faulty development.

Apnea: A temporary pause in one's breathing pattern. Sleep apnea consists of repeated episodes of temporary pauses in breathing during sleep.

Appendectomy: Surgical removal of the appendix.

Appendix: The worm-shaped pouch near the beginning of the large intestine.

Appetite suppressant: Drugs that decrease feelings of hunger and control appetite.

Aqueous humor: A watery fluid that fills the inside of the eyeball, providing nourishment to the eye and maintaining internal pressure in the eyeball.

Arteries: Blood vessels that carry blood from the heart to organs and tissues of the body.

Arteriosclerosis: Hardening of the arteries that can be caused by a variety of factors. Atherosclerosis is just one form of arteriosclerosis, but the two terms are often used interchangeably.

Artery: A blood vessel that carries blood from the heart to other parts of the body.

Arthrography: An imaging technique in which a dye is injected into a joint to make X-ray pictures of the inside of the joint easier to study.

Asperger syndrome: A type of autism that involves no problems with language.

Aspiration: Inhalation of food or saliva.

Astigmatism: A condition in which light from a single point fails to focus on a single point of the retina. The condition causes the patient to see a blurred image.

Ataxia: A condition in which balance and coordination are impaired.

Athetonia: A condition marked by slow, twisting, involuntary muscle movements.

Atopy: A condition in which people are more likely to develop allergic reactions, often because of the inflammation and airway narrowing typical of asthma.

Atrium: (plural: atria) One of the two upper chambers of the heart.

Audiometer: An instrument for testing a person's hearing.

Auditory nerve: A bunch of nerve fibers that carries sound from the inner ear to the brain.

Auditory canal: A tube that leads from the outside of the ear to the tympanic membrane.

Auricle: The external structure of the ear.

Autoimmunity: A condition in which the body's immune system produces antibodies in response to its own tissues or blood components instead of foreign particles or microorganisms.

Autonomic responses: Bodily responses that occur automatically, without the need for a person to think about it.

Autopsy: A medical examination of a dead body.

B

Bacillus Calmette-Guérin (BCG): A vaccine made from a weakened mycobacterium that infects cattle. It is used to protect humans against pulmonary tuberculosis and its complications.

Barium enema: A procedure in which a white liquid is injected into a patient's rectum in order to coat the lining of the colon so that X-ray photographs of the colon can be taken.

Becker muscular dystrophy (BMD): A type of muscular dystrophy that affects older boys and men and usually follows a milder course than Duchenne muscular dystrophy (DMD).

Benign: A growth that does not spread to other parts of the body, making recovery likely with treatment. Often used to describe noncancerous growths.

Binge: To consume large amounts of food without control in a short period of time.

Biofeedback: A technique in which a person learns to consciously control the body's response to a stimulus. Biofeedback enables a person to gain some control over involuntary body functions.

Biopsy: A procedure in which a small sample of tissue is removed and then studied under a microscope.

Blind spot: An area on the retina that is unable to respond to light rays.

Blood-brain barrier: A network of blood vessels between the neck and the brain that prevents many chemicals from passing into the brain.

Bone marrow: Soft, spongy material found in the center of bones from which blood cells are produced.

Bone marrow biopsy: A procedure by which a sample of bone marrow is removed and studied under a microscope.

Bone marrow transplantation: A process by which marrow is removed from the bones of a healthy donor and transferred to the bones of a person with some kind of blood disorder.

Bortadella pertussis: The bacterium that causes whooping cough.

Brain stem: A mass of nervous tissue that connects the forebrain and the cerebrum to the spinal cord.

Bronchi: Two large tubes that branch off the trachea and lead to the lungs; each tube is called a bronchus when referred to singularly. Also called bronchial tubes.

Bronchial tubes: Another name for bronchi. The major airways that lead to the lungs.

Bronchioles: Smaller extensions of the bronchi.

Bronchodilator: A substance that causes muscles in the respiratory system to relax, making breathing easier.

Bronchoscope: A device consisting of a long thin tube with a light and camera on the end for looking into a patient's airways and lungs.

BSA: Refers to "body surface area," a unit used in the treatment of burns to express the amount of the total body surface area covered by the burn.

C

C. botulinum: A very deadly bacteria that causes a disease known as botulism.

Calcium: An essential mineral with many important functions in the body, one of which is in the formation of bone.

Campylobacter jejuni (C. jejuni): A bacteria that is the leading cause of bacterial diarrhea in the United States. It occurs in healthy cattle, chickens, birds, and flies.

Carcinogen: Any substance capable of causing cancer.

Cardiovascular: A term that refers to the heart and blood system.

Carditis: Inflammation of the heart.

Caries: The medical term for tooth decay.

Carpal tunnel: A passageway in the wrist, created by bones and ligaments, through which the median nerve passes.

Carrier: A person whose body contains the organisms that cause a disease but who does not show symptoms of that disease.

Cartilage: Tough, elastic tissue that covers and protects the ends of bones.

Cataplexy: A sudden loss of muscular control that may cause a person to collapse.

Catatonic behavior: Behavior characterized by muscular tightness or rigidity and lack of response to the environment.

Catheter: A thin tube inserted into the patient's body, often into a vein or artery, to allow fluids to be sent into or taken out of the body.

Cavity: In dentistry, a hole or weak spot in tooth enamel caused by decay.

CD4: A type of protein molecule in human blood that is present on the surface of 65 percent of immune cells. The HIV virus infects cells that have CD4 surface proteins, and as a result, depletes the number of T cells, B cells, natural killer cells, and monocytes in the patient's blood. Most of the damage to an AIDS patient's immune system is done by the virus's destruction of CD4 lymphocytes.

Central nervous system: A system of nerve cells in the brain and the spinal cord.

Cephalosporin: A specific type of antibiotic used to treat many types of infections.

Cerebral thrombosis: Blockage of a blood vessel in the brain by a blood clot that formed in the brain itself.

Cerebral edema: Swelling of the brain caused by an accumulation of fluid.

Cerebral embolism: Blockage of a blood vessel in the brain by a blood clot that originally formed elsewhere in the body and then traveled to the brain.

Cerebrospinal fluid (CSF): Fluid made in chambers of the brain that flows over the surface of the brain and the spinal cord. CSF provides nutrients to cells of the nervous system and provides a cushion for the structures of the nervous system. It is often used to diagnose infections of the central nervous system (the brain and spinal cord).

Cerumen: Earwax.

Cervical traction: The process of using a mechanism to create a steady pull on the neck in order to keep it in the correct position while it heals.

CFTR: An abbreviation for cystic fibrosis transmembrane conductance regulator, a chemical that controls the amount of water in mucus.

Chelation therapy: Treatment with chemicals that bind to a poisonous metal and help the body quickly eliminate it.

Chemotherapy: A method of treating cancer using certain chemicals that can kill cancer cells.

Child abuse: Intentional harm done to infants and children, usually by parents or care givers.

Chlamydia: A family of microorganisms that causes several types of sexually transmitted diseases in humans.

Chloroquine: An antimalarial drug first used in the 1940s as a substitute for quinine, and still widely used in Africa because of its relatively low cost.

Cholesterol: A waxy substance produced by the body and used in a variety of ways.

Chorea: Involuntary movements that may cause the arms or legs to jerk about uncontrollably.

Chromosome: A structure located inside the nucleus (center) of a cell that carries genetic information.

Chronic: Recurring frequently or lasting a long time.

Cilia: Fine, hair-like projections that line the trachea and bronchi. Cilia wave back and forth, carrying mucus through the airways and clearing the airways of foreign materials.

Circadian rhythm: Any body pattern that follows a twenty-four-hour cycle, such as waking and sleeping.

Circumcision: The procedure in which the foreskin is removed from the penis.

Cirrhosis: A liver disorder caused by scarring of liver tissue.

Classic Kaposi's sarcoma: A form of Kaposi's sarcoma that usually affects older men of Mediterranean or eastern European background.

Clostridium tetani: The bacterium that causes tetanus.

Clonic phase: The stage of a grand mal seizure in which muscles alternately contract and relax.

Clotting factor: One of the chemicals necessary for blood clotting.

Cobb angle: A measure of the curvature of the spine, determined from measurements made on X-ray photographs.

Cognitive-behavioral therapy: A form of psychological counseling in which patients are helped to understand the nature of their disorder and reshape their environment to help them function better.

Colonoscopy: A procedure in which a long, thin tube is inserted through a patient's rectum into the colon to permit examination of the inner walls of the colon.

Colostomy: An opening created surgically that runs from the colon to the outside of the body to provide an alternative route for the evacuation of body wastes.

Comedo: A hard plug composed of sebum and dead skin cells that develops in the pores of the skin. The mildest form of acne.

Comedolytic: Drugs that break up comedos and open clogged pores.

Compulsion: A very strong urge to do or say something that usually cannot be resisted and is repeated again and again.

Computed tomography (CT) scan: A technique in which X-ray photographs of a particular part of the body are taken from different angles. The pictures are then fed into a computer that creates a single composite image of the internal (inside) part of the body. CT scans provide an important tool in the diagnosis of brain and spinal disorders, cancer, and other conditions.

Computerized axial tomography (CAT) scan: Another name for a computed tomography (CT) scan.

Condom: A thin sheath (covering) worn over the penis during sexual activity to prevent pregnancy and the spread of sexually transmitted diseases.

Conduct disorder: A behavioral and emotional disorder of childhood and adolescence. Children with a conduct disorder act inappropriately, infringe on the rights of others, and violate social rules.

Conductive hearing loss: Hearing loss that occurs in the external or middle ear.

Cone cells: Special cells in the retina responsible for color vision.

Congenital disorder: A medical condition that is present at birth.

Contact dermatitis: Inflammation of the skin caused by exposure to an allergen.

Contracture: A permanent shortening and tightening of a muscle or tendon causing a deformity.

Contrast hydrotherapy: A procedure in which a series of hot- and cold-water applications is applied to an injured area.

Contusion: A bruise.

Cornea: The transparent outer coating on the front of the eyeball.

Coronary: Referring to the heart.

Coronavirus: A type of virus that can cause the common cold.

Coxsackie virus: A virus that causes a disease known as herpangina.

Crabs: A slang term for pubic lice.

Crib death: Another name for sudden infant death syndrome.

Cryosurgery: The use of liquid nitrogen for the purpose of removing diseased tissue.

Cyanosis: A condition that develops when the body does not get enough oxygen, causing the skin to turn blue.

D

Debridement: The surgical removal of dead skin.

Decompression stops: Stops divers should make when returning to the surface to let the nitrogen in their blood dissolve safely out of their bodies. Charts developed by the U.S. Navy and other groups list the number of stops and the time to be spent at each stop.

Delusion: A fixed, false belief that is resistant to reason or factual disproof.

Dementia: Impaired intellectual function that interferes with normal social and work activities.

Densitometry: A technique for measuring the density of bone by taking photographs with low-energy X rays from a variety of angles around the bone.

Dentin: The middle layer of a tooth.

Dependence: A state in which a person requires a steady amount of a particular drug in order to avoid experiencing the symptoms of withdrawal.

Depot dosage: A form of medication that can be stored in the patient's body for several days or weeks.

Depression: A psychological condition with feelings of sadness, sleep disturbance, fatigue, and inability to concentrate.

Detoxification: The phase of treatment during which a patient gives up a substance and harmful chemicals are removed from his or her system.

Diaphragm: As a form of birth control, a thin rubber cap inserted into the vagina.

Diastolic blood pressure: Blood pressure exerted by the heart when it is resting between beats.

Digital rectal examination: A medical procedure in which a doctor inserts a lubricated gloved finger into the rectum to look for abnormal structures.

Dimercaprol (BAL): A chemical agent used in chelation therapy.

Diopter: The unit of measure used for the refractive (light bending) power of a lens.

Diplegia: Paralysis of the arm and leg on one side of the body.

Disease reservoir: A population of animals in which a virus lives without causing serious illness among the animals.

Distal muscular dystrophy (DD): A form of muscular dystrophy that usually begins in middle age or later, causing weakness in the muscles of the feet and hands.

Dominant gene: A form of a gene that predominates over a second form of the same gene.

Dopamine: A neurotransmitter that helps send signals that control movement.

DSM-IV: The *Diagnostic and Statistical Manual of Mental Disorders,* Fourth Edition, the standard reference book used for diagnosing and treating mental disorders.

Duchenne muscular dystrophy (DMD): The most severe form of muscular dystrophy, usually affecting young boys, beginning in the legs, and resulting in progressive muscle weakness.

Duodenum: The upper part of the small intestine, joined to the lower part of the stomach.

Dyslexia: Difficulty in reading, spelling, and/or writing words.

Dysthymic disorder: An ongoing, chronic depression that lasts two or more years.

Dystonia: Loss of the ability to control detailed muscle movement.

E

Echocardiogram: A test that uses sound waves to produce an image of the structure of the heart.

ECT: Electroconvulsive shock therapy, a method for using electric shocks to treat patients with mental disorders, such as bipolar disorder.

Edetate calcium disodium (EDTA calcium): A chemical agent used in chelation therapy.

Electrocardiogram: A test that measures the electrical activity of the heart to determine whether it is functioning normally.

Electroencephalogram (EEG): A test used to measure electrical activity of the brain to see if the brain is functioning normally.

Electrolytes: Salts and minerals present in the body that produce electrically charged particles (ions) in body fluids. Electrolytes control the fluid balance in the body and are important in muscle contraction, energy generation, and almost all major biochemical reactions in the body.

Electromagnetic radiation (ER): Radiation that travels as waves at the speed of light.

Electromyography: A test used to measure how well a nerve is functioning.

Enamel: The hard, outermost layer of a tooth.

Encephalopathy: A brain disorder characterized by loss of memory and other mental problems.

Endemic: The widespread occurrence of a disease over a given area that lasts for an extended period of time.

Endoscope: An instrument consisting of a long, narrow tube that can be inserted down a patient's throat to study the health of a patient's digestive system.

Enema: The injection of liquid into the intestine through the anus. This procedure is used either to induce a bowel movement or to coat the lining of the colon so that X-ray photographs can be taken of the colon.

Enzymes: Chemicals present in all cells that make possible the biological reactions needed to keep a cell alive.

Epidemic: An outbreak of a disease that spreads over a wide area in a relatively short period of time.

Epidermis: The outer layer of skin.

Epithelium: The layer of cells covering the body's outer and inner surfaces.

Epstein-Barr virus (EBV): A virus that causes mononucleosis and other diseases.

***Escherichia coli* (*E. coli*):** A bacteria that commonly causes food poisoning, most often from food products derived from cows, especially ground beef.

Estrogen: A female hormone with many functions in the body, one of which is to keep bones strong.

Eustachian tube: A passageway that connects the middle ear with the back of the throat.

Evoked potential test (EPT): A test that measures the brain's electrical response to certain kinds of stimulation, such as light in the eyes, sound in the ears, or touch on the skin.

Extrapulmonary: Outside of the lungs.

F

Facioscapulohumeral muscular dystrophy (FSH): A form of muscular dystrophy that begins in late childhood to early adulthood; affects both men and women; and causes weakness in the muscles of the face, shoulders, and upper arms.

Fecal occult blood test: A laboratory test designed to find blood in feces.

Fibrin: A thick material formed over an injured section of a blood vessel by the process of blood clotting.

Fibromyalgia: Pain, tenderness, and stiffness in muscles.

Fistula: An abnormal tubelike passage in tissue.

Flashback: A sudden memory of an event that occurred months or years earlier.

Fluoride: A chemical compound that is effective in preventing tooth decay.

Fragile X syndrome: A genetic condition involving the X chromosome that results in mental, physical, and sensory problems.

Frequency: The rate at which a wave vibrates in space.

Frostbite: A medical condition in which some part of the body has become frozen.

Fungus: A large group of organisms that includes mold, mildew, rust fungi, yeast, and mushrooms, some of which may cause disease in humans and other animals.

G

Ganglioside: A fatty substance found in brain and nerve cells.

Gangrene: Death and decay of body tissue.

Gastrointestinal system: The digestive system, consisting of the stomach and intestines.

Gel electrophoresis: A laboratory test that separates different types of molecules from each other.

Gene: A chemical unit found in all cells that carries information telling cells what functions they are to perform.

General autoimmune disorder: An autoimmune disorder that involves a number of tissues throughout the body.

Genetic disorder: A medical problem caused by one or more defective genes.

Genital: Having to do with the organs of the reproductive system.

Gingiva: The outer layer of the gums.

Ginkgo: An herb obtained from the ginkgo tree, thought by some alternative practitioners to be helpful in treating patients with Alzheimer's disease.

Glucose: A type of sugar present in the blood and in cells that is used by cells to make energy.

Gonorrhea: A sexually transmitted disease caused by the *Gonococcus* bacterium that affects the mucous membranes, particularly in the urinary tract and genital area. It can make urination painful and cause puslike discharges through the urinary tract.

Grand mal: An alternate term used for tonic-clonic epilepsy.

Granules: Small packets of reactive chemicals stored within cells.

Gray (Gy): A unit used to measure damage done to tissue by ionizing radiation.

H

Hairy leukoplakia of the tongue: A white area of diseased tissue on the tongue that may be flat or slightly raised. It is caused by the Epstein-Barr virus and is an important diagnostic sign of AIDS.

Hallucination: A perception of objects (or sounds) that have no reality. Seeing or hearing something that does not actually exist.

Helicobacter pylori: A bacterium that lives in mucous membranes and is responsible for the development of ulcers.

Hemiplegia: Paralysis of one side of the body.

Hemodialysis: A mechanical method for cleansing blood outside the body.

Hemoglobin: A molecule found in blood that gives blood its red color. Hemoglobin is responsible for transporting oxygen through the blood stream.

Hemorrhage: Heavy or uncontrollable bleeding.

Herpes virus: A group of viruses that cause many different infections in the human body, including cold sores and infections of the genital area.

Histamine: A chemical released by mast cells that activates pain receptors and causes cells to leak fluids.

Hormone replacement therapy (HRT): A method of treating osteoporosis by giving supplementary doses of estrogen and/or other female hormones.

Hormone therapy: Treatment of cancer by slowing down the production of certain hormones.

Hormones: Chemicals that occur naturally in the body and control certain body functions.

Human immunodeficiency virus (HIV): A transmissible virus that causes AIDS in humans. Two forms of HIV are now recognized: HIV-1, which causes most cases of AIDS in Europe, North and South America, and most parts of Africa; and HIV-2, which is chiefly found in West African patients. HIV-2, discovered in 1986, appears to be less virulent than HIV-1 and may also have a longer latency period.

Human papilloma virus (HPV): A family of viruses that cause hand, foot, flat, and genital warts.

Hydrocephalus: An abnormal accumulation of cerebrospinal fluid (CSF) in the brain.

Hyperbaric chamber: A sealed compartment used to treat decompression sickness, in which air pressure is first increased and then gradually decreased.

Hyperopia: Farsightedness. A condition in which vision is better for distant objects than for near ones.

Hypersomnia: The need to sleep excessively; a symptom of dysthymic and major depressive disorder.

Hyperthermia: The general name for any form of heat disorder.

Hyperventilation: Deep, heavy breathing.

Hypotonia: A condition in which muscles lack strength.

I

Iatrogenic: Caused by a medical procedure.

Iatrogenic Kaposi's sarcoma: A form of Kaposi's sarcoma that develops in people who have had organ transplants and are taking immunosuppressant drugs.

Ideal weight: Weight corresponding to the appropriate, healthy rate for individuals of a specific height, gender, and age.

Idiopathic epilepsy: A form of epilepsy for which no cause is known.

Immune system: A system of organs, tissues, cells, and chemicals that work together to fight off foreign invaders, such as bacteria and viruses.

Immunization: The process of injecting a material into a person's body that protects that person from catching a particular infectious disease.

Immunodeficient: A condition in which the body's immune response is damaged, weakened, or is not functioning properly.

Immunotherapy: Treatment of cancer by stimulating the body's immune system.

Incubation period: The time it takes for symptoms of a disease to appear after a person has been infected.

Infestation: A situation in which large numbers of organisms come together in a single area.

Inflammation: The body's response to tissue damage that includes heat, swelling, redness, and pain.

Inflammatory bowel disease: A group of disorders that affect the gastro-intestinal (digestive) system.

Insomnia: Difficulty in falling asleep or in remaining asleep.

Insulin: A hormone (type of protein) produced by the pancreas that makes it possible for cells to use glucose in the production of energy.

Intestinal perforation: A hole in the lining of the intestine that allows partially digested foods to leak into the abdominal cavity.

Intracerebral hemorrhage: Bleeding that occurs within the brain.

Intraocular pressure (IOP): The pressure exerted by aqueous humor (clear liquid) inside the eyeball.

Ionizing radiation (IR): Any form of radiation that can break apart atoms and molecules and cause damage to materials.

J

Jaundice: A yellowing of the skin, often caused by a disorder of the liver.

Jet lag: A temporary disruption of the body's sleep/wake rhythm caused by high-speed air travel through different time zones.

Joint: A structure that holds two or more bones together.

K

Karyotype: The specific chromosomal makeup of a particular organism.

Ketoacidosis: A condition that results from the build-up of toxic chemicals known as ketones in the blood.

Koplik's spots: Tiny white spots on a reddish bump found inside of the mouth that are a characteristic marker for measles.

L

Lactobacillus acidophilus: A bacterium found in yogurt that changes the balance of bacteria in the intestine in a beneficial way.

Laparoscopy: A procedure in which a tube with a small light and viewing device is inserted through a small incision near the navel, allowing a surgeon to look directly into the patient's abdomen.

Laparotomy: A surgical procedure that allows a surgeon to view the inside of the abdominal cavity.

Larva: An immature form of an organism.

Larynx: The part of the airway between the pharynx and trachea, often called the voice box.

Laser: A device for producing very intense beams of light of a single color. Used in surgery to cut and/or dissolve tissues.

Latency: A period during which a disease-causing organism is inactive but not dead.

Lens: In the eye, a transparent, elastic, curved structure that helps focus light on the retina.

Lesion: Any change in the structure or appearance of a part of the body as the result of an injury or infection.

Ligament: Tough, fiber-like tissue that holds bones together at joints.

Limb-girdle muscular dystrophy (LGMD): A form of muscular dystrophy that begins in late childhood to early adulthood, affects both men and women, and causes weakness in the muscles around the hips and shoulders.

Lumbar puncture: A procedure in which a thin needle is inserted into the space between vertebrae in the spine and a sample of cerebrospinal fluid is withdrawn for study under a microscope.

Lumpectomy: A procedure in which a cancerous lump is removed from the breast.

Lymph nodes: Small round or oval bodies within the immune system. Lymph nodes provide materials that fight disease and help remove bacteria and other foreign material from the body.

Lymphocyte: A type of white blood cell that is important in the formation of antibodies and that can be measured to monitor the health of AIDS patients.

Lymphoma: A cancerous tumor in the lymphatic system that is associated with a poor prognosis in AIDS patients.

M

Macrophage: A large white blood cell, found primarily in the bloodstream and connective tissue, that helps the body fight off infections by ingesting the disease-causing organism. HIV can infect and kill macrophages.

Magnetic resonance imaging (MRI): A procedure that uses electromagnets and radio waves to produce images of a patient's internal tissue and organs. These images are not blocked by bones, and can be useful in diagnosing brain and spinal disorders and other diseases.

Malignant: Describes a tumor that can spread to other parts of the body and that poses a serious threat to a person's life.

Malnutrition: A condition in which a person is not eating enough of the right kinds of foods.

Mammogram: An X-ray photograph of the breast.

Mandible: The scientific term for the lower jaw.

Mania: A mental condition in which a person feels unusually excited, irritated, or happy.

Mantoux test: Another name for the purified protein derivative (PPD) test, which is used to determine whether a person has been infected with the tuberculosis bacterium.

Mast cells: A type of immune system cell that is found in the lining of the nasal passages and eyelids. It displays a type of antibody called immunoglobulin type E (IgE) on its cell surface and participates in the allergic response by releasing histamine from intracellular granules.

Mastectomy: Surgical removal of a breast.

Meconium ileus: A condition that appears in newborn babies with cystic fibrosis, in which the baby's first bowel movement is abnormally dark, thick, and sticky.

Median nerve: A nerve that runs through the wrist and into the hand, providing feeling and movement to the hand, thumb, and fingers.

Melanocyte: A specialized skin cell that produces melanin, a dark pigment (color) found in skin.

Melatonin: A hormone thought to control the body's natural sleep rhythms.

Meninges: The three-layer membranous covering of the brain and spinal cord.

Menopause: The end of menstruation.

Menstruation: The discharge of menses (a bloody fluid) from the uterus of women who are not pregnant that occurs approximately every four weeks from puberty to menopause.

Metabolism: A series of chemical reactions by which cells convert glucose to energy.

Metastasis: The process by which cancer cells travel from one area of the body to another.

Methadone: A chemical given to heroin addicts to help them overcome their addiction.

Miliary tuberculosis: A form of tuberculosis in which the bacillus spreads throughout the body producing many thousands of tubercular lesions.

Miscarriage: When a human fetus is expelled from the mother before it can survive outside of the womb.

MMR vaccine: A vaccine that contains separate vaccines against three diseases: measles, mumps, and rubella.

Monocyte: A large white blood cell that is formed in the bone marrow and spleen. About 4 percent of the white blood cells in normal adults are monocytes.

Mosaic: Medically, a condition in which an individual cell may contain more than one type of chromosomal composition, with forty-six chromosomes in one cell, for example, and forty-seven chromosomes in another cell, which causes relatively mild symptoms of Down's syndrome.

Motor function: A body function controlled by muscles.

Motor neuron: A nerve cell that controls a muscle.

Mucolytic: Any type of medication that breaks up mucus and makes it flow more easily.

Mucus: A mixture of water, salts, sugars, and proteins, which has the job of cleansing, lubricating, and protecting passageways in the body.

Myalgia: Muscle pain.

Myalgic encephalomyelitis: An inflammation of the brain and spinal cord.

Myelin: A layer of tissue that surrounds nerves and acts as an insulator.

Myelograph: A test in which a dye is injected into the spinal column to allow examination of the spine with X rays or a computed tomography (CT) scan.

Myocardial infarction: The technical term for heart attack.

Myopia: Nearsightedness. A condition in which far away objects appear fuzzy because light from a distance doesn't focus properly on the retina.

Myotonic dystrophy: A form of muscular dystrophy that affects both men and women and causes generalized weakness in the face, feet, and hands.

N

Narcolepsy: A sleep disorder characterized by sudden sleep attacks during the day and often accompanied by other symptoms, such as cataplexy, temporary paralysis, and hallucinations.

Narcotic: A drug that relieves pain and induces sleep.

Natural killer cells: Cells in the immune system that help fight off infections.

Necrosis: Abnormal death of body tissues.

Nervous tic: An involuntary action, continually repeated, such as the twitching of a muscle or repeated blinking.

Neural tube: A structure that forms very early in the life of a fetus and eventually develops into the central nervous system of the body.

Neurasthenia: Nervous exhaustion.

Neurofibrillary tangle: Twisted masses of peptides (fragments of protein fibers) that develop inside brain cells of people with Alzheimer's disease.

Neuron: A nerve cell.

Neurotransmitter: A chemical found in the brain that carries electrical signals from one nerve cell to another nerve cell.

Nitrogen: A tasteless, odorless gas that makes up four-fifths of Earth's atmosphere.

Nits: The eggs produced by head or pubic lice.

Nonsteroidal anti-inflammatory drugs (NSAIDs): A group of drugs, including aspirin, ibuprofen, and acetaminophen, used to treat pain and fever.

Nucleoside analogues: A medication that interferes when HIV tries reproduce by making copies of itself inside cells.

O

Obsession: A troubling thought that occurs again and again and causes severe distress in a person.

Oculopharyngeal muscular dystrophy (OPMD): A form of muscular dystrophy that affects adults of both sexes and causes weakness in the muscles of the eyes and throat.

Opiate blockers: Drugs that interfere with the action of natural opiates, substances that cause sleepiness and numbness.

Opportunistic infection: An infection by organisms that usually don't cause infection in people whose immune systems are working normally.

Optic nerve: A nerve at the back of the eyeball that carries messages from the retina to the brain.

Organ specific disorder: An autoimmune disorder in which only one type of organ is affected.

Ossicles: Tiny bones located within the middle ear responsible for transmitting sound vibrations from the outer ear to the inner ear.

Osteoarthritis: A type of arthritis that weakens the joint cartilage. It is most common among the elderly.

Otosclerosis: A disorder in which the bones of the middle ear become joined to each other.

P

Pancreas: A gland located behind the stomach that produces insulin.

Paralysis: The inability to move one's muscles.

Paranoia: Excessive or irrational suspicion or distrust of others.

Penicillin: A specific type of antibiotic used to treat many types of infections.

Peptic ulcer: A general name referring to ulcers in any part of the digestive system.

Pericardium: The membrane surrounding the heart.

Peristalsis: Periodic waves of muscular contractions that move food through the digestive system.

Peritonitis: Inflammation of the membranes that line the abdominal wall.

Persistent generalized lymphadenopathy (PGL): A condition in which HIV continues to produce chronic painless swellings in the lymph nodes during the latency period.

Petit mal: An alternative term for absence epilepsy.

Pharynx: The part of the throat that lies between the mouth and the larynx, or voice box. It connects the nose and mouth with the upper part of the digestive system.

Phenylketonuria (PKU): A genetic disorder in which a person's body is unable to break down the amino acid phenylalanine, causing damage to the brain.

Physiological dependence: A condition in which a person's body requires the intake of some substance, without which it will become ill.

Plaque: Generally refers to a build-up of some substance. The fatty material and other substances that form on the lining of blood vessels are called plaque. Patches of scar tissue that form in areas where myelin tissue has been destroyed are also called plaque. Dental plaque is a thin, sticky film composed of sugars, food, and bacteria that cover teeth.

Platelet: A type of blood cell involved in the clotting of blood.

Pleural: Having to do with the membrane that surrounds the lungs.

Polyps: Small, abnormal masses of tissue that can form on the lining of an organ.

Polysomnograph: An instrument used to measure a patient's body processes during sleep.

Positron emission tomography (PET): A diagnostic technique that uses radioactive materials to study the structure and function of organs and tissues within the body.

Primary progressive: A form of multiple sclerosis in which the disease continually becomes worse.

Prion: A form of protein that can cause an infectious disease.

Process addiction: A condition in which a person is dependent on some type of behavior, such as gambling, shopping, or sexual activity.

Prodrome: A period of time during which certain symptoms signal the beginning of a disease.

Prophylactic: Referring to a treatment that prevents the symptoms of a condition from developing.

Protease inhibitors: The second major category of drug used to treat AIDS. They work by suppressing the replication of the HIV virus.

Protein: A type of chemical compound with many essential functions in the body, one of which is to build bones.

Psychological dependence: A condition in which a person requires the intake of some substance in order to maintain mental stability.

Psychosis: Extremely disordered thinking accompanied by a poor sense of reality.

Psychosocial therapy: Any means by which a trained professional holds interviews with a patient and tries to help that patient better understand himself or herself and the reasons for his or her thoughts and actions.

Psychotic disorder: A mental disorder characterized by delusions, hallucinations, and other symptoms indicating a loss of contact with the real world.

Pulmonary: Relating to the lungs.

Pulmonary function test: A test that measures the amount of air a patient can breath in and out.

Pulmonary hypertension: High blood pressure in the arteries and veins associated with the lungs.

Pulp: The soft, innermost layer of a tooth.

Purge: To rid the body of food by vomiting, the use of laxatives, or some other method.

Purified protein derivative (PPD): A substance injected beneath the skin to see whether a person presently has or has ever had the tubercle bacillus.

Q

Quadriplegia: Paralysis of both arms and both legs.

Quinine: One of the first successful treatments for malaria, derived from the bark of the cinchona tree.

R

Rad: A unit once used to measure the amount of damage done to tissue by ionizing radiation, now replaced by the gray.

Radial keratotomy (RK): A surgical procedure in which the shape of the cornea is changed in order to correct myopia.

Radiation: Energy transmitted in the form of electromagnetic waves or subatomic particles.

Radiation therapy: Treatment that uses high-energy radiation, like X rays, to treat cancer.

Radical mastectomy: Surgical removal of an entire breast along with the chest muscles around the breast and all the lymph nodes under the arm.

Radioactive isotope: A substance that gives off some form of radiation.

Radiotherapy: Treatment of a disease using some form of radiation, such as X rays.

Radon: A radioactive gas that occurs naturally and is often found in the lower levels of buildings.

Rash: A spotted pink or red skin condition that may be accompanied by itching.

Recessive gene: A form of a gene that does not operate in the presence of a dominant form of the same gene.

Reconstructive surgery: A medical procedure in which an artificial breast is created to replace the breast removed during a mastectomy.

Rectum: The lower part of the digestive system from which solid wastes are excreted.

Red blood cells: Blood cells that carry oxygen from the lungs to the rest of the body.

Reduction: The restoration of a body part to its original position after it has been displaced, such as during a fracture.

Refraction: The bending of light waves as they pass through a dense substance, such as water, glass, or plastic.

Relapse: A reoccurrence of a disease.

Relapsing-remitting: A form of multiple sclerosis in which symptoms appear for at least twenty-four hours and then disappear for a period of time.

Rem: An older unit used to measure the amount of damage done to tissue by ionizing radiation, now replaced by the sievert.

Renal: Relating to the kidneys.

Resorption: The process by which the elements of bone are removed from bone and returned to the body.

Respiratory system: The nose, tonsils, larynx, pharynx, lungs, and other structures used in the process of breathing.

Restless leg syndrome: A condition in which a patient experiences aching or other unpleasant sensations in the calves of the legs.

Retina: A thin membrane at the back of the eyeball that receives light rays that pass through the eyeball and transmits them to the optic nerve.

Rhabdovirus: The virus that causes rabies.

Rhinovirus: A type of virus that can cause the common cold.

RICE: The term stands for the program of rest, ice, compression, and elevation that is recommended for treating tendinitis.

Rickets: A condition caused by the deficiency of certain minerals, including vitamin D and calcium, causing abnormal bone growth.

S

Salmonella: A bacteria that commonly causes food poisoning, most often from poultry, eggs, meat, and milk.

Scald: A burn caused by a hot liquid or steam.

Scoliometer: A tool for measuring the amount of curvature in a person's spine.

Screening: Using a test or group of tests to look for some specific medical disorder.

Sebum: An oily material produced by sebaceous glands that keeps the skin moist.

Secondary progressive: A form of multiple sclerosis in which a period of relapses and remissions is followed by another period in which the disease becomes progressively worse without improvement.

Secondhand smoke: Smoke that someone inhales after it is exhaled by another person.

Sedative: A substance that calms a person. Sedatives can also cause a person to feel drowsy.

Seizure: A convulsion; a series of involuntary muscular movements that alternate between contraction and relaxation.

Selective serotonin reuptake inhibitors (SSRIs): A class of drugs used to reduce depression.

Semen: A white fluid produced by the male reproductive system that carries sperm.

Seminal vesicles: The organs that produce semen.

Senile plaque: Deposits that collect inside the brain cells of people with Alzheimer's disease.

Sensory hearing loss: Hearing loss that occurs in the inner ear, auditory nerve, or brain.

Serotonin: An important neurotransmitter in the brain.

Shigella: A bacterium that grows well in contaminated food and water, in crowded living conditions, and in areas with poor sanitation. It is transmitted by direct contact with an infected person or with food that has been contaminated by an infected person.

Shingles: A disease that causes a rash and a very painful nerve inflammation. An attack of chickenpox eventually gives rise to shingles in about 20 percent of the population.

Shock: A life-threatening condition that results from low blood volume due to loss of blood or other fluids.

Sickle cell: A red blood cell with an abnormal shape due to the presence of an abnormal form of hemoglobin.

Sievert (Sv): A unit used to measure the amount of damage done to tissue by ionizing radiation.

Sigmoidoscopy: A medical procedure in which a doctor looks at the rectum and lower colon through a flexible lighted instrument called a sigmoidoscope.

Silicosis: A disease of the lungs caused by inhaling fine particles of sand.

Skin graft: A surgical procedure in which dead skin is removed and replaced by healthy skin, usually taken from elsewhere on the patient's own body.

Sleep disorder: Any condition that interferes with sleep. The American Sleep Disorders Association has identified eighty-four different sleep disorders.

Somnambulism: Also called sleepwalking, it refers to a range of activities a patient performs while sleeping, from walking to carrying on a conversation.

Spasm: A contraction of the muscles that can cause paralysis and/or shaking.

Spastic: A condition in which muscles are rigid, posture may be abnormal, and control of muscles may be impaired.

Sphygmomanometer: An instrument used to measure blood pressure.

Spinal cord: A long rope-like piece of nervous tissue that runs from the brain down the back.

Spinal transection: A complete break in the spinal column.

Spirometer: An instrument that shows how much air a patient is able to exhale and hold in his or her lungs as a test to see how serious a person's asthma is and how well he or she is responding to treatment.

Spondylosis: Arthritis of the spine.

Sputum: Secretions produced inside an infected lung. When the sputum is coughed up it can be studied to determine what kinds of infection are present in the lung.

Staphylococcus aureas: A bacteria that causes food poisoning, commonly found on foods that are kept at room temperature.

Staphylococcus: A class of bacteria found on human skin and mucous membranes that can cause a variety of infectious diseases.

Streptococcus: A class of bacteria that causes a wide variety of infections.

Stem cells: Immature blood cells formed in bone marrow.

Steroids: A category of naturally occurring chemicals that are very effective in reducing inflammation and swelling.

Stimulant: A substance that makes a person feel more energetic or awake. A stimulant may increase organ activity in the body.

Stress test: An electrocardiogram taken while a patient is exercising vigorously, such as riding a stationary bicycle.

Subarachnoid hemorrhage (SAH): Loss of blood into the subarachnoid space, the fluid-filled area that surrounds brain tissue.

Subdural hematoma: An accumulation of blood in the outer part of the brain.

Substance addiction: A condition in which a person is dependent on some chemical substance, such as cocaine or heroin.

Substantia nigra: A region of the brain that controls movement.

Succimer (Chemet): A chemical agent used to remove excess lead from the body.

Symptomatic epilepsy: A form of epilepsy for which some specific cause is known.

Synovial fluid: A fluid produced by the synovial membranes in a joint that lubricates the movement of the bones in the joint.

Synovial membrane: A membrane that covers the articular capsule in a joint and produces synovial fluid.

Syphilis: A sexually transmitted disease that can cause sores and eventually lead to brain disease, paralysis, and death.

Systemic treatment: A form of treatment that affects the whole body.

Systolic blood pressure: Blood pressure exerted by the heart when it contracts (beats).

T

T-cells: Lymphocytes that originate in the thymus gland. T-cells regulate the immune system's response to infections, including HIV.

Tartar: Plaque that has become hardened and attached to the tooth surface.

Temporal bones: The bones that form the right and left sides of the skull.

Tendon: A tough, rope-like tissue that connects muscle to bone.

Tennis elbow: A form of tendinitis that occurs among tennis players and other people who engage in the same movement of the elbow over and over again.

Testosterone: A male sex hormone.

Thermal burns: Burns caused by hot objects or by fire.

Thoracentesis: A procedure for removing fluids from the pleural space by inserting a long, thin needle between the ribs.

Throat culture: A sample of tissue taken from a person's throat for analysis. The culture is often taken by swiping a cotton swab across the back of the throat.

Thrombolytic: Capable of dissolving a blood clot.

Thrombosis: The formation of a blood clot.

Thyroid: An organ that controls a number of important bodily functions.

Tic: A muscular contraction or vocal sound over which a patient has very little control.

Tinea capitis: Scalp ringworm; a fungal infection of the scalp.

Tinea corporis: Scientific name for body ringworm, a fungal infection of the skin that can affect any part of the body except the scalp, feet, and facial area.

Tinea cruris: An fungal infection that affects the groin and can spread to the buttocks, inner thighs, and external genitalia; also called "jock itch."

Tinea unguium: Ringworm of the nails; a fungal infection that usually begins at the tip of a toenail.

Tissue plasminogen activator (tPA): A substance that dissolves blood clots in the brain.

Tolerance: The ability of a body to endure a certain amount of a substance that had previously been too much for it to tolerate.

Tonic phase: The stage of a grand mal seizure in which muscles become rigid and fixed.

Tonometer: A device used to measure intraocular pressure in the eyeball.

Tonsillectomy: A surgical procedure to remove the tonsils.

Tonsils: Oval-shaped masses of lymph gland tissue located on both sides of the back of the throat.

Toxic dilation of the colon: An expansion of the colon that may be caused by inflammation due to ulcerative colitis.

Toxin: A poison.

Trachea: The windpipe, extending from the larynx (the voice box) to the lungs.

Traction: The process of placing an arm or leg bone, or group of muscles under tension by applying weights to them in order to keep them in alignment while they heal.

Tranquilizers: Drugs that help a person to calm down.

Transcutaneous electrical nerve stimulation: A procedure in which mild electrical currents are used to stimulate nerves in order to prevent the transmission of pain messages in the body.

Translocation: A condition in which a piece of one chromosome breaks off and becomes attached to another chromosome.

Tretinoin: A drug that increases the rate at which skin cells are formed and die.

Triglyceride: A type of fat.

Trimester: Three months. Often used to refer to one third of a woman's pregnancy.

Trisomy: A condition in which three identical chromosomes, rather than two, are matched with each other.

Tumor: A mass or lump of tissue made of abnormal cells.

Twelve-step program: A plan for overcoming an addiction by going through twelve stages of personal development.

Tympanic membrane: A thin piece of tissue between the external ear and the middle ear.

U

Ulcer: An open wound in the skin or mucous membrane that is usually sore and painful.

Ultrasound test: A medical procedure in which a sound wave is transmitted into a pregnant woman's womb. The reflections produced from the sound wave can be studied for the presence of abnormalities in a fetus.

Ultraviolet (UV) light: A naturally occurring part of ordinary sunlight that may, under some circumstances, have beneficial effects in curing certain medical disorders.

Urethra: The tube through which the bladder empties to the exterior of the body.

V

Vaccine: A substance that causes the body's immune system to build up resistance to a particular disease.

Varicella-zoster immune globulin (VZIG): A substance that can reduce the severity of chickenpox symptoms.

Varicella-zoster virus: The virus that causes chickenpox and shingles.

Variola: The virus that causes smallpox. The only two small samples of variola that remain on Earth are being stored in two separate research laboratories.

Varivax: A vaccine for the prevention of chickenpox.

Vasodilator: Any drug that causes a blood vessel to relax.

Vector: An animal that transmits an infectious agent, such as a virus, from one animal to another animal.

Vector-borne disease: A disease transferred from one organism to another by means of a third organism, such as an insect or tick.

Ventricle: One of the two lower chambers of the heart.

Vertebrae: Bones that make up the spinal column.

Virus: A very small organism that can live only within a cell and that can cause some form of disease.

Volume reduction surgery: A surgical procedure in which damaged portions of a patient's lung are removed to make it easier for the patient to use healthy parts of the lung to get the oxygen needed for ordinary functioning.

Voluntary muscle: A muscle under a person's conscious control.

W

Wasting Syndrome: A progressive loss of weight and muscle tissue caused by AIDS.

White blood cells: Blood cells that fight invading organisms, such as bacteria and viruses.

Withdrawal: The process by which a person adjusts to the absence of some substance or activity to which he or she has become addicted.

X

X rays: A kind of high-energy radiation that can be used to take pictures of the inside of the body, to diagnose cancer, or to kill cancer cells.

Research and Activity Ideas

The following research and activity ideas are intended to offer suggestions for complementing science and health curricula, to trigger additional ideas for enhancing learning, and to suggest cross-disciplinary projects for library and classroom use.

Disease graph: Different environments create different opportunities for diseases to spread. Obtain current data for your city or county on occurrences of a disease such as rabies or lyme disease or a condition such as asthma. Create a graph that compares the number of outbreaks in urban areas with the number in rural areas. If there are differences, brainstorm some of the environmental factors that may be causing such differences.

Public service announcement: Choose a disease or disorder and write a public service announcement that would appear on television to inform people about the condition. Your ad should include information about symptoms, warn of risk factors, mention current treatments, and dispel any myths that are associated with the disease. Record the public service announcement using a video camera or present it in class.

Geographic study: Different parts of the world often face unique challenges in controlling diseases. Choose two different countries with different cultures and environments. Find out what the top five health concerns are in each country. For each one, determine the major risk factors. Discuss what aspects of the culture or the environment may be increasing the incidences of these diseases in each country.

Disease transmission: With a group of five to eight people choose one daily activity that you will act out. This could be going to the grocery store, going through the lunch line at school, playing a game, or going out to dinner. Assign each person a role in the activity. Choose one player who will be infected with a contagious disease, such as influenza. Coat that person's hands with flour. Act out the scene as realistically as possible. At the end of the scene, note how many other players have flour on themselves and how many places the ill person left his or her germs.

Diabetic diet: Research the dietary requirements of a person with diabetes. Keep a food diary for two days, recording everything you eat. Examine how your eating habits would have to change if you had diabetes. What foods couldn't you have eaten? What might you have to eat more of?

AIDS risk factors: What are some of the myths about the transmission of AIDS? Choose five activities sometimes incorrectly thought to be risk factors for contracting AIDS. For each myth give the scientific reasons that the activity does not put one at risk of contracting AIDS.

The following Web sites offer many more research and activity ideas as well as interactive activities for students:

The American Museum of Natural History: Infection, Detection, Protection. http://www.amnh.org/explore/infection/smp_index.html

Cool Science for Curious Kids. http://www.hhmi.org/coolscience/

The Gateway to Educational Materials. http://thegateway.org/index1/SubjectIndex.html#health

Newton's Apple®. http://ericir.syr.edu/Projects/Newton/index.html

The University of Arizona. The Biology Project: An Online Interactive Resource for Learning Biology. http://www.biology.arizona.edu/

WNET School. http://www.wnet.rog/wnetschool

SICK!

*Diseases and
Disorders,
Injuries and
Infections*

ACNE

Acne is a common skin disease characterized by pimples on the face, chest, and back. It occurs when the pores of the skin become clogged with oil, dead skin cells, and bacteria.

DESCRIPTION

The medical term for acne is acne vulgaris. It is the most common of all skin diseases, affecting about seventeen million Americans. Acne can occur at any age, but it is most common among adolescents. Nearly 85 percent of people between the ages of twelve and twenty-five develop acne. Up to 20 percent of women over twenty-five develop mild acne. The disease is also sometimes found in newborns.

Acne is a disease of the sebaceous (pronounced see-BAY-shus) glands. These glands lie just beneath the surface of the skin. They produce an oil called sebum, which keeps the skin moist. At puberty, a person's body may begin to produce an excess of sebum. Puberty is the period of life when a person's sex hormones become active. The male sex hormone called androgen causes an over-production of sebum.

ACNE IS THE MOST COMMON OF ALL SKIN DISEASES, AFFECTING ABOUT SEVENTEEN MILLION AMERICANS.

When excess sebum combines with dead skin, a hard plug, or comedo (pronounced KO-mee-do), is formed. The comedo can block skin pores. Two types of comedos can occur. They are known as whiteheads and blackheads.

More serious forms of acne develop when bacteria invade blocked pores. A pimple forms when sebum, bacteria, skin cells, and white blood cells are released into tissue around the pore. The pimple may then become inflamed. Inflamed pimples near the skin are called papules. Those that form deeper in the skin are called pustules. The most severe type of acne occurs when cysts (closed sacs) or nodules (hard swellings) form.

Acne often causes scarring of the skin. This occurs when new skin cells form to replace damaged cells. The new skin is usually not formed very easily, causing an unevenness that produces scars. Acne occurs most commonly on the face, chest, shoulders, and back because those are the places that sebaceous cells occur.

CAUSES

The exact cause of acne is not known, however, several risk factors have been identified.

- **Age.** Because of the effect of sex hormones, teenagers are quite likely to develop acne.
- **Cosmetics.** Make-up and hair sprays that contain oils can make acne worse.
- **Diet.** Acne is not caused by diet, but some foods can make the disease more serious.
- **Disease.** Hormonal disorders can increase the severity of acne problems in girls.
- **Drugs.** Acne can develop as a result of using certain drugs, such as tranquilizers, antibiotics, oral contraceptives, and anabolic steroids. Steroids are synthetic hormones that may sometimes be abused by athletes to increase the size of their muscles.
- **Environment.** Acne can become worse as a result of exposure to oils, greases, and polluted air. Sweating in hot weather can also make the condition worse.
- **Gender.** Boys are more likely to develop acne and tend to have more serious cases than girls.
- **Heredity.** Acne is more common in some families than in others.
- **Hormonal changes.** Acne can flare up during menstruation, pregnancy, and menopause. Menopause is the period in a woman's life when her body stops producing certain hormones.

WORDS TO KNOW

Androgen: A male sex hormone found in both males and females.

Anti-androgen: A drug that slows down the production of androgens.

Antibiotic: A drug that kills bacteria.

Comedo: A hard plug that develops in the pores of the skin composed of sebum and dead skin cells. The mildest form of acne.

Comedolytic: Drugs that break up comedos and open clogged pores.

Isotretinoin: A drug that decreases sebum production and dries up acne pimples.

Sebum: An oily material produced by sebaceous glands that keeps the skin moist.

Tretinoin: A drug that increases the rate at which skin cells are formed and die.

- **Personal hygiene.** Strong soaps, hard scrubbing, and picking at pimples can make acne worse.
- **Stress.** Emotional stress can contribute to acne.

SYMPTOMS

Acne is often not apparent to an observer. Inflamed pores, however, can cause pain or itching. The most troubling aspect of acne for many people is the scarring that can occur. And, while acne may not be very noticeable, individuals tend to be sensitive about their appearance. Teenagers especially may become concerned about the way other people react to them.

DIAGNOSIS

People with acne are often treated by family doctors. More serious cases are referred to a dermatologist (a specialist in skin disorders) or an endocrinologist (a specialist in hormonal disorders).

Because of its appearance, acne is not difficult to diagnose. A doctor takes a complete medical history, which includes questions about skin, diet, medication use, and other factors associated with risk for acne. He or she conducts a physical examination of the face, upper neck, chest, shoulders, back, and other affected areas. The doctor determines the number and type of blemishes, whether they are inflamed or not, whether they are deep or near the surface of the skin, and whether there is scarring or skin discoloration.

Laboratory tests are not done unless the patient appears to have a hormonal disorder. In that case, blood tests and other tests may be ordered. Most insurance plans cover the cost of diagnosing and treating acne.

TREATMENT

Acne treatment consists of reducing sebum production, removing dead skin cells, and killing bacteria. Treatment methods differ depending on how serious the acne is.

Topical Drugs

Topical drugs are applied directly to the affected areas of the skin. They are available in the

ANTI-ACNE DRUGS	
Brand Name (Generic Name)	**Possible Common Side Effects Include:**
Accutane (isotretinoin)	Dry skin, dry mouth, conjunctivitis
Benzamycin	Dry and itchy skin
Cleocin T (clindamycin phosphate)	Dry skin
Desquam-E (benzoyl peroxide)	Itching, red and peeling skin
Erythromycin topical (A/T/S, erycette, t-stat)	Burning, dry skin, hives, red and peeling skin
Minocin (minocycline hydrochloride)	Headache, hives, diarrhea, peeling skin, vomiting
Retin-A (tretinoin)	Darkening of the skin, blistering, crusted, or puffy skin

(Reproduced by permission of Stanley Publishing)

form of creams, gels, lotions, or pads. They are used primarily to treat mild forms of acne in which there is little or no inflammation.

One group of topical drugs used for acne includes antibiotics. These drugs kill the bacteria that contribute to the disease. Another group of drugs is called comedolytics (pronounced KO-mee-do-LIE-tiks). These drugs loosen hard plugs and open pores. Still another group of drugs works by increasing the rate at which new skin cells form. These drugs prevent the formation of new comedos.

Topical drugs are applied once or twice a day after washing with mild soap. Treatment may have to continue anywhere from a few weeks to a few months to a few years. Side effects such as mild redness, peeling, irritation, dryness, and an increased sensitivity to sunlight may occur.

Oral Drugs

Oral drugs are taken by mouth. Doctors sometimes prescribe oral antibiotics for moderate cases of acne. These antibiotics prevent the formation of new comedos and reduce inflammation. They are usually taken once a day

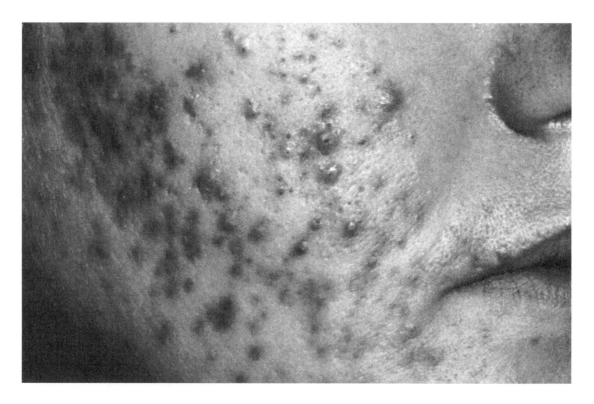

A close-up of clinical acne. (© 1991 National Medical Slide. Reproduced by permission of Custom Medical Stock Photo.)

for two to four months. Side effects may include allergic reactions, stomach upset, vaginal yeast infections, dizziness, and tooth discoloration.

A drug that is used for severe cases of acne is isotretinoin (pronounced i-so-TRET-uh-no-un, trade name Accutane). This drug reduces the production of sebum and the stickiness of skin cells. It is used when cysts and nodules are present. The drug may be used alone or with other topical or oral antibiotics.

Isotretinoin treatment usually lasts for four or five months. It is effective in about 60 percent of all patients. If the acne reappears, another course of treatments may be necessary. Some side effects that may accompany the use of isotretinoin include nosebleeds, dry skin, a temporary worsening of the acne, vision disorders, and increased production of liver enzymes, blood fats, and cholesterol. It may also cause birth defects and cannot, therefore, be used by pregnant women.

Women who do not respond to any of these treatments may be given another type of oral drug, an anti-androgen. Anti-androgens reduce the production of androgen and therefore reduce the formation of comedos. Certain types of oral contraceptives are also effective as anti-androgens.

The most serious forms of acne require other types of drugs, including oral corticosteroids, or anti-inflammatory drugs. These drugs are often used for the treatment of a form of acne known as acne fulminans, which occurs mostly among adolescent males. They are also used with acne that produces numerous deep, inflamed nodules that heal with scarring.

Other Treatments

Several surgical or medical treatments may be used to reduce acne or the scars caused by the disease.

- **Chemical peel.** A chemical known as glycolic acid is first applied to the skin. When it dries, it is peeled off, taking the top layer of skin with it. This treatment helps reduce scarring.
- **Collagen injection.** Shallow scars are filled in by injecting collagen, a skin protein, beneath the scars.
- **Comedo extraction.** A special tool is used to remove a comedo from a pore.
- **Dermabrasion.** The affected skin is first frozen with a chemical spray. Then it is removed with a brush or sandpaper-like instrument.
- **Intralesional injection.** Anti-inflammatory drugs are injected directly into inflamed pimples.
- **Punch grafting.** Deep scars are removed and the area repaired with small skin grafts.

Alternative Treatment

Alternative treatments for acne focus on proper hygiene and diet. Patients are advised to keep their skin clean and oil-free. They are also encouraged to eat a well-balanced diet high in fiber, zinc, and raw fruits and vegetables. They should also avoid alcohol, dairy products, caffeine, sugar, smoking, processed foods, and foods high in iodine, such as table salt.

Some doctors recommend the use of herbs to supplement the diet. Some herbs that have been used in the treatment of acne include burdock root, red clover, and milk thistle. Additional nutrients that may help to control acne include B-complex vitamins and chromium. Chinese herbal treatments that are recommended include cnidium seed and honeysuckle flower. Another herbal treatment is tea tree oil. The proper dose of these substances can be recommended by physicians or nutritionists.

PROGNOSIS

Acne cannot be cured. However, it can be controlled in about 60 percent of patients with the drug isotretinoin. Improvement usually takes at least two months, and the problem may recur after treatment has been stopped. Inflammatory acne that results in the formation of scars may require one of the more aggressive treatments already described.

PREVENTION

There are no sure ways to prevent acne. However, the following steps tend to reduce flare-ups of the condition:

- Gently wash—do not scrub—the affected areas once or twice every day.
- Avoid rough cleansers.
- Use makeup and skin moisturizers that do not produce comedos.
- Shampoo often and wear hair away from the face.
- Eat a well-balanced diet and avoid foods that trigger flare-ups.
- Give dry pimples a limited amount of sun exposure unless otherwise directed by your doctor.
- Do not pick or squeeze pimples.
- Reduce stress.

FOR MORE INFORMATION

Books

Balch, James F., and Phyllis A. Balch. "The Disorders: Acne." in *Prescription for Nutritional Healing,* edited by Amy C. Tecklenburg, et al. Garden City, NY: Avery Publishing Group, 1997.

Bark, Joseph P. *Your Skin: An Owner's Guide.* Englewood Cliffs, NJ: Prentice Hall, 1995.

Chu, Tony, and Anne Lovell. *The Good Skin Doctor: A Leading Dermatologist's Guide to Beating Acne.* London: Thorson's, 1999.

Silverstein, Alvin, Robert Silverstein, and Virginia Silverstein. *Overcoming Acne: The How and Why of Healthy Skin Care.* New York: William Morrow & Company, 1992.

Periodicals

Billings, Laura. "Getting Clear." *Health Magazine* (April 1997): pp. 48–52.

Christiano, Donna. "Acne Treatment Meant for Grown-Ups." *American Health* (October 1994): pp. 23–24.

"Clearly Better New Treatments Help Adult Acne." *Prevention Magazine* (August 1997): pp. 50–51.

"Pimple Control Pill?" *Prevention Magazine* (May 1997): p. 132.

Organizations

American Academy of Dermatology. 930 N. Meacham Road., Schaumburg, IL 60173–6016. (847) 330–0230. http://www.aad.org.

ADDICTION

DEFINITION

Addiction is a dependence on a substance, such as the drug heroin, or a type of behavior, such as gambling. The dependence is so strong that it may seem as if the person is unable to break away from the dependence.

DESCRIPTION

At one time, the term "addiction" was used almost exclusively for substance addiction. That is, addicts were thought of as people who were totally dependent on drugs such as heroin, cocaine, nicotine, or alcohol. That form of addiction is now known as "substance addiction."

Experts also recognize that people can become addicted to certain behaviors. Some individuals may develop a dependence on gambling, shopping, sexual activity, eating, or many other activities. Addictions of this kind are sometimes called "process addictions."

The costs associated with addiction cannot be calculated. They go beyond the actual dollar amount that individuals spend. Addictions cause enormous personal harm to not only the addict, but to their families and friends as well. People who become addicted to drugs may develop any number of health problems. They may also experience personality changes and lose the ability to interact with other people socially.

Addicts may have trouble staying in school or holding a job. If they do hold a job, they may pose a certain risk to their co-workers, to their customers, and to any individuals with whom they interact. For example, a truck driver who is addicted to alcohol may pose a serious safety threat to other drivers on the road.

Addiction is also responsible for a host of societal problems. Because many addictions are very expensive, addicts may turn to crime in order to get the money they need. The business of providing addicts with the substances and activities they require has become a huge enterprise. Casino operators, tobacco and alcohol companies, and other operations are kept in steady business.

CAUSES

Addiction is a very complex behavior. Humans have been trying to understand its causes for many years. At one time, moral weakness was accepted as the primary reason for addiction. According to this theory, some people do not have the moral strength to withstand an addiction. Although still believed by some members of the general public, this theory is no longer accepted by professionals.

Today, researchers understand that a variety of factors can contribute to making a person an addict. Many events in a person's background may

WORDS TO KNOW

Detoxification: Withdrawal; the process by which a person gives up a substance or activity to which he or she has become addicted.

Impairment: An inability to carry on normal everyday functions because of an addiction.

Methadone: A chemical given to addicts to help them overcome their addiction to heroin.

Physiological dependence: A condition in which a person's body requires certain behaviors or the intake of some substance, without which it will become ill.

Process addiction: A condition in which a person is dependent on some type of behavior, such as gambling, shopping, or sexual activity.

Psychological dependence: A condition in which a person requires certain activities or the intake of some substance in order to maintain mental stability.

Substance addiction: A condition in which a person is dependent on some chemical substance, such as cocaine or heroin.

Tolerance: The ability of a body to endure a certain amount of a substance that had previously been too much for it to tolerate.

Twelve-step program: A plan for overcoming an addiction by going through twelve stages of personal development.

Withdrawal: The process by which a person adjusts to the absence of some substance or activity to which he or she has become addicted.

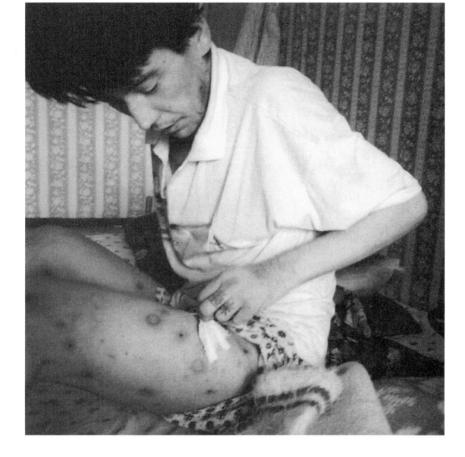

An opium addict peals gauze off an infected sore, caused by injecting opium up to ten times a day. (Reproduced by permission of AP/Wide World Photos)

lead him or her to begin using addictive substances. Some of these events include:

- Use of illegal substances by family members and friends.
- Poor family upbringing where love, warmth, praise, and acceptance are lacking.
- Lack of direction from the family about the proper ways to get along with others.
- Poverty, poor living conditions, or isolation from other people.
- Failure in school.
- Failure to develop the ability to get along with peers.
- Growing up in a neighborhood in which drug use is common and widely accepted.
- Frequent family moves to new homes.

• Medical use of prescription drugs for legitimate reasons. For example, a doctor may prescribe a drug to an individual suffering from back pain. While the drug is intended to alleviate the pain, it may also contain some addictive side effects. Such drug use is carefully monitored by the physician, but it is also up to the patient to use the drug only as prescribed.

Addictions grow stronger over time for two reasons. First, a person's body may become biologically dependent on the substance or behavior. That is, the body may begin to need and expect that it will receive a certain substance each day or each hour. If it does not receive that substance, it responds by becoming ill. When this happens, the person is said to be physiologically dependent on the substance or activity.

IN MANY CASES, ADDICTIONS INVOLVE BOTH PHYSIOLOGICAL AND PSYCHOLOGICAL ASPECTS.

This explanation has been used for addictive behavior as well as addictive substances. Some types of behavior cause a person to become very excited. Their body chemistry may actually

Counseling is often used to help people overcome their addictions. Both individual and group counseling are common treatments for addiction. (© 1994 Joseph R. Siebert, Ph.D. Reproduced by permission of Custom Medical Stock Photo.)

change as they win a jackpot or make another sexual conquest. Over time, body chemistry may demand repetition of the activities that produced this level of excitement.

People can also become psychologically addicted to substances and activities. That is, the substance or activity makes them feel happy, more self-confident, or better in some other way. In order to keep experiencing these feelings, they believe they must continue to use the substance or activity that gave them these feelings. In this case, a person is said to be psychologically dependent. In many cases, addictions involve both physiological and psychological aspects.

SYMPTOMS

All forms of addictions have some common symptoms, including:

- **Loss of control.** Addicts are unable to manage their behavior or their use of a substance. They may decide to quit the behavior or using the substance one day and then fall back into the habit the next day.
- **Tolerance.** In most forms of addiction, a person needs more and more of the substance or behavior over time. Early in an addiction, a person may need only one "hit" of heroin a day. A few months later, he or she may need two, six, or a dozen "hits" to get the same response.
- **Impairment.** Addicts often continue to use a substance or demonstrate a behavior even when they know the undesirable effects it may have. For example, a gambling addict may continue to wager money even though he or she has lost everything in previous gambling experiences.

DIAGNOSIS

Diagnosis of an addiction may be made by a medical doctor or by a mental health professional. Often, patients go for help because they feel they can no longer deal with their addictive behavior by themselves. Sometimes family or friends intervene and bring the patient for diagnosis and treatment. In some cases, individuals are brought to the attention of professionals because of legal problems related to their addiction.

The standards used for diagnosing addiction include the three symptoms listed under *Symptoms*. A person who displays these three symptoms is diagnosed as being addicted to some substance or type of behavior.

TREATMENT

There are many treatments available for people who suffer from addiction. These treatments are designed to deal with one or both forms of addiction: physiological and psychological. For example, people who are addicted to certain substances must often go through withdrawal therapy. Withdrawal therapy involves placing patients in a protected area where they are no longer allowed to use and where they have no access to the substance to which they are addicted.

This form of withdrawal therapy is sometimes called "drug detoxification." The term means that the toxins (poisons) in a person's system caused by drug addiction are being removed from the body.

Withdrawal therapy can be very difficult. The person's body may still be expecting its daily ration of the abusive substance. When the substance is not provided, the body may react strongly. Nausea, vomiting, pain, and hallucinations are common side effects of withdrawal therapy. In some cases, patients must be physically restrained to help them get through this period.

Medications are also available for treating addictions. Perhaps the best known example is methadone. Methadone is a chemical that has many properties similar to heroin. For example, it is addictive, just as heroin is. But methadone does not have the narcotic effects of heroin. A narcotic is a substance that dulls the senses and makes a person drowsy and sleepy. People who are addicted to heroin may be treated by giving them methadone instead. Ideally, the methadone treatment can very slowly be reduced until the patient is no longer addicted to either drug.

Various forms of counseling are also used to treat addictions. The theory behind counseling is that people become addicts because of serious problems in their lives. If those problems can be resolved, they may be less inclined to depend on addictive substances or behavior.

In some cases, one-on-one counseling may work best. An addict meets regularly with a trained mental health worker, and the two discuss the patient's life and try to find solutions to problems that may have led to addiction. Group counseling is another option. People with common addictions may meet with a professional counselor to discuss their problems.

Perhaps the best-known examples of group counseling are the so-called 12-step programs. The original 12-step program was Alcoholics Anonymous (AA). The term "12-step" comes from the stages of recovery through which AA members are expected to pass. The AA 12-step model is now used by other groups working to overcome other types of addiction.

Alternative Treatment

Acupuncture (a Chinese therapy technique where fine needles puncture the body) has been used to decrease withdrawal symptoms. Meditation and yoga have been suggested to help control behavior addictions.

PROGNOSIS

The prognosis for addictions is varied. Many factors are involved in determining whether a person can recover from an addiction, including:

- The substance or activity to which a person is addicted
- The reasons for the addiction
- The length of time the addiction has existed
- The patient's desire to be cured of the addiction
- The amount and type of support available to the addict

Medications may be successful in treating the immediate symptoms of some addictions. But recovery is likely to be partial and temporary unless underlying issues that led to the addiction have been resolved.

PREVENTION

One way to prevent addictions is to eliminate the substances and activities to which one may become addicted. One major thrust of the drug prevention program in the United States is to prevent illegal drugs from entering the country. People who support this method of prevention argue that if illegal drugs are not available, people cannot become addicted to them. Similarly, people who are concerned about addictions to gambling argue that legal gambling should not be permitted. They claim that if gambling casinos do not exist, people are less likely to become addicted to them.

Another approach to prevention is to deal with the kinds of problems that lead to addiction. People who grow up in warm, supportive, healthy, financially secure environments may be less likely to become dependant on certain substances and activities to achieve happiness or security. In this regard, improving family structures, home life, and social institutions is an important step in preventing addictions.

See also: Alcoholism.

FOR MORE INFORMATION

Books

Carnes, Patrick. *Out of the Shadows: Understanding Sexual Addiction.* Center City, MN: Compcare Publications, 1992.

Horvath, A. Thomas, Reid K. Hester, and G. Alan Marlatt. *Sex, Drugs, Gambling & Chocolate: A Workbook for Overcoming Addictions.* San Luis Obispo, CA: Impact Publishers, 1999.

Landau, Elaine. *Hooked: Talking about Addictions*. Brookfield, CT: Millbrook Press, 1995.

Peel, Stanton, and Archie Brodsky, with Mary Arnold. *The Truth about Addiction and Recovery*. New York: Simon and Schuster, 1991.

Smith, Miriam, et al. *Addiction: The 'High' That Brings You Down*. Hillsdale, NJ: Enslow Publishers, 1997.

West, James W., and Betty Ford. *The Betty Ford Center Book of Answers: Help for Those Struggling with Substance Abuse and for the People Who Love Them*. New York: Pocket Books, 1997.

Organizations

Al-Anon Family Groups, PO Box 182, Madison Square Station, New York, NY 10159. http://www.al-anon-alateen.org.

Center for Substance Abuse Prevention, 1010 Wayne Avenue, Suite 850, Silver Springs, MD 20910. (800) 729–6686.

National Institute on Drug Abuse, Department of Health and Human Services, 200 Independence Avenue SW, Washington, DC 20201. (301) 443–3673.

Web sites

"About Drug Addiction and Drug Abuse." [Online] http://www.addiction2.com/faq.htm (accessed on October 5, 1999).

"Addiction Resource Guide." [Online] http://www.hubplace.com/addictions (accessed on October 5, 1999).

"Alcoholism/Drug/Teen/Gambling Treatment Information."

[Online] http://www.robertperkinson.com (accessed on March 27, 1999).

"Gambling Addiction." [Online] http://addictionrecov.org/addicgam.htm (accessed on March 27, 1999).

The National Center on Addiction and Substance Abuse at Columbia University. [Online] http://www.casacolumbia.org (accessed on June 15, 1999).

The National Clearinghouse for Alcohol and Drug Information. [Online] http://www.health.org (accessed on October 5, 1999).

AIDS

DEFINITION

AIDS is the abbreviation for acquired immune deficiency syndrome. The disease is caused by a virus known as the human immunodeficiency virus, or HIV. The disease was first recognized in the United States in 1981.

A person can be infected with HIV without developing AIDS. The virus can remain in a person's body for many years without causing serious health problems. During this period, the virus is said to be latent, or inactive. Eventually, however, most people who are infected with HIV do develop AIDS. Treatment of HIV patients involves trying to slow or stop the virus from spreading in the body's cells and treating or preventing diseases that develop when a person's immune system has been damaged by the virus.

DESCRIPTION

AIDS is considered one of the most serious public health problems in modern history. In 1998 the U.S. Centers for Disease Control and Prevention (CDC) estimated that between 650,000 and 900,000 Americans were HIV-positive. HIV-positive means that a person has been infected with the virus. The CDC estimates that as of 1998 some 300,000 Americans were living with AIDS.

Nearly half of all AIDS patients are gay or bisexual men. About one quarter are intravenous drug users. An intravenous drug user is someone who takes drugs illegally by means of injection with a hypodermic needle. About 18 percent of AIDS patients are women. In addition, between one thousand and two thousand children are born infected with HIV each year.

AIDS IS CONSIDERED ONE OF THE MOST SERIOUS PUBLIC HEALTH PROBLEMS IN MODERN HISTORY.

AIDS is a far worse problem in some parts of the world than it is in others. The World Health Organization (WHO) estimates that 32.2 million adults and 1.2 million children worldwide were infected with HIV or AIDS as of 1998. Most of these cases occur in the developing countries of Asia and Africa.

At one time, people were concerned that HIV could be transmitted by casual contact, such as shaking hands or eating in the same room with an infected person. Scientists now know that the virus is never passed during casual contact of this kind. HIV *can* be transmitted in several ways:

SEXUAL CONTACT. HIV can be transmitted any time two people exchange bodily fluids, such as semen or blood. Most forms of sexual contact involve some exchange of bodily fluids. The risk of contracting the virus increases if an individual has a high number of different sexual partners or practices unsafe sex. Unsafe sex refers to having sexual contact without using any method to prevent the exchange of bodily fluids. In the United States and Europe, most cases of sexually transmitted HIV infection occur during homosexual contact, that is, between two people of the same gender. In Africa, Asia, and other parts of the world, HIV is transmitted primarily through heterosexual contact, that is, between two people of opposite genders.

EXPOSURE TO CONTAMINATED BLOOD OR BLOOD PRODUCTS.
Early in the HIV epidemic, the virus was sometimes transmitted during blood transfusions. Blood taken from one person with the HIV infection was given to a second person for medical treatment, he or she also received the virus. Hemophiliacs (pronounced hee-muh-FIH-lee-ak; see hemophilia entry), people who require blood transfusions quite often, were especially at high risk for HIV infection.

In the 1980s, new rules were adopted for the screening of donated blood. Since that time, the rate of HIV infections from contaminated blood and blood products has been greatly reduced. However, HIV infection is still spread by this method among illegal drug users. These men and women often share the same needle with each other. When they do so, the blood from one person is easily transferred to a second person. If the first person is infected with HIV, the virus may be passed on.

NEEDLE STICKS. Health professionals sometimes poke themselves accidentally with a needle when drawing blood from a patient. If the patient is infected with HIV, the health professional may receive the virus from the nee-

WORDS TO KNOW

Acute retroviral syndrome: A group of symptoms resembling mononucleosis that are the first sign of HIV infection in 50 to 70 percent of all patients and 45 to 90 percent of women.

AIDS dementia complex: A type of brain dysfunction caused by HIV infection that causes confusion, difficulty thinking, and loss of muscular coordination.

Antibody: A specific protein produced by the immune system in response to a specific foreign protein or particle called an antigen.

Antigen: Any substance that stimulates the body to produce antibody.

Autoimmunity: A condition in which the body's immune system (the system that fights disease and infection) produces antibodies in response to its own tissues or blood components instead of foreign particles or microorganisms.

CD4: A type of protein molecule in human blood that is present on the surface of 65 percent of immune cells. The HIV virus infects cells that have

CD4 surface proteins, and as a result, depletes the number of T cells, B cells, natural killer cells, and monocytes in the patients blood. Most of the damage to an AIDS patient's immune system is done by the virus's destruction of CD4 lymphocytes.

Hairy leukoplakia of the tongue: A white area of diseased tissue on the tongue that may be flat or slightly raised. It is caused by the Epstein-Barr virus and is an important diagnostic sign of AIDS.

Hemophilia: Any of several hereditary blood coagulation disorders occurring almost exclusively in males. Because blood does not clot properly, even minor injuries can cause significant blood loss that may require a blood transfusion, with its associated minor risk of infection.

Human immunodeficiency virus (HIV): A transmissible virus that causes AIDS in humans. Two forms of HIV are now recognized: HIV-1, which causes most cases of AIDS in Europe, North and South America, and most parts of Africa; and HIV-2, which is chiefly found in West African patients. HIV-2, discovered in 1986, appears to be less virulent that HIV-1 and may also have a longer latency period.

dle stick. The risk of transmitting the virus this way is very small (virtually zero) when health professionals use standard procedures for drawing blood and handling needles.

PREGNANCY AND BIRTH. A woman infected with HIV can transmit the virus to her unborn child. The virus passes through the amniotic fluid (the fluid surrounding the unborn baby) and into the child's bloodstream. A young baby can also get the virus from an infected woman during breast feeding.

CAUSES

AIDS develops when HIV attacks and destroys certain types of cells that are part of the immune system. The immune system consists of all those cells, tissues, and substances that protect the body from infection by foreign bodies, such as bacteria. An important element of the immune system is a group of white blood cells that include helper T cells, macrophages (pronounced MAK-ruh-fages), and monocytes (pronounced MON-uh-sites). These cells attack foreign bodies and prevent them from causing disease and infection.

Immunodeficient: A condition in which the body's immune response is damaged, weakened, or is not functioning properly.

Kaposi's sarcoma: A cancer of the connective tissue that produces painless purplish red or brown blotches on the skin. It is a major indication that a patient has AIDS.

Latent period: Also called incubation period, the time between infection with a disease-causing agent and the development of the disease.

Lymphocyte: A type of white blood cell that is important in the formation of antibodies and that can be used to monitor the health of AIDS patients.

Lymphoma: A cancerous tumor in the lymphatic system that is associated with a poor prognosis in AIDS patients.

Macrophage: A large white blood cell, found primarily in the bloodstream and connective tissue, that helps the body fight off infections by ingesting the disease-causing organism. HIV can infect and kill macrophages.

Monocyte: A large white blood cell that is formed in the bone marrow and spleen. About 4 percent of the white blood cells in normal adults are monocytes.

Nucleoside analogues: A medication that interferes when HIV tries to make copies of itself inside cells.

Opportunistic infection: An infection by organisms that usually don't cause infection in people whose immune systems are working normally.

Persistent generalized lymphadenopathy (PGL): A condition in which HIV continues to produce chronic painless swellings in the lymph nodes during the latency period.

Protease inhibitors: The second major category of drug used to treat AIDS that works by suppressing the replication of the HIV virus.

T Cells: Lymphocytes that originate in the thymus gland. T cells regulate the immune system's response to infections, including HIV. CD4 lymphocytes are a subset of T lymphocytes.

Wasting Syndrome: A progressive loss of weight and muscle tissue caused by AIDS.

After it enters the body, HIV attaches itself to a certain part of these cells called the CD4 protein. The virus then takes command of the chemical changes that take place within the cell. It orders the cell to start making copies of the HIV virus. It eventually causes the cell's death. As the cell dies, it breaks apart and releases many new copies of the HIV. The new HIV cells then travel through the bloodstream and attack other white blood cells.

As white blood cells die, the immune system becomes weaker. The body is no longer able to fight back against infection. Infections that would normally be relatively harmless, such as the common cold (see common cold entry), can become life-threatening to someone who is HIV positive.

SYMPTOMS

A person who has been infected with HIV is likely to pass through three stages of the disease. Not all individuals experience all of the stages.

Acute Retroviral Syndrome

Acute retroviral syndrome is a term used to describe a group of symptoms that can resemble mononucleosis (pronounced MON-o-NOO-klee-O-siss; see infectious mononucleosis entry). Mononucleosis is a flu-like infection. Its symptoms include fever, fatigue, muscle aches, loss of appetite, upset stomach, weight loss, skin rash, headache, and swollen lymph nodes. These symptoms occur in 50 to 70 percent of all men who are HIV positive and in 45 to 90 percent of all women with the infection. The symptoms develop between one and six weeks after infection and last for two to three weeks.

Latency Period

After entering a person's lymph nodes, the virus becomes latent. Latency means that the virus is still present in the body, but that there are no signs of infection. Therefore, a person may appear to be perfectly healthy even though blood tests show that the virus is present.

HIV infection has an unusually long latency period. It may last for ten years or more. During this period, the virus continues to reproduce itself in the lymph nodes. As a result, certain abnormal conditions and symptoms may develop. These include the following:

- Persistent Generalized Lymphadenopathy (PGL). As HIV continues to reproduce, it can cause swelling of the lymph nodes known as persistent generalized lymphadenopathy (pronounced lim-fad-uhn-AP-uh-thee). The nodes become larger, but are usually not sore or painful. The lymph nodes most commonly affected are those in the neck, jaw, groin, and armpits. PGL affects between 50 to 70 percent of all patients during latency.

- Constitutional Symptoms. Many patients will develop low-grade fevers, fatigue, and general weakness. The virus may also cause a loss of appetite, a decrease in the body's ability to absorb food, and an increased rate of metabolism, the process by which the body converts food to energy. These changes result in a condition called wasting in which a person continually loses weight and energy.
- Other Symptoms. At any time during the course of HIV infection, the virus may cause problems with organs and tissues throughout the body. A common problem is a yeast infection in the mouth known as thrush. Ulcers and open sores can also develop in the mouth. The virus can also damage the digestive system. Patients may develop diarrhea or malnutrition as a result. The virus can also destroy cells in the lungs, kidneys, and nervous system. Damage to the nervous system leads to a general loss of strength, loss of reflexes, and feelings of numbness or burning sensations in the feet or lower legs.

Late-stage AIDS

Late-stage AIDS is the period of HIV infection when the virus has become very active and has started to cause massive damage to the immune system. One sign of late-stage AIDS is a sharp decrease in the number of white blood cells known as CD4 lymphocytes. The patient also begins to have more frequent and more serious medical problems, such as infectious diseases and cancers (see cancer entry). The infections that occur are called opportunistic infections. That term means that foreign bodies, such as bacteria, have taken advantage of the bodies weakened immune systems.

CD4 cell counts are an important indication of the course of the HIV infection. Doctors use these counts to determine how far the disease has developed and what treatments to use. About 10 percent of those individuals infected with HIV never reach this final stage of disease. Researchers do not know why these individuals are more resistant to the virus than others who do develop late-stage AIDS.

AIDS dementia (pronounced dih-MEN-sha) complex usually occurs late in the progress of AIDS. It is marked by loss of reasoning ability, loss of memory, inability to concentrate, listlessness, and unsteadiness in walking. Scientists do not understand how HIV causes AIDS dementia. There are no treatments for the condition.

Patients in late-stage AIDS may develop inflammation of the muscles, especially in the hip area. They may experience pain in their joints similar to those that occur with arthritis (see arthritis entry). Thrush and ulcers (open sores) in the mouth continue to occur during the late stages of AIDS. Another common condition of this stage is hairy leukoplakia (pronounced loo-ko-PLA-kee-uh) of the tongue. Hairy leukoplakia is characterized by a white area on the tongue that may be flat or slightly raised.

Patients with late-stage AIDS may develop a form of cancer known as Kaposi's (pronounced kuh-PO-seez) sarcoma (KS). KS is a form of skin cancer characterized by reddish-purple blotches or patches. The disease may also occur in the digestive tract or lungs. KS is one of the most common causes of death in AIDS patients.

DIAGNOSIS

HIV infection can be difficult to diagnosis. Its symptoms are often similar to those of other diseases. To aid doctors in diagnosing the disease, the CDC has drawn up a list of thirty-four conditions to look for. These conditions can be used to decide which of three categories a patient falls into. Those categories include the following:

- Definite diagnosis with or without laboratory evidence of HIV infection.
- Definite diagnosis with laboratory evidence of HIV infection.
- Probable diagnosis with laboratory evidence of HIV infection.

Many symptoms discovered during a physical examination suggest the possibility of HIV infection. Some of these are more reliable predictors than others. Hairy leukoplakia of the tongue and KS are examples of strong predictors of HIV infection.

The presence of HIV infection is always confirmed with one or more blood tests. The first of these tests is called an enzyme-linked immunosorbent assay (ELISA). A person who tests positive on an ELISA test is then given a second blood test. That test is called a Western blot or immunofluorescence (pronounced im-yuh-no-flur-ES-uhnts) assay (IFA). A combination of the ELISA and Western blot test is 99.9 percent accurate in diagnosing HIV infection. In rare cases where doubt still exists, a third test is available, the polymerase (pronounced POL-uh-muh-raze) chain reaction (PCR) test.

A variety of tests are available to track the course of HIV infection. Among these are blood counts that measure the number and kind of white blood cells present. Tests also track the development of opportunistic infections, such as damage to the nervous system, and cancers.

TREATMENT

Treatment for AIDS involves the following:

- Prophylactic Treatment for Opportunistic Infections. Prophylactic (pronounced pro-fuh-LAK-tik) treatment is treatment given to prevent disease. Certain symptoms, such as persistent weight loss, low white blood cell counts, and the presence of thrush, are used to determine when prophylactic treatments should be given. Three drugs used in treatment are

AZT shown at 25-times enlargement. (Reproduced by permission of AP/Wide World Photos)

trimethoprim-sulfamethoxazole (pronounced tri-METH-o-prim SULL-fuh-meth-OCK-suh-zole), dapsone, and pentamidine (pronounced pen-TAM-uh-deen).

- Treatment of Opportunistic Infections and Cancers. These treatments are often made more difficult because the organisms that cause the diseases may become resistant to the usual drugs used to kill them. In such cases, doctors have to look for other drugs with which to treat the infections. Both radiation therapy and chemotherapy (pronounced kee-mo-THAIR-uh-pee) can be used to treat some types of infections and forms of cancer.

- Anti-retroviral Treatment. Anti-retroviral treatments make use of drugs that attack and destroy the virus itself rather than treating the infections and diseases it causes. The first successful drugs of this kind were nucleoside analogues. A nucleoside analogue is a chemical that interferes when the virus tries to make copies of itself inside cells. If the virus cannot reproduce in cells, it cannot continue to damage white blood cells. The best known of these drugs is zidovudine (pronounced zie-DOE-vyoo-deen), sometimes called azidothymidine (pronounced AZE-ih-do-thi-mih-deen) or AZT.

One of the most serious problems in developing treatments for AIDS is that HIV mutates (changes) rapidly. In a short period of time, it can become resistant to drugs that could once kill it. As those drugs become ineffective against the disease, new ones must be found to replace them.

In 1997, the first of a new class of drugs was approved for use with AIDS patients. This class of drugs is the protease inhibitors and includes saquinavir (pronounced suh-KWIN-uh-ver). The protease inhibitors are now used by themselves or in combination with nucleoside analogues to kill the virus.

Stimulation of Blood Cell Production

Many AIDS patients have very low levels of white and red blood cells. People with low red blood cell counts often suffer from anemia (see anemia entry), a condition that causes weakness, exhaustion, and generally poor health. People with low white blood cell counts are unable to fight off infections. To protect AIDS patients against these conditions, drugs may be given to stimulate the production of both red and white blood cells.

Alternative Treatment

For many years, doctors were able to offer AIDS patients little assistance in treating their disease. As a result, patients became very interested in alternative forms of treatment. Among those treatments were a variety of Chinese and Western herbal medicines and specialized diets designed to strengthen the immune system. Patients also tried nonphysical methods, such as visualization. In visualization, a person tries to imagine what a virus looks like and what kind of battle is going on in his or her body. By this method, the person believes that he or she may have some control over that battle.

Patients have tried a variety of pain control techniques as well. These have included hydrotherapy (the use of water baths and treatments), acupuncture (a Chinese therapy technique where fine needles puncture the body), meditation, and chiropractic (pronounced KIRE-uh-prak-tik; therapy that involves manipulation of the spine).

PROGNOSIS

At present there is no cure for AIDS. At one time, however, a diagnosis of HIV infection was thought to be a death sentence. Today, that situation has changed. The development of new drugs and new ways of using those drugs has made it possible to prolong the life of an AIDS patient. Since the introduction of drug cocktails (the combining of two or more drugs) in the treatment of HIV infection, the death rate from AIDS in the United States and other developed countries has dropped dramatically.

The situation is quite different in some countries because the drugs used to treat AIDS are very expensive. People who are HIV positive in developing nations are seldom able to afford the expense of taking such drugs. The AIDS epidemic is, therefore, still out of control in most parts of the world.

PREVENTION

The ultimate goal of many AIDS researchers is to find a vaccine against the virus. If such a vaccine were found, people could be protected against the disease as they are against measles, mumps, and other infectious diseases. As of 1999 more than a dozen different vaccines were being tested.

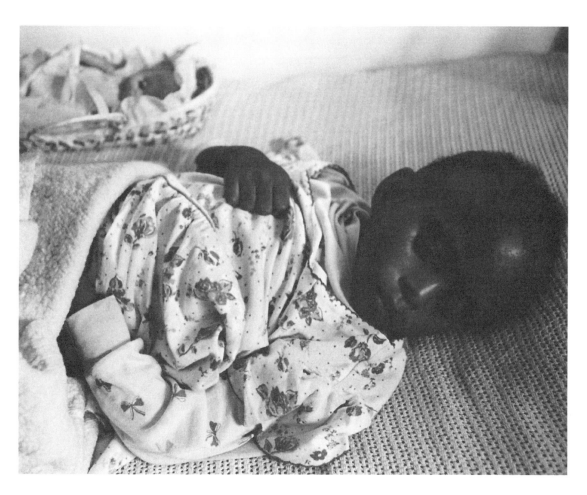

This seven-year-old Kenyan girl, looking much younger due to her illness, is suffering from pneumonia due to HIV complications. (Reproduced by permission of AP/Wide World Photos)

Until a vaccine is developed, the best protection against AIDS is to avoid contracting the HIV virus by doing the following:

- Limiting the number of sexual partners and practicing safer sex. The fewer partners one has and the better one knows those partners, the less the risk of HIV infection. The risk of transmitting the virus can also be reduced by some simple practices, such as using a condom.
- Avoiding the sharing of needles among intravenous drug users.
- Making plans to use one's own blood when major surgery is planned. By doing so, there is no risk of contracting HIV from the blood of an infected donor.
- Observing normal and standard procedures for handling needles and blood products by health care professionals. These procedures include the wearing of face masks and gloves when working with patients.
- Having an HIV test as soon as one suspects that he or she may have been infected with the virus. In general, the sooner one knows that infection has occurred, the more effective treatment can be.

FOR MORE INFORMATION

Books

Check, William A. *AIDS: The Encyclopedia of Health.* New York: Chelsea House Publishers, 1998.

Newton, David E. *AIDS Issues: A Handbook.* Hillside, NJ: Enslow Publishers, 1992.

Silverstein, Alvin, Virginia B. Silverstein, and Laura Silverstein Nunn. *AIDS: An All-About Guide for Young Adults.* Hillside, NJ: Enslow Publishers, 1999.

Organizations

AIDS Action. 1875 Connecticut Avenue NW, Washington, DC 20009. (202) 986–1300. http://www.aidsaction.org.

American Foundation for AIDS Research (AmFAR). 120 Wall Sreet, 13th floor, New York, NY 10005. (212) 806–1600. http://www.amfar.org.

Gay Men's Health Crisis, Inc. 129 West 20th Street, New York, NY 10011–0022. (212) 807–6655.

National AIDS Hot Line. (800) 342–AIDS (English); (800) 344–SIDA (Spanish); (800) AIDS–TTY (hearing impaired).

Web sites

AVERT-AIDS Education and Research Trust. [Online] http://www.avert.org (accessed on June 15, 1999).

HIV InSite: Gateway to AIDS Knowledge. [Online] http://HIVinsite.ucsf.edu (accessed on October 7, 1999).

ALCOHOLISM

DEFINITION

Alcoholism is the popular term for two disorders: alcohol abuse and alcohol dependence. The key element of these disorders is that a person's use of alcohol has repeatedly caused problems in his or her life. Alcoholism has serious consequences on a person's health and personal life, on family and friends, and on society at large.

DESCRIPTION

The effects of alcoholism on the body are quite far-reaching. Alcohol abuse can result in poor nutrition, memory disorders, difficulty with walking and balance, liver disease, high blood pressure, muscle weakness, heart problems, anemia (a blood disorder that causes weakness and fatigue; see anemias entry), problems with blood clotting, low resistance to infections, disorders of the digestive system, problems with the pancreas, low blood sugar, high blood fat content, reduced sexual abilities, reproductive problems, and weak bones.

Alcoholism can also lead to a number of personal problems, including depression, unemployment, family problems, and child abuse. The effects of alcoholism also extend to society at large. For example, alcohol is a contributing factor in about half of all deaths from motor vehicle accidents. The condition also causes or contributes to other social issues, such as homelessness, murder, suicide, injury, and violent crime. According to some estimates, more than $130 billion are spent each year in the United States to deal with alcohol-related problems.

ALCOHOL IS A CONTRIBUTING FACTOR IN ABOUT HALF OF ALL DEATHS FROM MOTOR VEHICLE ACCIDENTS.

CAUSES

Most scientists believe that alcoholism is caused by a number of factors including the physical make-up of a person, the environment in which they grew up, and other social and psychological reasons. One of the most important of these factors is heredity. Studies have shown that children who are born to alcoholic parents are four times more likely to become alcoholics than children who are not from alcoholic backgrounds. This trend holds true even when the children are raised away from their biological parents. Current research is being developed to identify other factors that contribute to alcoholism.

alcoholism

The symptoms of alcoholism can be broken down into two major categories: symptoms of acute (immediate) alcohol use and symptoms of chronic (long-term) alcohol use.

Acute Effects of Alcohol Use

Any amount of alcohol that a person consumes goes quickly to the brain. There it exerts a numbing effect. An individual may experience mild mood swings, or have trouble walking or maintaining balance. He or she may not be able to speak clearly and may lose coordination. The loss of coordination accounts for the high rate of accidents involving alcoholism.

As the level of alcohol in a person's blood increases, physical problems become more serious. Heart and respiration (breathing) rates slow down. At high enough alcohol levels, a person may fall into a coma and even die.

Chronic Effects of Alcohol Use

Long-term use of alcohol can affect virtually every organ system of the body:

- **Blood.** Alcohol can cause changes in all kinds of blood cells. It can reduce the production of white blood cells, for example, which weakens a person's immune system. This means that an individual loses the ability to fight off disease and infection. Blood platelets (pronounced PLATE-lit; blood cells that help blood clot) can also be damaged, increasing the risk of bleeding.

- **Gastrointestinal system.** Alcohol exerts its effects on nearly every part of the digestive system. It can damage muscles in the stomach lining, allowing stomach acid to flow upwards and back into the esophagus (pronounced ee-SAH-fuh-guss). This action causes pain and bleeding in the esophagus, which is the tubal passage through which food moves from the throat to the stomach.

- **Heart.** High levels of alcohol in the blood can cause a number of problems in the heart and circulatory system. Heart size tends to increase, heart muscles become weaker, and abnormal heart rhythms begin to appear. All of these changes increase the risk of stroke (the blocking of a brain blood vessel by means of a blood clot; see stroke entry).

- **Liver.** Alcohol interferes with a number of important chemical reactions that take place in

WORDS TO KNOW

Dependence: A state in which a person requires a steady amount of a particular drug in order to avoid experiencing the symptoms of withdrawal.

Detoxification: The phase of treatment during which a patient stops drinking, and harmful chemicals are removed from his or her system.

Tolerance: The condition under which a drug user becomes physically accustomed to a particular quantity of a drug, such as alcohol.

Withdrawal: Those signs and symptoms experienced by a person who has become physically dependent on a drug, exhibited when the drug's dosage is decreased or discontinued.

the liver. In order to combat this problem, the liver begins to enlarge and fill in with fat and scar tissue. These materials interfere with the liver's normal function and result in the diseases cirrhosis (pronounced suh-RO-suss) and hepatitis (pronounced hep-uh-TIE-tuss; see hepatitis entry). Both conditions can be fatal.

- **Nervous system.** Heavy drinking can cause blackouts and loss of memory. By some estimates 30 to 40 percent of all men in their teens and twenties have experienced an alcoholic blackout. Over time, alcohol abuse can also cause sleep disturbances and numbness and tingling in the arms and legs. Two major diseases of the nervous system are associated with alcohol abuse: Wernicke's syndrome and Korsakoff's syndrome. Both are caused by low thiamine (pronouonced THIE-uh-min), or B-vitamin, levels produced by excessive consumption of alcohol.

- **Reproductive system.** Heavy drinking has a tendency to reduce the size of both testicles and ovaries, the reproductive organs in men and women, respectively. As a result, there is a reduction in the number of sperm and eggs produced, which makes becoming pregnant more difficult.

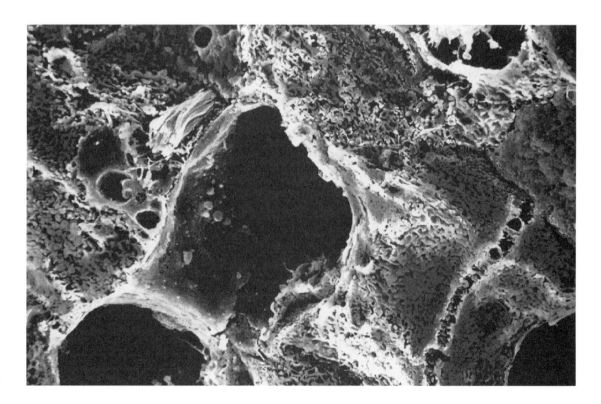

A magnified image of liver cirrhosis, a disease caused by drinking too much alcohol. (© Prof. P. Motta/Dept of Anatomy/University of "La Sapienza," Rome/Science Photo Library, National Audubon Society Collection. Reproduced by permission of Photo Researchers, Inc.)

Alcohol can also cause a condition called pancreatitis (pronounced PANG-kree-uh-TIE-tis), which is an inflammation of the pancreas. Damage to the pancreas, in turn, can result in bouts of diarrhea, diabetes (see diabetes entry), and other serious and painful conditions. If left untreated, a person may eventually lose their ability to produce the enzymes the body needs to digest food and may even die.

Babies born to women who consumed alcohol during their pregnancy may develop a condition known as fetal alcohol syndrome. This disorder may cause facial defects, reduced intelligence, and long-term behavioral problems in the child.

DIAGNOSIS

A number of factors may lead a doctor to suspect that an individual is an alcoholic. First, a person may seem to be accident-prone because they repeatedly report unexplained accidents and injuries. In some cases, an alcoholic's family may intervene and alert a physician. In other instances, an individual may realize the need for medical attention. The problem rests not so much with the amount of alcohol a person consumes, but with how alcohol consumption affects the person's well-being, job, educational goals, relationships, and family life.

One technique used by some doctors is called the CAGE questionnaire. It consists of four questions about the patient's drinking patterns:

- Have you ever tried to *Cut* down on your drinking?
- Have you ever been *Annoyed* by anyone's comments about your drinking?
- Have you ever felt *Guilty* about your drinking?
- Do you ever need an *Eye-opener* (a morning drink of alcohol) to start the day?

Based on personal interviews and family history, a doctor may diagnose one of two forms of alcoholism: alcohol dependence or alcohol abuse. In the case of alcohol dependence, a person literally seems to depend on alcohol consumption to get through a day. Some characteristics of alcohol dependence include the following:

- Increasing tolerance for alcohol, meaning that a person has become accustomed to consuming a certain amount of alcohol each day and must gradually increase that amount over time.
- Inability of a person to stop drinking without experiencing unpleasant physical and psychological effects.
- A tendency to over drink, meaning that a person consistently drinks more alcohol than he or she really intended or is unable to stop once he or she begins.

- Inappropriate drinking patterns, which include setting aside large blocks of time to drink, drinking instead of performing expected tasks such as attending school or work, or continuing to drink even when the person realizes that his or her job, education, or relationships are being affected.

Alcohol abuse leads to physical, medical, legal, or other kinds of problems as a result of alcohol consumption. A person who abuses alcohol may experience:

- Physical endangerment, such as driving while drunk
- Legal difficulties
- Problems in personal relationships or at work

Physical Signs of Alcoholism

Some surface signs of excessive alcohol consumption include broken capillaries (small blood vessels) on the face, a raspy voice, trembling hands, and chronic diarrhea. Upon further physical examination, a doctor may uncover some additional physical signs of alcoholism. Such signs include a visible network of enlarged veins just under the skin around the navel, fluid in the abdomen, a yellowish tone to the skin, decreased size of the testicles, and poor nutritional health. Laboratory studies may reveal an increase in the size of red blood cells, a reduced number of white blood cells, and an increase in the number of certain liver enzymes.

TREATMENT

Treatment of alcoholism takes place in two steps: detoxification and rehabilitation. Detoxification involves helping a person to stop drinking and ridding his or her body of the harmful (toxic) effects of alcohol.

Detoxification and Withdrawal

Detoxification is often difficult because a person's body becomes accustomed to the intake of alcohol. When alcohol is no longer available, the body goes through a period known as withdrawal. The ease and success of withdrawal depends on the person's prior drinking habits. The amount of alcohol consumed on a regular basis and the length of time the person has been drinking determines the difficulty of the withdrawal process.

Mild withdrawal symptoms may include nausea, achiness, diarrhea, difficulty in sleeping, excessive sweating, trembling, and anxiety. These symptoms often disappear in less than a week. Patients going through a mild withdrawal usually require no medical attention other than observation to see that their symptoms do not become worse.

An individual who has been dependent on alcohol for a long period of time may experience more serious withdrawal symptoms. Such symptoms include fever, increased heart rate, high blood pressure, seizures, and halluci-nations, which may take the form of delirium tremens (DT). A person suffer-ing from DT has uncontrollable shaking, panic attacks (see panic disorders entry), and severe hallucinations. DT usually begin about three to five days after the patient's last drink and may last up to a week. During this time, the patient must be monitored.

Patients going through serious withdrawal generally require medical at-tention. For example, they are often given sedatives to avoid the potentially life-threatening consequences of high blood pressure, rapid heart rate, and seizures.

Rehabilitation

Rehabilitation may involve the use of both medications and recovery pro-grams. Some chemicals act as a deterrent to drinking because when they in-teract with alcohol they produce nausea, vomiting, and other unpleasant phys-ical effects. One drug that has been used with some positive results is disulfiram (pronounced di-SUL-fuh-ram; trade name Antabuse). Drugs by themselves are often not very effective, however, since they do not deal with some of the rea-sons that may have contributed to a person becoming an alcoholic.

Recovery programs help alcoholics to understand why they abuse alco-hol and to find ways to avoid drinking in the future. Some of the most ef-fective rehabilitation programs involve peer groups in which recovering al-coholics meet regularly and provide support for each other. Perhaps the best known of these groups is Alcoholics Anonymous (AA). The AA recovery pro-gram is based on a 12-step model. These steps include the need to recognize the destructive power that alcohol has over an alcoholic's life, the damage that alcoholism has done to others involved personally or professionally with the alcoholic, and the need to turn to a higher power for help in overcom-ing the problem.

Alternative Treatment

The lives of alcoholics and those around them are quite stressful. Whether stress leads to alcoholism or is a direct result of alcoholism is up for debate. In either case, stress-relieving therapies may help a person avoid alcohol con-sumption. These therapies include massage, meditation, and hydrotherapy (water therapy).

The harmful physical effects of alcoholism can also be treated by alter-native therapies. Vitamins and mineral supplements, for example, can be used to treat malnutrition. The herb known as milk thistle is thought to protect the liver. Other herbs, such as lavender, skullcap, chamomile, peppermint, and yarrow, are believed by some to help an alcoholic through withdrawal. Acupuncture (a Chinese therapy technique where fine needles puncture the body) has also been recommended to decrease withdrawal symptoms and to prevent a return to drinking.

PROGNOSIS

Recovery from alcoholism is a life-long process. In fact, people who have suffered from alcoholism are encouraged to refer to themselves as recovering alcoholics, rather than recovered alcoholics. Probably because alcoholism is believed to be an inherited condition, the risk of returning to an alcoholic lifestyle never completely disappears.

The prognosis for many alcoholics is fairly good. Studies of alcoholics who have the support of family and friends, who are otherwise healthy, and who are motivated, indicate that 60 percent give up drinking for at least one year and, in many cases, for a lifetime.

PREVENTION

Prevention must begin at an early age. In the vast majority of cases, alcoholics begin drinking during their teenage years. Educational programs need to be aimed especially at those known to be at risk—those whose parents or other relatives are alcoholics. Efforts to develop effective prevention programs of this kind continue to be an issue within the United States's educational system.

FOR MORE INFORMATION

Books

Holmes, Pamela. *Alcohol.* Austin, TX: Steck Vaughn Library Division, 1991.

Pringle, Laurence. *Drinking: A Risky Business.* New York: William Morrow & Company, 1997.

Organizations

Al-Anon Family Groups, PO Box 182, Madison Square Station, New York, NY 10159. http://www.al-anon-alateen.org.

American Council on Alcoholism. 2522 Saint Paul Street, Baltimore, MD 21218. (410) 889–0100. http://www.aca-usa.org.

National Alliance on Alcoholism and Drug Dependence, Inc. 12 West 12th Street, New York, NY 10010. (212) 206–6779.

Web sites

Alcoholism—Home Page. [Online] http://www.alcoholism.about.com (accessed on June 15, 1999).

Alcoholism.Net. [Online] http://www.alcoholism.net (accessed on June 15, 1999).

ALLERGIES

DEFINITION

Allergies are abnormal reactions of the immune system to substances that are otherwise harmless.

DESCRIPTION

Allergies are among the most common medical disorders. By some estimates more than one in every five Americans suffer from some form of allergy. This statistic holds true throughout the world. Allergies are the single most common reason for absence from school, and they are the major cause of hours lost from work.

An allergy is a type of immune reaction. Normally, the immune system protects the body against harmful invaders, like bacteria and viruses. These invaders carry distinctive markers on their outside surface called antigens (pronounced an-TIH-juns). The immune system produces special molecules called antibodies when it finds an antigen. The antibodies attach themselves to the antigens. The antigen-antibody combination sets off a series of changes in the body, which protect the body from infection and disease.

This same sequence of events can also occur with harmless invaders, such as dust and pollen. This response by the immune system is known as an allergy. The markers on the otherwise harmless invaders are known as allergens (pronounced AL-er-jins).

Allergens can enter the body through four main routes: the nose and mouth, the gastrointestinal (digestive) tract, the skin, and the circulatory (blood) system.

- Allergens in the air can cause hay fever (see hay fever entry), asthma (pronounced AZ-muh; see asthma entry), or conjunctivitis (pink eye; see conjunctivitis entry).
- Allergens in food can cause itching and swelling of the lips and throat, cramps, and diarrhea. If they get into the blood, the allergens

WORDS TO KNOW

Allergen: A substance that causes an allergic reaction.

Anaphylaxis: An increased sensitivity to an allergen causing dilation (expansion) of blood vessels and tightening of muscles. Anaphylaxis can result in sharp drops in blood pressure, difficulty in breathing, and death if left untreated.

Antibody: A chemical produced by the immune system in response to an antigen.

Asthma: A lung condition in which airways become narrowed, causing wheezing, coughing, and shortness of breath.

Contact dermatitis: Inflammation of the skin caused by exposure to an allergen.

Histamine: A chemical released by mast cells that causes cells to become leaky and irritates nerve cells, causing pain.

Mast cells: A type of cell that makes up the immune system that releases histamine when stimulated by immunoglobin type E, a molecule released by white blood cells.

can cause hives or more serious reactions. Hives are red, itchy blotches on the skin. Food allergens can also cause anaphylaxis (pronounced a-neh-feh-LAK-siss). Anaphylaxis (or anaphylactic shock) is a life-threatening condition in which tissues swell up and begin to close the throat. A person may go into convulsion or a coma.

• Allergens that come into contact with the skin can cause reddening, itching, and blistering. This condition is called contact dermatitis (pronounced der-muh-TIE-tis). Skin reactions can also occur when allergens enter the body through other routes, such as the mouth or nose.

• Allergens can enter the body through bites and stings or drug administration (injections or shots). In such cases, the allergens go directly into the bloodstream. They are then carried to other parts of the body where they can exert their effects.

People with allergies are not equally sensitive to all allergens. A person may be allergic to some kinds of food but not affected by breathing in dust or pollen. Sensitivity to allergens can also change over time. A person may become more (or less) allergic to certain allergens as he or she grows older.

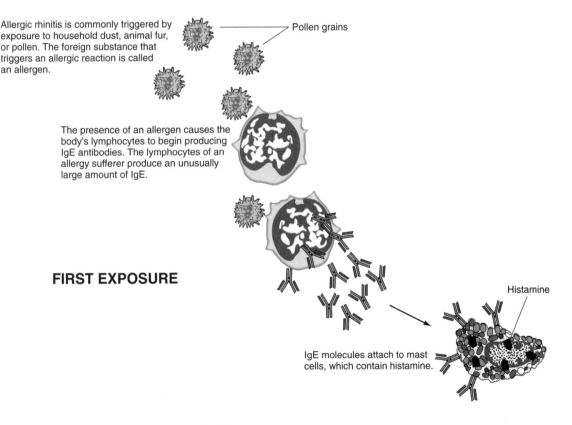

Allergic rhinitis is commonly triggered by exposure to household dust, animal fur, or pollen. The foreign substance that triggers an allergic reaction is called an allergen.

Pollen grains

The presence of an allergen causes the body's lymphocytes to begin producing IgE antibodies. The lymphocytes of an allergy sufferer produce an unusually large amount of IgE.

FIRST EXPOSURE

Histamine

IgE molecules attach to mast cells, which contain histamine.

Allergy flow chart. (Illustration by Hans & Cassidy)

allergies

When allergens enter the body, they set off a series of reactions. The first of these reactions occurs when the allergens come into contact with lymphocytes (pronounced LIM-fuh-sites), a type of white blood cells. Lymphocytes produce a special kind of marker molecule known as immunoglobulin (pronounced IM-yuh-no-GLOB-yuh-lin) type E (IgE). IgE molecules search out and attach themselves to a second kind of cell, called mast cells.

Mast cells manufacture a chemical known as histamine (pronounced HISS-tuh-meen). When IgE molecules attach themselves to a mast cell, the cell begins to release large amounts of histamine into blood vessels, nerves, and other tissue around it. Histamine causes changes in the cells with which it comes into contact. For example, it causes blood vessels to become leaky. Fluid escapes from the blood vessel, causing swelling and redness in surrounding tissue.

Histamine also causes nerve cells to become more sensitive, producing pain and irritation. All of these changes result in the familiar symptoms of an allergic reaction: redness, swelling, pain, and itching.

Common Allergens

The most common allergens in the air are:

- Animal fur and dander (dry skin that is shed)
- Cigarette smoke
- Dust
- House mites
- Mold spores (seeds)
- Plant pollen
- Solvents (chemicals used in cleaning)

Common food allergens include:

- Eggs
- Fish and shellfish
- Food additives
- Milk
- Nuts, especially peanuts, walnuts, and Brazil nuts
- Wheat

The following types of drugs often cause allergic reactions:

- Flu vaccines
- Gamma globulin (pronounced GA-muh GLAH-byu-lun), which are used to treat infectious diseases such as measles (see measles entry) and hepatitis (see hepatitis entry)

CAN YOU INHERIT ALLERGIES?

Specific kinds of allergies are not inherited. But the tendency to develop *some* kinds of allergies can be. This pattern is thought to result from the body's tendency to produce IgE. The more IgE the body produces, the more likely a person is to have allergies. IgE is a hereditary trait. Some people's bodies naturally produce more or less of the chemical, a trait they can pass on to their children.

If neither parent has allergies, the chance of a child developing an allergy is no more than 20 percent. If one parent has allergies, the chance rises to as high as 50 percent. If both parents have allergies, the chance can be as high as 75 percent.

- Penicillin and other antibiotics

Common causes of contact dermatitis include the following:

- Latex products (such as rubber gloves)
- Nickel or nickel alloys
- Poison ivy, poison oak, and poison sumac

Insects or other animals whose bites or stings can cause allergies include the following:

- Bees, wasps, hornets, and yellow jackets
- Fleas
- Mosquitoes

SYMPTOMS

Symptoms depend on the specific kind of allergic reaction. Allergens in the air can cause an itchy, runny nose with post-nasal drip. Post-nasal drip occurs when fluid runs out of the back of the nose into the throat. When this happens, the throat can become scratchy and irritated. The thin membrane around the eye can also become irritated by allergens in the air. When this happens, the eye becomes red and itchy and begins to produce tears. Severe reaction to allergies may cause a disease called asthma. The symptoms of asthma include wheezing, coughing, and shortness of breath.

Food allergens can cause a variety of symptoms depending on a person's sensitivity to the allergen and the part of the body to which it goes. In the mouth and throat, an allergen can cause swelling and tingling in the lips, tongue, or throat. In the stomach, it can cause nausea, cramps, and diarrhea.

Contact dermatitis is marked by red, itchy skin that may develop skin blisters that ooze fluid.

Allergic reactions that spread throughout the body can occur with any kind of allergen. They tend to be more common, however, with allergens that enter the bloodstream through an insect bite or injection. Anaphylaxis is one of the most dangerous of these reactions.

DIAGNOSIS

Diagnosis of allergies usually occurs in two steps. First, a doctor takes a medical history of the patient. He or she tries to find some connection between an allergic reaction and a particular allergen, such as a specific food or insect bite.

Second, direct tests can be carried out to discover the allergens to which a patient might be sensitive. In skin patch tests, for example, small amounts of many different allergens are placed directly on a person's skin. Any reaction that occurs to an allergen indicates that the person is allergic to that allergen.

TREATMENT

A large number of prescription and over-the-counter drugs are available for treating allergic reactions. Most of these work by interfering with the action of histamine on cells. Other drugs counteract the effects of histamine. They stimulate other systems or reduce immune responses in general.

Antihistamines

Antihistamines prevent histamine from exerting its effect on nasal (nose) cells. They can be used after an allergic reaction has begun. But they are more effective if used preventively, before symptoms appear. Many people take an antihistamine every day, whether they feel uncomfortable or not.

A wide variety of antihistamines is available. They are among the most widely sold of all drugs. Older types of antihistamines often caused drowsiness as a side effect. Included among these drugs are diphenhydramine (pronounced DIE-fen-HI-druh-meen, trade name Benadryl), chlorpheniramine (pronounced KLOR-fen-er-uh-meen, trade name Chlor-trimeton), brompheniramine (pronounced BROM-fen-er-uh-meen, trade name Dimetane), and clemastine (pronounced KLEM-uh-steen, trade name Tavist).

Newer antihistamines do not cause drowsiness. They are available by prescription and include drugs such as astemizole (pronounced a-STEM-uh-zole, trade name Hismanal), loratadine (luh-RAT-uh-deen, trade name Claritin), and

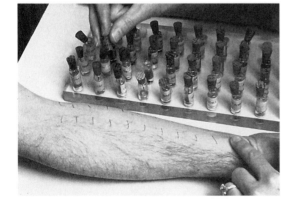

Allergy scratch test. (Reproduced by permission of Custom Medical Stock Photo)

fexofenadine (pronounced fex-o-FEN-uh-deen, trade name Allegra). One of the most popular antihistamines was terfenadine (pronounced tir-FEN-uh-deen, trade name Seldane), the original non-drowsiness medication. It was taken off the market by its manufacturers in 1998 because questions about its safety had arisen. In addition, a safer alternative, fexofenadine, had become available.

Decongestants

Decongestants have the opposite reaction on blood vessels from that of histamines. They cause the blood vessels to constrict and hold fluid better. Therefore, they reduce the swelling, itchiness, and redness usually caused by histamine.

Decongestants can be taken in the form of nasal sprays or pills. They should be used with caution as they can produce side effects such as headaches, increased blood pressure and heart rate, and agitation. If used for too long a period of time, they can also cause a rebound effect. In a rebound effect, the nasal passages become even more swollen and tender than they were originally.

Topical Corticosteroids

Topical corticosteroids (pronounced KOR-ti-ko-steer-oids) are drugs used directly on the skin that reduce inflammation of mucous membranes, the tissues that line the nose, mouth, and other body openings. Topical corticosteroids tend to work more slowly and last longer than other allergy medications. A person generally starts to apply these drugs before an allergic reaction (such as hay fever) begins. The drugs can provide an extended period of protection, throughout the period during which the allergen is present.

Mast Cell Stabilizers

Mast cell stabilizers prevent mast cells from releasing histamine, which means they prevent the symptoms of allergies from developing. The most common mast cell stabilizer is cromolyn (pronounced KRO-muh-lun) sodium. The drug is often taken year-round in the form of a nose or throat spray.

Immunotherapy

Immunotherapy is also known as desensitization. This treatment takes the form of a series of injections (shots) taken over long periods of times (months or years). The shots contain a chemical that reduces the ability of IgE to cause allergic reactions. The amount of this chemical in the injection is gradually increased over time.

The effects of immunotherapy often do not show up for long periods of time. With about 20 percent of all patients, they are never very effective. The most serious possible side effect of a desensitization injection is anaphylactic shock.

Bronchodilators

Allergic reactions in the lungs cause airways to tighten, which makes it difficult for a person to breathe. Bronchodilators (pronounced brong-ko-die-LATE-urs) are substances that reverse this action. They cause air passages to dilate, or become more open, so that air flows more easily through them.

Bronchodilators are commonly used in serious asthma attacks. They are administered through nose or throat sprays. In the most serious cases, these drugs can be injected directly into the bloodstream. Some commonly used bronchodilators are adrenaline (pronounced uh-DREN-uh-lin), albuterol (pronounced al-BYOO-tuh-rol), various steroids, and theophylline (pronounced thee-OFF-uh-lin), a component of coffee and tea.

Treatment of Contact Dermatitis

Calamine lotion and corticosteroid creams can reduce the discomfort and itching of contact dermatitis. Overuse of corticosteroids can, however, lead to dry and scaly skin.

Treatment of Anaphylaxis

Anaphylaxis is one of the most serious conditions relating to allergic reactions. A person who goes into anaphylactic shock must be treated very quickly or he or she may die. The standard treatment for anaphylaxis is an injection of adrenalin, also known as epinephrine (pronounced EP-uh-nef-rin). People who are at risk for anaphylaxis often carry with them an Epi-pen, a small needle containing a dose of adrenalin.

Alternative Treatment

The most effective alternative to medical treatment for allergies is to avoid the allergens that cause them. A person who is allergic to peanuts, for example, should avoid eating peanuts or foods that contain them.

In addition, a number of natural products have been found to be effective in treating allergic reactions. Products that have been suggested as alternatives for each of the medical treatments that have been discussed include:

- **Antihistamines:** Vitamin C and the natural product known as hesperidin (pronounced he-SPER-i-din).
- **Decongestants:** Vitamin C, the amino acid N-acetylcysteine (pronounced uh-seet-uhl-SIS-tuh-een), and the minerals iron phosphate and potassium chloride.
- **Mast cell stabilizers:** The natural products hesperidin and quercetin (pronounced KWER-si-tin).
- **Immunotherapy:** The herbs echinacea (ek-i-NAY-see-uh) and milk-vetch root (astragalus, pronounced uh-STRAG-uh-luhs).
- **Bronchodilators:** The herbs ephedra (pronounced i-FED-ruh), khellin (pronounced KEL-un), and cramp bark.

Alternative Treatment of Contact Dermatitis

The use of certain herbs taken internally or applied directly to the skin has been recommended as a treatment for the pain and itching of contact dermatitis. One treatment consists of a paste containing jewelweed or chickweed applied to the skin. A cream containing calendula (pronounced KUH-len-juh-luh) sometimes relieves a rash. The use of certain drinks or pills made of herbs may also be effective against contact dermatitis.

PROGNOSIS

Some allergies become less severe over time, while others become more serious. Anaphylaxis and asthma are the most serious problems associated with allergies. Either can result in death if not properly treated.

PREVENTION

The best approach for dealing with allergies is to find out which allergens cause sensitivity and then avoid them to the greatest extent possible. If one is allergic to certain foods, for example, those foods must be avoided. Allergens carried through the air can be the most difficult to avoid. The best approach is to keep a house as clean as possible, to avoid animals that cause allergic reactions, and to be aware of other housekeeping activities that will reduce the number of allergens to which one is exposed.

See also: Hay fever.

FOR MORE INFORMATION

Books

Novick, N. L. *You Can Do Something about Your Allergies.* New York: Macmillan, 1994.

Weil, A. *Natural Health, Natural Medicine: A Comprehensive Manual for Wellness and Self-Care.* Boston: Houghton Mifflin, 1995.

Organizations

American Academy of Allergy, Asthma, and Immunology. (800) 822–2762. http://www.aaaai.org.

National Institute of Allergy and Infectious Diseases. Building 31, Room 7A-50, 31 Center Drive, MSC 2520, Bethesda, MD 20892–2520. http://www.niaid.nih.gov.

Web sites

The On-Line Allergy Center. [Online] http://www.onlineallergycenter.com (accessed on October 5, 1999).

ALZHEIMER'S DISEASE

DEFINITION

Alzheimer's (pronounced ALTS-hih-merz) disease (AD) is the most common form of dementia (pronounced dih-MEN-sha). Dementia is a disease of the nervous system characterized by loss of certain mental abilities. This loss is severe enough to interfere with normal activities and lasts at least six months. AD is not present at birth but usually develops during old age. It is marked by a decline in mental functions such as memory, reasoning, and the ability to plan.

DESCRIPTION

A person with AD usually has a gradual decline in mental functions. The first stages include a slight loss in memory, such as the inability to remember the names of people or objects. As the disease develops, a person loses the ability to carry out familiar tasks, to reason, and to exercise judgment. Moods, personality, and ability to communicate may also be affected.

People with AD typically die within eight years of their diagnosis. Some individuals may die within a year of diagnosis, others may live as long as twenty years. AD is the fourth leading cause of death among adults in the United States after heart disease, cancer, and stroke.

Between two and four million Americans have AD. That number is expected to reach fourteen million by the middle of the twenty-first century. The reason for this growth is that the U.S. population as a whole is aging (there are more older people than younger people).

One form of AD, called early-onset AD, affects people in their forties and fifties. But the majority of AD patients are older than sixty-five. About 3 percent of those between ages sixty-five and seventy-four have the disease compared to 19 percent of those between ages seventy-five and eighty-four, and 47 percent of those over the age of eighty-four.

WORDS TO KNOW

Dementia: Impaired intellectual function that interferes with normal social and work activities.

Donepezil hydrochloride (Aricept): A drug approved for use with AD patients that increases brain activity.

Ginkgo: An herb obtained from the ginkgo tree, thought by some alternative practitioners to be helpful in treating AD patients.

Neurofibrillary tangle: Twisted masses that develop inside brain cells of people with AD.

Senile plaque: Deposits that collect inside the brain cells of people with AD.

Tacrine (Cognex): A drug that may help improve memory in people with mild to moderate cases of Alzheimer's disease.

CAUSES

The causes of AD are currently not known. Research has produced some strong leads, however, and made possible the development of some promising experimental treatments. This research has been based largely on autopsies of people who have died from AD. These autopsies show that brain cells responsible for learning, reasoning, and memory have been damaged. They have become clogged with two kinds of abnormal structures known as neurofibrillary (pronounced noor-o-FIB-ruhl-ary) tangles and senile plaques.

No one knows how these structures cause AD, but researchers have some theories. They think the structures keep brain cells from functioning normally, which prevents the transmission of brain signals from one cell to another.

This discovery has led to the development of one class of drugs for the treatment of AD. These drugs increase the amount of neurotransmitters produced in the brain. Neurotransmitters are chemicals that carry signals between brain cells. The first two drugs of this kind were approved for use by the U.S. Food and Drug Administration (FDA) in January 1998.

What triggers the formation of tangles and plaques is not known. But researchers are pursuing some possible leads. First, inflammation in the brain may be a factor. A class of drugs known as nonsteroidal anti-inflammatory drugs (NSAIDs) may prevent inflammation and reduce the risk of AD.

Free radicals are another factor in the formation of tangles and plaques. Free radicals are very active chemicals that form in the brain and damage brain cells. Chemicals known as antioxidants react with and destroy free radicals. Vitamin E is a naturally occurring antioxidant.

Genetic factors seem to be important in the development of AD. Scientists have discovered certain gene defects that appear to be related to the disease. They have found that mutations (changes) in certain genes are connected with some forms of AD. However, research in this area is at a very early stage. Little information that can be used for treatment of the disease has been uncovered.

In spite of how little is known about the causes of AD, a number of risk factors have been identified. The most obvious of these factors is age. The older a person is, the more likely he or she will be to develop AD. Another risk factor is heredity. People whose family members have had AD, Down's syndrome (see down's syndrome entry), or Parkinson's disease (see Parkinson's disease entry) are more likely to develop Alzheimer's disease than those whose families do not have this history. People who have hypothyroidism

 The Alzheimer's Association has developed a list of ten warning signs of AD:

- Memory loss that affects job skills.
- Difficulty in performing familiar tasks.
- Problems with language.
- Confusion about time and place.
- Poor or diminished judgment.
- Problems with abstract thinking.
- Misplacing of things.
- Changes in mood or behavior.
- Changes in personality.
- Loss of initiative.

(reduced levels of thyroid in the blood) or have experienced head injuries are also at relatively high risk for AD.

Environmental factors have sometimes been proposed as possible causes for AD. For example, the ingestion of aluminum was once thought to be a possible factor in the disease. So far, scientific studies have not been able to confirm the role of any environmental factor in causing AD.

SYMPTOMS

The earliest symptom of Alzheimer's disease is memory loss. Older people often worry that they may have AD because they forget more easily. But memory loss by itself is not an indication that a person has Alzheimer's disease. Some memory loss is a natural part of growing old.

With AD patients, however, memory loss is progressive and, eventually, so serious that they cannot function normally. In the early stages, memory loss may simply mean that the person has forgotten where he or she left the

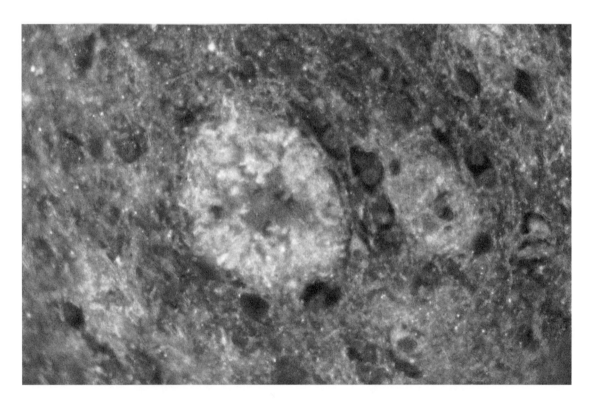

Diseased brain tissue from an Alzheimer's patient showing senile plaques, seen as darker spots surrounded by lighter halos. (Photograph by Cecil Fox/Science Source. Reproduced by permission of the National Audubon Society Collection/Photo Researchers, Inc.)

car keys. Over time, the problem becomes so serious that he or she can no longer remember where the car is parked or how to drive it.

As AD progresses, other symptoms appear. Patients can no longer perform routine tasks, like tying shoes or eating. Many patients develop sleep disorders or become confused or disturbed in the evening. These symptoms are sometimes referred to as "sunsetting." In the final stages of the disease, patients have problems eating, communicating with others, and controlling their bladder or bowels.

Other forms of mental disorders can cause any of these symptoms. In fact, about 20 percent of those who are first suspected of having AD turn out to have some other disorder. For that reason, it is essential that a person who experiences any of the symptoms discussed see a doctor for a thorough examination.

AS ALZHEIMER'S DISEASE PROGRESSES, PATIENTS CAN NO LONGER PERFORM ROUTINE TASKS, LIKE TYING SHOES OR EATING.

DIAGNOSIS

Diagnosis of AD is difficult. Its symptoms are similar to those of other diseases and to those of the normal aging process. For example, loss of memory and depression (see depressive disorder entry) are symptoms of AD, but they are also typical changes that take place as a person gets older.

The only way to be absolutely sure that a person has AD is to perform an autopsy of the brain after death. The autopsy will reveal tangles and plaques that characterize AD. But this method of diagnosis is of no value to a living person.

The main approach used in diagnosing AD is to rule out other disease possibilities. To do so, a doctor uses three methods: physical examination, medical history, and a variety of tests. A physical examination is used to make sure the patient is not suffering from some other medical problem, such as an infection or a mild stroke (see stroke entry). A medical history reveals changes in the patient's behavior. It also includes questions about drugs the patient is taking and other factors that may account for AD-like symptoms. Blood and urine tests, brain scans, and other tests are used to find out if other medical conditions exist that are causing the patient's abnormal behavior.

TREATMENT

There is currently no cure and virtually no medical treatment for Alzheimer's disease. Steps can be taken, however, to make an AD patient more comfortable and to protect him or her from potential dangers posed by the disease. Both physical and emotional support can be provided for the patients who are able to do less and less for themselves.

Caregivers also need assistance. Looking after a person with AD can be discouraging and exhausting. The caregiver needs support to prevent anger, despair, and burnout. Provisions also need to be made for the financial and legal problems that arise as an AD patient is less able to think and plan clearly.

Drugs

The two drugs currently approved for use with AD patients are tacrine (pronounced tak-REEN, trade name Cognex) and donepezil (pronounced do-NEP-uh-zil) hydrochloride (trade name Aricept). Both are neurotransmitters, which increase the ability of brain cells to communicate with each other. In this way, they provide some help in improving a person's ability to think and to perform normal daily activities.

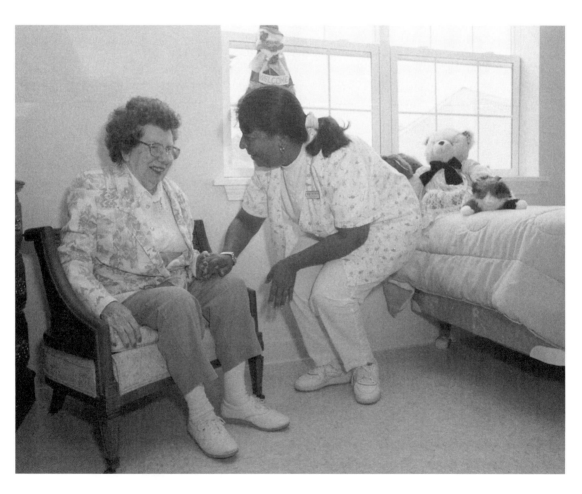

Some communities now offer full-time assisted living centers that cater exclusively to Alzheimer's patients. (Reproduced by permission of AP/Wide World Photos)

Tacrine has limited effects on patients in the early stages of AD. While it may delay their admission to a nursing homes by a few months, it is quite expensive and has side effects such as nausea, vomiting, diarrhea, stomach pain, indigestion, and skin rash. Donepezil has two advantages over tacrine: it has fewer side effects and has to be taken only once a day rather than three times a day.

Doctors sometimes prescribe other drugs for AD patients. Several preliminary studies have been made on older women who take the hormone estrogen, which is used to prevent osteoporosis (pronounced OSS-tee-o-puh-ROS-sis; see osteoporosis entry), or weakening of the bones. These studies show that women who take estrogen have lower rates of AD, and that those who do develop AD have slower disease progression and less severe symptoms.

Other early studies show promise in delaying the onset and even the risk of developing AD. The regular use of nonsteroidal anti-inflammatory drugs (NSAIDs) may reduce the risk of developing AD. Two antioxidants, selegiline and vitamin E, are also thought to delay the onset (beginning) of AD in some people.

Care and Safety of Individuals with Alzheimer's

As the course of AD develops, individuals require more and more care. At first, the problems are relatively simple. Perhaps they lose the ability to select appropriate clothing or comb their hair. Gradually, however, they may not be able to eat, wash, or otherwise take care of themselves.

Ensuring that people with AD eat properly is one problem. Sometimes they may simply not feel hungry or forget how to prepare foods for themselves. In advanced stages of the disease, they may have difficulty in swallowing, which means they ultimately will require the use of a feeding tube.

Eventually, many people with AD become incontinent, that is, they lose control of their bowels and bladder. Problems with incontinence are among the most difficult for family members to deal with, often convincing the family to have the AD patient moved to a nursing home where regular, professional care is available.

If a person with AD remains in the home, they should be provided with a calm, non-threatening environment. Regular exercise is also important. Professional help may be necessary to deal with emotional problems, such as anxiety, depression, and hallucinations.

AD patients must also be protected from a variety of physical hazards. They usually can no longer take long walks by themselves or drive a car. Safety devices such as grab bars in the bathroom, bed rails on the bed, and wider door openings may be needed. Electrical appliances may have to be unplugged when not in use, and the hot water heater thermostat adjusted to prevent the individual from being burned.

Care for the Caregiver

Family members and others who care for a person with AD have a difficult and stressful job that becomes even harder over time. It is not unusual for caregivers to develop feelings of anger, resentment, guilt, and hopelessness. Depression is a common problem among caregivers.

For many caregivers, the most helpful way of dealing with these feelings is a support group. Support groups consist of other AD caregivers and professional counselors. Caregivers have an opportunity to discuss their thoughts and feelings with others in the same situation. Contact numbers of AD support groups can be obtained from the Alzheimer's Association and from local social service agencies, the patient's physician, or drug companies that supply medications used to treat AD.

Outside Help, Nursing Homes, and Government Assistance

The problems of caring for an AD patient often become too much for family members. In such cases, a variety of outside care is usually available. For example, some local community agencies will bring a hot meal to the patient's home each day. Some adult day-care businesses exist where the patient can spend the day under professional supervision.

Eventually, temporary outside help may not be enough. In such cases, the family may decide to move the patient to a nursing home. This decision is usually extremely hard for both the patient and the family. It can also be very expensive. In addition, the most suitable home for the patient may be located at some distance from the family home, making regular visits difficult.

Several federal governmental programs can help with the cost of care for an AD patient. These include Social Security Disability, Medicare, and Supplemental Security income. These programs do not pay for long-term nursing home stays, but they may help with the cost of care, medication, and other expenses. Information about these programs can be obtained from local Social Security and Medicare offices.

Nursing home care can also be paid for through a variety of private insurance programs. In general, these programs tend to be expensive and are not available to many people with limited incomes.

Alternative Treatment

Ginkgo extract has been suggested as a possible treatment for AD patients. Some people think the herb may help relieve the symptoms of dementia. A natural product called acetylcarnitine (pronounced uh-setl-KAR-nuh-teen) has also been proposed as a method for improving the function of brain cells. At present, there is little scientific evidence for the effectiveness of either product. Other nutritional supplements, such as vitamin B_{12}, and folic acid have been recommended for the maintenance of good mental health.

PROGNOSIS

Alzheimer's is sometimes the immediate and direct cause of death. More often, patients die from conditions that result from their generally poor and deteriorating health. Pneumonia, cancer (see cancer entry), stroke, and heart disease (see heart attack and atherosclerosis entries) are the most common of these conditions. On average, people with AD live eight years beyond their diagnosis. Some die as soon as a year after diagnosis, while others survive up to twenty years.

PREVENTION

There is currently no approved method for preventing Alzheimer's disease. There is some hope that some of the drugs mentioned, such as estrogen, NSAIDs, and vitamin E, may be useful. Additional research is being conducted to provide more information.

FOR MORE INFORMATION

Books

Gillick, Muriel R. *Tangled Minds: Understanding Alzheimer's Disease and Other Dementias.* New York: E. P. Dutton, 1998.

Gray-Davidson, Frena. *The Alzheimer's Sourcebook for Caregivers: A Practical Guide for Getting Through the Day.* Los Angeles, CA: Lowell House, 1996.

Larkin, Marilynn. *When Someone You Love Has Alzheimer's: What You Must Know, What You Can Do, What You Should Expect.* New York: Dell Publishing, 1995.

Nelson, James Lindemann, and Hilde Lindemann Nelson. *Alzheimer's: Answers to Hard Questions for Families.* San Diego, CA: Main Street Books, 1997.

Powell, Lenore S., with Katie Courtice. *Alzheimer's Disease: A Guide for Families.* Reading, MA: Addison-Wesley Publishing Company, 1993.

Williams, Carol Lynch. *If I Forget, You Remember.* New York: Delacorte Press, 1998.

Organizations

Alzheimer Association. 919 North Michigan Avenue, Suite 1000, Chicago, IL 60611. (800) 272–3900. (312) 335–8882. http://www.alz.org.

National Institute of Aging. Alzheimer's Education and Referral Center. (800) 438–4380.

Web sites

Alzheimers.com [Online] http://www.alzheimers.com (accessed on June 15, 1999).

AMYOTROPHIC LATERAL SCLEROSIS

DEFINITION

Amyotrophic lateral sclerosis (ALS; pronounced ay-MY-eh-TRO-fik LA-ter-el skler-OH-sis) is a neurodegenerative disease. A neurodegenerative disease is one in which nerve cells are damaged or killed. In the case of ALS, the nerve cells that are damaged are motor neurons. Motor neurons are nerve cells that control movement. ALS is also known as motor neuron disease and Lou Gehrig's disease. Lou Gehrig (1903–41) was a famous baseball player who died of the disease.

DESCRIPTION

Under normal circumstances, muscles move because of messages sent from the brain through the spinal cord to the muscles. These messages are carried by motor neurons. In ALS, those motor neurons die off and messages from the brain to the muscles do not flow normally. Muscles do not respond when they are supposed to or as well as they should.

The death of motor neurons affects voluntary muscles. These muscles are controlled by conscious thought. They include muscles in the legs, arms, and trunk. These muscles normally move when a person wants them to move. As ALS develops, a person loses that control over these muscles.

ALS normally does not affect other kinds of muscles, such as those in the heart or digestive system. It also has no effect on the brain. Thus, ALS patients can usually think normally, although they lose the ability to move.

ALS affects approximately thirty thousand people in the United States. About five thousand new cases are diagnosed each year. Most cases occur in people between the age of forty and seventy. Men are slightly more likely to develop ALS than women.

ALS usually progresses slowly. In about half of all patients, it causes death within three years. About 80 percent of all patients die in less than five years, and a small number (about 10 percent) survive more than eight years.

WORDS TO KNOW

Aspiration: Inhalation of food or saliva.

Motor neuron: A nerve cell that controls a muscle.

Riluzole (Rilutek): The first drug approved for the treatment of ALS.

Voluntary muscle: A muscle under a person's conscious control.

CAUSES

No one knows what causes ALS. One or more factors cause motor neurons in the brain

ALS is also known as Lou Gehrig's disease, after the famous baseball player who died of the disease in 1941. (Reproduced by permission of Archive Photos)

and spinal cord to begin dying off. Nerve signals can no longer travel from the brain to the muscles. The patient is unable to move normally and he or she becomes weaker. Disturbed nerve messages can cause abnormal muscle movements that result in twitching and spasms. As muscle cells are not used, they begin to die off. The amount of muscle tissue decreases, causing a condition known as wasting.

Researchers have been unsuccessful in finding the cause of motor neuron death. There is some evidence that free radicals may be involved. Free radicals are very active chemicals that can damage living cells. Defective enzymes may also be a factor in the death of motor neurons. An enzyme is a naturally occurring chemical needed for many chemical reactions that occur in the body. Additional research is now being conducted to find out more about the cause or causes of ALS.

Two major forms of ALS are known: familial and sporadic. About 10 percent of all ALS cases are familial. As the name suggests, familial ALS is thought to be caused by genetic factors. Scientists have found that 15 percent of the people with familial ALS have a mutation (change) in a gene known as SOD-1. A parent with this mutated gene can pass it on to his or her children.

Sporadic ALS has no known cause. Certain chemical factors in the body, such as free radicals, may be involved. Or it, too, may result from genetic factors.

SYMPTOMS

The earliest sign of ALS is usually weakness in the arms or legs. This weakness tends to be more apparent on one side of the body than the other. Leg weakness may first become apparent by an increased frequency of stumbling on uneven pavement or difficulty in climbing stairs. Arm weakness may lead to difficulty in grasping or holding a cup, for instance, or loss of coordination in fingers.

Less commonly, the earliest sign of ALS is weakness in muscles of the mouth. This condition makes it difficult for the patient to chew, swallow and speak. He or she may become hoarse or tired after speaking or may have slurred speech.

Over time, ALS spreads to all voluntary muscle groups in the body. Later symptoms include loss of the ability to walk, to use the arms and hands, to speak clearly or at all, to swallow, and to hold up one's head. Weakness in the muscles of the respiratory (breathing) system can make breathing, coughing, and swallowing difficult. These conditions can result in the inhaling of foods or saliva (aspiration) which, in turn, can cause lung infections. Such infections are a common cause of death in ALS patients.

Respiratory problems can be reduced by inserting a mechanical ventilator in the person's throat. This breathing device can extend the patient's life, although muscle weakness and wasting are not reduced. Toward the end of the disease, ALS patients may be able to communicate only by means of eye blinks or a computer-assisted device.

OVER TIME, ALS SPREADS TO ALL VOLUNTARY MUSCLE GROUPS IN THE BODY.

DIAGNOSIS

The diagnosis of ALS begins with a complete medical history, physical examination, and neurological (nervous system) examination. An electromyogram (EMG; pronounced ih-LECK-tro-my-oh-gram) is part of the neurological exam. An EMG measures muscle function and tells how much damage has already occurred in motor neurons. A variety of blood and urine tests, X rays, and brain scans may also be conducted to rule out diseases other than ALS. ALS is rarely misdiagnosed after a review of all these factors.

TREATMENT

There is no cure for ALS. There are also no treatments that can significantly alter the course of the disease. In 1998 a new drug, riluzole (trade name Rilutek) was approved for use with ALS patients. The drug somewhat reduces the loss of muscle strength. It can extend the life of an ALS patient for an average of three months. No other drug or vitamin has been found to

Renowned scientist Stephen Hawking suffers from amyotrophic lateral sclerosis.
(Reproduced by permission of AP/Wide World Photos)

have any effect on the progress of ALS.

Physical therapy can often help a patient maintain strength, retain range of motion, and promote general health. Stretching exercises and swimming are often a part of these routines. Drugs can sometimes be helpful in treating certain symptoms of ALS, such as cramping.

Various health specialists can be of help in dealing with specific problems encountered by ALS patients. An occupational therapist, for example, can help design solutions to the patient's movement and coordination problems. He or she can also help design special devices and home modifications to improve the patient's mobility.

Speech therapists can train an ALS patient to deal with problems of swallowing and speaking. A nutritionist can help patients design diets that will be easier to swallow and yet still be nutritious.

In later stages of the disease, mechanical ventilators may be necessary. Mechanical ventilators help patients to breathe more easily and can help prevent aspiration. They can be inserted through the mouth or nose or though an opening in the throat. Modern mechanical ventilators are small and portable. They allow ALS patients some degree of freedom and mobility. Under the best of circumstances, ventilators are somewhat awkward and unpleasant devices. Some ALS patients choose to use them for only short periods of time or not at all.

Most ALS patients eventually require full-time nursing care. This care is not difficult to learn and can often be provided by family members. The physical and emotional burden for caregivers, however, can be enormous. They must learn to be aware of and to find ways of dealing with their own needs as well as those of the patient.

Support groups can help caregivers in this regard. Support groups consist of other people also working with ALS patients as well as professional counselors. Support groups are sponsored by both the ALS Society and the Muscular Dystrophy Association.

Alternative Treatment

There is no scientific evidence that any form of alternative therapy has been successful in treating ALS. A number of vitamins, herbal remedies, and other natural products have been tried but, thus far, none appears to have any success. As the causes of the disease are better understood, it is possible that some alterative therapies may be found to provide relief from the disease.

PROGNOSIS

ALS usually progresses rapidly and leads to death from respiratory infection within three to five years. The disease progresses most slowly in those who are young and have their first symptoms in the arms and legs.

PREVENTION

There is no known way to prevent ALS or to alter its course.

FOR MORE INFORMATION

Books

Atkinson, David R., and Debbie Atkinson. *Hope Springs Eternal: Surviving a Chronic Disease.* Virginia Beach, VA: Are Press, 1999.

Horn, Robert, III. *How Will They Know If I'm Dead?: Transcending Disability and Terminal Illness.* Boca Raton, FL: Saint Lucie Press, 1996.

The Muscular Dystrophy Association. *When a Loved One Has ALS: A Caregiver's Guide.* Tucson, AZ: The Muscular Dystrophy Association, 1997.

Schwartz, Morrie. *Letting Go: Morrie's Reflections on Living While Dying.* New York: Dell Books, 1997.

Organizations

The ALS Association. 27001 Agoura Road, Suite 150, Calabasas Hills, CA 91301–5104. (800) 782–4747. http://www.alsa.org.

The Muscular Dystrophy Association. 3300 East Sunrise Drive, Tucson, AZ 85718. (520) 529–2000; (800) 572–1717. http://www.mdausa.org.

Web sites

"Amyotrophic Lateral Sclerosis (ALS)." *National Institute of Neurological Disorders and Stroke.* [Online] http://www.ninds.nih.gov (accessed on June 15, 1999).

ANEMIAS

DEFINITION

Anemia is a condition characterized by abnormally low levels of red blood cells.

anemias

Cells require a constant supply of oxygen in order to stay healthy. Oxygen is delivered to cells by red blood cells, which pick up oxygen in the lungs. They carry the oxygen to cells through the bloodstream.

The oxygen-carrying molecule in red blood cells is hemoglobin (pronounced HEE-muh-glo-bin). Hemoglobin is a large, complex molecule. It contains an atom of iron at its center. Iron attaches itself easily to oxygen atoms. It is the iron in hemoglobin that actually carries oxygen to cells.

Anemia develops when the body has an insufficient supply of red blood cells and hemoglobin. When that happens, cells do not get the oxygen they need and begin to die off. A variety of medical problems may develop.

Types of Anemia

More than four hundred different kinds of anemia have been identified. Many of them are rare. Some are mild medical problems, while others are moderate or serious. Some are so serious that they may cause death. A few of the most common forms of anemia include the following.

IRON DEFICIENCY ANEMIA. Iron deficiency anemia is the most common form of anemia in the world. In the United States the condition primarily affects young children and women. About 240,000 children between the ages of one and two have the condition. About 3.3 million women of child-bearing age have iron deficiency anemia.

The onset (beginning) of iron deficiency anemia is gradual. There may be no symptoms at first. As the name suggests, iron deficiency anemia occurs when the body does not have enough iron to make all the red blood cells it needs. Red blood cells die off faster than they can be made by the body.

FOLIC ACID DEFICIENCY ANEMIA. Folic acid is a member of the vitamin B family. It is used in the production of new red blood cells. Some people do not get enough folic acid in their normal diet, so their bodies are unable to produce enough red blood cells. In other cases, the body may not be able to properly use the folic acid eaten.

Folic acid deficiency anemia occurs most often in infants and teenagers. Some important sources of folic acid are cheese, eggs, fish, green vegetables, meat, milk, and yeast. Smoking can also interfere with the body's ability to use folic acid.

WORDS TO KNOW

Aplastic: Having incomplete or faulty development.

Diabetes mellitus: A medical disorder caused by the inability of a person's cells to use sugar correctly.

Hemoglobin: A molecule found in red blood cells that contains an iron atom and that helps transport oxygen from the lungs to cells throughout the body.

VITAMIN B$_{12}$ DEFICIENCY ANEMIA. Like folic acid, vitamin B$_{12}$ is used to make red blood cells. The vitamin is found in meat and vegetables. Some symptoms of vitamin B$_{12}$ deficiency anemia are loss of muscle control, loss of feeling in the arms and legs, soreness of the tongue, and weight loss.

The most common form of vitamin B$_{12}$ deficiency anemia is called pernicious anemia. People between the ages of fifty and sixty are at highest risk for pernicious anemia. Some conditions that can lead to pernicious anemia are eating disorders (see anorexia nervosa and bulimia entries), poor nutrition, diabetes mellitus (pronounced DI-uh-BEE-teez MEH-luh-tuss; see diabetes mellitus entry), stomach problems, and thyroid disease.

HEMOLYTIC ANEMIA. Hemolytic (pronounced HEE-muh-lit-ik) anemia occurs when red blood cells are destroyed faster than they are made. In some cases, an infection can cause this problem. In other cases, the body's own immune system destroys the red blood cells. Some symptoms of hemolytic anemia include pain, shock, gallstones, an enlarged spleen, and other serious health problems.

THALASSEMIAS. Thalassemias (pronounced thal-uh-SEE-mee-uhs) are caused by the body's inability to manufacture enough red blood cells. The condition is a genetic disorder, meaning that parents who have a gene for the condition may pass it to their children. Genes are chemical units in the body that tell cells what functions to perform. In people who have defective thalassemia genes, cells have lost the instructions needed to produce red blood cells.

AUTOIMMUNE HEMOLYTIC ANEMIAS. An autoimmune disorder is one in which a person's immune system attacks its own body. The normal function of the immune system is to protect the body against foreign invaders, such as bacteria and viruses. But the immune system can sometimes become confused. It thinks that parts of the body are a foreign invader. In the case of autoimmune hemolytic anemias, the immune system attacks red blood cells, killing them just as it would destroy bacteria or viruses.

SICKLE CELL ANEMIA. Sickle cell anemia (see sickle cell anemia entry) is a genetic disorder. Cells receive genes that give them the wrong

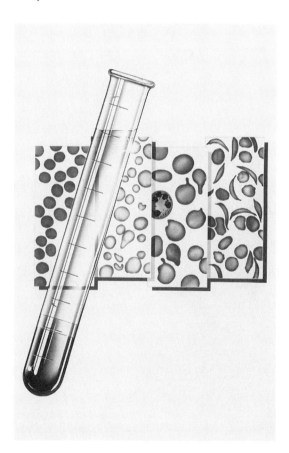

An illustration of normal red blood cells (left) and those in three different types of anemia (from left), iron deficiency anemia, megaloblastic anemia, and sickle cell anemia. (Reproduced by permission of John Bavosi and Custom Medical Stock Photo)

instructions for making red blood cells. Red blood cells are normally shaped like plump doughnuts. In sickle cell anemia, the cells are curved with sharp points. These cells easily stick to each other. They also stick to the walls of blood vessels. Clumps of sickled red blood cells can collect in a vein or artery and block it. This condition can cause pain, weakness, and, in extreme cases, death.

APLASTIC ANEMIA. Aplastic anemia is a serious form of anemia that can lead to death. The body makes too few of all kinds of blood cells: red blood cells, white blood cells, and platelets (pronounced PLATE-lits). Platelets are blood cells that help blood to clot. Aplastic anemia may be caused by a recent severe illness, long-term exposure to industrial chemicals, and the use of certain types of medication.

CAUSES

Anemia is caused primarily by one of three conditions. The first is bleeding. Bleeding results in the loss of red blood cells from the body. The second condition is a decreased rate of red blood cell production. Red blood cells are not produced as fast as they die off. The third condition is an increased rate of red blood cell destruction. Red blood cells die off faster than they can be replaced by the body.

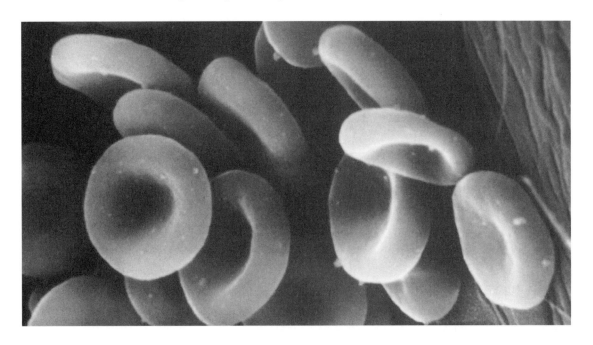

Magnified red blood cells floating inside a blood vessel. (Photograph by Dennis Kunkel. Reproduced by permission of Phototake NYC.)

Of these factors, bleeding is the most common cause of anemia. Bleeding can be a chronic or acute problem. A chronic problem is one that lasts for a long period of time. An acute problem is one that comes on suddenly and is quite severe. Some common causes of chronic bleeding include:

- Cancer (see cancer entry)
- Gastrointestinal (digestive system) tumors
- Other diseases and disorders of the digestive system
- Heavy menstrual flow
- Hemorrhoids
- Nosebleeds
- Stomach ulcers (see ulcer entry)
- Long-term alcohol abuse (see alcoholism entry)

Acute blood loss is usually the result of:

- Childbirth
- Injury
- A ruptured blood vessel
- Surgery

SYMPTOMS

Some common symptoms of mild anemia include weakness, fatigue, and a "run-down" feeling. Other signs include pale skin and a lack of color in the creases of the palm, gums, nail beds or lining of the eyelids. Someone who is weak, tires easily, is often out of breath, and feels faint or dizzy may have severe anemia. Other symptoms of anemia include:

- Chest pain, often accompanied by a choking sensation
- A strong desire to eat ice, paint, or dirt
- Headache
- Loss of memory or the ability to concentrate
- Inflammation of the tongue or mouth
- Insomnia (inability to sleep)
- Irregular heartbeat
- Loss of appetite
- Nails that are dry, brittle, or ridged
- Rapid breathing
- Sores in the mouth, throat, or rectum
- Sweating
- Swelling of the hands and feet
- Excessive thirst
- Ringing in the ears
- Unexplained bleeding or bruising

Additional symptoms related to pernicious anemia include:

- Problems with movement or balance
- Tingling in the hands and feet
- Confusion, depression, and memory loss

DIAGNOSIS

The first step in diagnosing anemia is usually to take a medical history. Since some forms of anemia are inherited, a doctor will especially want to discover if the condition has occurred with other members of the family.

The best way of diagnosing anemia is with a blood test. A sample of the patient's blood is taken with a needle. The sample is then studied under a microscope. The number, size, and shape of red blood cells can then be determined. This information tells whether the patient has anemia and, if so, what kind.

TREATMENT

Treatment differs for each type of anemia. Iron deficiency, folic acid deficiency, and vitamin B_{12} deficiency anemias are all nutritional problems. That is, the patient is not getting enough of certain essential nutrients through his or her diet. Problems of this kind can often be solved with nutritional sup-

---

MEETING YOUR NEEDS FOR IRON

Four groups of people have a greater-than-normal need for iron: infants, growing boys and girls, women who are menstruating, and pregnant women. Infants often lack iron because they drink primarily milk, and milk contains no iron. Growing boys and girls often don't get enough iron in their daily diet to keep up with their developing bodies. Menstruating women need extra iron because of the blood they lose during menstruation. And pregnant women lack sufficient iron because of the blood needed by their growing fetus.

These conditions are recognized in the U.S. government's Recommended Dietary Allowances (RDAs). An RDA is the amount of a vitamin or mineral that a person needs to take in each day in order to stay healthy. The RDA for iron for in-

fants one year of age is 15 mg (milligrams) per day. This number drops to 10 mg a day for boys and girls between the ages of three and eleven. During the teen years, however, the RDA for iron increases to 18 mg per day.

That standard stays the same for women until they reach menopause (the period when menstruation stops). It then drops to 10 mg per day again. For pregnant women, however, the RDA ranges from 30 to 60 mg per day. It is during this period that the human body needs iron more than any other time in life.

Most people can get all the iron they need by choosing the right foods. Beef, kidney, liver, beans, clams, peaches, and soybeans are all rich in iron. But pregnant women find it nearly impossible to get enough iron from their diet. They usually have to take iron pills in order to avoid anemia.

---

plements. The patient may need to take vitamin or mineral supplements that provide the missing nutrient. Patients should also be sure to eat foods that contain the vitamins and minerals needed to prevent anemia, including:

- Almonds
- Broccoli
- Dried beans
- Dried fruits
- Enriched breads and cereals
- Lean red meat
- Liver
- Potatoes
- Rice
- Shellfish
- Tomatoes

More serious forms of anemia may require surgery. Bleeding ulcers and certain types of stomach disorders are examples of anemias that may be treated surgically. In some cases, blood transfusions may be required. People who have lost large numbers of red blood cells may require a transfusion in order to avoid serious complications of anemia.

The most extreme form of treatment in such cases is a bone marrow transplant. All blood cells are made in bone marrow. Marrow is a fatty tissue found in the center of bones. People whose bodies make too few red blood cells may need a bone marrow transplant. Marrow from a healthy person is injected into the patient's bones. If successful, the healthy marrow begins producing red blood cells.

There is no cure for sickle cell anemia, autoimmune hemolytic anemia, and some other forms of anemia, therefore, treatment for these forms of anemia has two goals. First, steps should be taken to avoid complications. For example, a person with sickle cell anemia may require immunizations (shots) to protect against influenza, pneumonia, and other infectious diseases. Second, efforts should be made to relieve symptoms as much as possible. People with hemolytic anemia, for example, may be given shots of corticosteroids (pronounced kor-tih-ko-STIHR-oids), which help reduce inflammation and swelling that often accompany this condition.

Alternative Treatment

Practitioners often follow traditional medical treatments in dealing with anemia. That is, they may recommend nutritional supplements to replace lost iron or to improve general health. Certain iron-rich herbs may also be recommended. These herbs include yellow dock root, dandelion, parsley, and nettle.

Herbs may also be suggested to improve digestion. Improved digestion ensures that iron in foods is more likely to be absorbed by the body. Some herbs recommended for this purpose include gentian, anise, caraway, cumin, linden, and licorice.

Traditional Chinese treatments for anemia include:

- Acupuncture, which is a therapy technique where fine needles puncture the body, to improve the health of the spleen
- Asian ginseng, to restore energy
- Dong quai, an herb used to control heavy menstrual bleeding
- A mixture of dong quai and Chinese foxglove, to clear a pale complexion

PROGNOSIS

Prognosis differs for various kinds of anemia. Deficiency anemias usually improve after three to six weeks of treatment. Patients should continue taking supplements for six months to make sure the body has enough iron. Periodic tests may be necessary to make sure that the anemia has not returned.

Pernicious anemia cannot be cured. However, its symptoms can be treated with regular shots of vitamin B_{12}. This treatment usually works very quickly, often within a matter of minutes. There is also no cure for sickle cell anemia. Many patients, however, are able to lead reasonably normal lives with proper treatment.

Aplastic anemia can sometimes be cured with a bone marrow transplant. Thalassemias usually require no treatment. People are able to live normal lives with all but the most severe forms of the disease.

PREVENTION

Inherited forms of anemia cannot be prevented. Parents can often find out if they carry the genes for anemia. With this information, they can decide if they want to have children and pass those genes on to them.

Eating a well-balanced diet and avoiding excessive amounts of alcohol is a simple method to protect against deficiency forms of anemia. To be safe, a person can take nutritional supplements to ensure that he or she is getting enough iron.

Some methods of preventing specific types of anemia include:

- Avoiding lengthy exposure to industrial chemicals and drugs known to cause aplastic anemia
- Not taking medications or eating foods that may cause hemolytic anemia
- Receiving regular B_{12} shots to prevent pernicious anemia

See also: Sickle cell anemia.

FOR MORE INFORMATION

Books

Beshore, George W., ed. *Sickle Cell Anemia.* New York: Franklin Watts, 1994.

Uthman, Ed. *Understanding Anemia.* Jackson: University Press of Mississippi, 1998.

Organizations

Aplastic Anemia Foundation of America. P.O. Box 613, Annapolis, MD 21404. (800) 747–2620. http://www.aplastic.org.

ANOREXIA NERVOSA

DEFINITION

Anorexia nervosa is an eating disorder that occurs primarily among girls and women. It is characterized by a fear of gaining weight, self-starvation, and a distorted view of body image. The condition is usually brought on by emotional disorders that lead a person to worry excessively about the appearance of his or her body. There are generally two types of anorexia: one is characterized by strict dieting and exercising; the other type includes binging and purging. Binging is the act of eating abnormally large amounts of food in a short period of time. Purging is the use of vomiting or other methods, such as laxatives, to empty the stomach. An individual who suffers from anorexia is called anorexic.

DESCRIPTION

Anorexia nervosa was first classified as a psychiatric (mental) disorder in 1980 and has since become a growing problem in the United States. The number of cases has doubled since 1970, and experts now estimate that 0.5 to 1 percent of all white females may be anorexic. About 90 percent of all anorexics are female, although the number of males with the disorder is growing. The most common age at which the disorder first appears is fourteen to eighteen years. However, anorexia nervosa may begin later in life; some cases of the disorder have been documented in infants. Studies indicate that the disorder is increasing among women of all races and social classes in the United States.

WORDS TO KNOW

Amenorrhea: Absence of menstrual periods.

Binge eating: A pattern of eating large quantities of food in a short period of time.

Purging: The use of vomiting or other techniques to empty the stomach of food.

Anorexia nervosa is a very dangerous disorder. It has a very high rate of mortality (death). In addition, it can cause some serious long-term health effects. These effects include a reduced rate of growth, dental problems, constipation, stomach rupture, anemia (see anemia entry), loss of kidney function, heart problems, and osteoporosis (weakening of the bones; see osteoporosis entry).

CAUSES

The exact cause of anorexia nervosa is not known. However, a combination of factors are believed to contribute to the disorder.

Social Influences

American society places high value on thinness among women. Many consider being thin an essential part of beauty and young girls often think that they must be slender to be attractive. Being thin is also equated with social success. Images of girls and women in mass media (magazines, television, and movies) have been blamed, in part, for reinforcing such stereotypes. Some girls become anorexic as a form of copy-cat behavior. They imitate the actions of other women whom they admire. Extreme dieting may be one of these behaviors.

Occupational Goals

Some occupations traditionally expect women be slender. Dancers, fashion models, gymnasts, and actresses are often expected to be very thin. A young girl who aims for these careers may decide to pursue an extreme weight-loss program.

Genetic and Biological Factors

Anorexia nervosa seems to run in some families. Women whose mothers or sisters have the disorder are more likely to develop the condition than those who do not have relatives with anorexia nervosa.

Psychological Factors

One factor possibly leading to anorexia nervosa is the way a person looks at the world. Many theories have been developed to explain how an individual's view of the world may lead to the disorder. Anorexia nervosa has been interpreted as:

- A fear of growing up. By becoming anorexic, a young girl may be able to remain a child.

Dancers, gymnasts, and other female athletes often feel pressure to be very thin. The pressure sometimes leads to eating disorders such as anorexia nervosa. (© 1996 P. Stocklein. Reproduced by permission of Custom Medical Stock Photo.)

- Reaction to sexual assault or abuse.
- A desire to remain weak and passive in the belief that men will find this attractive.
- A drive to be perfect in every part of life, whether it be school work or weight control.

• Response to family problems.
• Biological or psychological problems caused by incorrect feeding experiences at an early age.

SYMPTOMS

The symptoms of anorexia nervosa vary widely. In some people, they are very severe. In others, they are quite mild. In most cases, anorexics tend to have very thin bodies, dry or yellowish skin, and very low blood pressure. Young girls often have amenorrhea (pronounced a-men-uh-REE-uh), the failure to menstruate. They may also experience abdominal pain, constipation, and lack of energy. Chills, the growth of downy body hair, and damaged tooth enamel (from vomiting) are other symptoms of the condition.

DIAGNOSIS

Anorexia nervosa is often difficult to diagnose for a number of reasons. Most people with the disorder deny that they have a problem. They may not get professional help until a family member intervenes and takes them to a doctor.

A physical examination and medical history will be conducted by the physician. Other possible causes for symptoms must first be ruled out. Brain tumors, diseases of the digestive tract, and other conditions can produce symptoms similar to those of anorexia nervosa. Blood tests, urinalysis, and other tests can be used to eliminate other possibilities.

Some psychiatric conditions also produce symptoms like those of anorexia nervosa. Doctors may use certain written tests to distinguish between these disorders and anorexia nervosa. The Eating Attitudes Test and the Eating Disorder Inventory are two such tests.

TREATMENT

Treatment of anorexia nervosa is often quite complicated. The patient may have to deal with immediate problems as well as long-range ones. A variety of professional helpers may be needed. They may include psychiatrists or psychologists, dietitians, and medical specialists in other areas. Treatment is often difficult because of a patient's attitude. He or she may refuse to take the steps necessary to be cured of the disorder.

Hospital Treatment

Serious cases of anorexia nervosa may require hospital treatment. Some symptoms that may lead to hospitalization include:

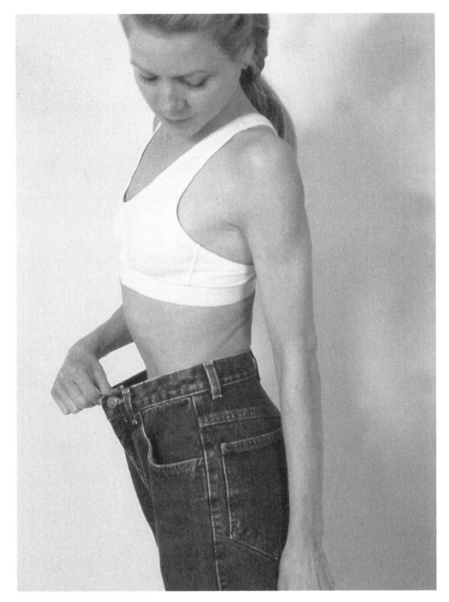

Anorexia nervosa is characterized by a fear of gaining weight, self-starvation, and a distorted self-image. (© 1993 B. Bodine. Reproduced by permission of Custom Medical Stock Photo.)

- A weight of 40 percent or more below normal, or weight loss of 30 pounds or more over a three-month period
- Severely disturbed metabolism (body reactions by which energy is produced)
- Severe binging and purging
- Signs of mental disorders

- Severe depression or risk of suicide
- Family crisis

Hospital treatment has two objectives. First, the patient is given the opportunity to eat on a more normal schedule. In extreme cases, it may be necessary to force-feed the patient. Second, he or she is provided with group or individual counseling. The purpose of counseling is to help the patient understand the reasons for his or her disorder.

Outpatient Treatment

Patients whose health is not seriously at risk can be treated on an outpatient basis. Outpatient services are provided in a hospital or doctor's office. The patient comes in for help but then goes home after the session is over. Most outpatient services for anorexics involve counseling. The counseling can be done on an individual basis or in groups. In some cases family therapy can be helpful. Family therapy helps relatives of the anorexic to understand their role in the patient's problems.

Medications

Drugs can sometimes by used to treat the psychological aspect of anorexia nervosa. They may help patients become less depressed, less anxious, and better able to think clearly about his or her problems.

PROGNOSIS

According to the best estimates available, about half of all anorexics make a good physical and social recovery. About three-quarters gain weight. On a long-term basis, about 10 percent of all anorexics eventually die from the disorder. The most frequent causes of death are starvation, imbalances of chemicals in the body, heart failure, and suicide.

PREVENTION

Anorexia nervosa is likely to remain a problem until overall changes in society occur. As long as thinness is an ideal, anorexics will exist. Educational programs in the schools and discussions at home can help young people to think about and develop positive attitudes toward food, weight control, and body image.

FOR MORE INFORMATION

Books

Hall, Lindsey, and Monika Ostroff. *Anorexia Nervosa: A Guide to Recovery.* Carlsbad, CA: Gurze Design & Books, 1998.

Hornbacher, Marya. *Wasted: A Memoir of Anorexia and Bulimia.* New York: Harpercollins, 1999.

Robbins, Paul R. *Anorexia and Bulimia.* Hillside, NJ: Enslow Publishers, 1998.

Organizations

American Anorexia/Bulimia Association. 165 West 46th Street, Suite 1108, New York, NY 10036. (212) 575–6200.

Anorexia Nervosa and Related Eating Disorders. PO Box 5102, Eugene, OR 97405. (541) 344–1144.

Center for the Study of Anorexia and Bulimia. 1 W. 91st Street, New York, NY 10024. (212) 595–3449.

Eating Disorder Awareness & Prevention. 603 Steward St., Suite 803, Seattle, WA 98101. (206) 382–3587.

National Association of Anorexia Nervosa and Associated Disorders. Box 7, Highland Park, IL 60035. (708) 831–3438.

National Eating Disorders Organization. 6655 South Yale Avenue, Tulsa, OK 74136. (918) 481–4044.

National Institute of Mental Health Eating Disorders Program. Building 10, Room 3S231. 9000 Rockville Pike, Bethesda, MD 20892. (301) 496–1891.

Web sites

"Anorexia." *Healthtouch.com* [Online] http://www.healthtouch.com/level1/leaflets/115207/115207.htm (accessed on June 15, 1999).

Anorexia Nervosa and Related Eating Disorders, Inc. [Online] http://www.anred.com (accessed on June 15, 1999).

"A Teen Guide to Eating Disorders." [Online] http://kidshealth.org (accessed on October 5, 1999).

"Understanding Eating Disorders." [Online] http://www.ndmda.org (accessed on June 15, 1999).

APPENDICITIS

DEFINITION

Appendicitis (pronounced uh-pen-di-SIE-tis) is the inflammation of the appendix, a worm-shaped pouch near the beginning of the large intestine. The appendix has no known function in the body, but it can become diseased. Appendicitis is a medical emergency. If the condition is left untreated, the appendix may rupture and cause a potentially fatal infection.

DESCRIPTION

appendicitis

Appendicitis is the most common abdominal emergency among children and young adults. One person in fifteen develops appendicitis in his or her lifetime. The frequency of appendicitis is highest among males between the ages of ten and fourteen and among females between the ages of fifteen and nineteen. The disease is rare among the elderly and in children under the age of two.

The main symptom of appendicitis is increasingly severe pain in the abdomen. Many different conditions can cause abdominal pain, so an accurate diagnosis of appendicitis can be difficult. A prompt diagnosis is important, however. A delay can result in perforation (rupture) of the appendix. When this happens, the infected contents of the appendix spill into the abdomen. A serious infection known as peritonitis (pronounced per-i-tuh-NIE-tiss) may result.

ONE PERSON IN FIFTEEN DEVELOPS APPENDICITIS IN HIS OR HER LIFETIME.

Other conditions produce symptoms similar to those of appendicitis, especially among women. An example is endometriosis (pronounced en-do-mee-tree-O-suhs), an infection of the lining of the uterus, or pelvic inflammatory disease, an infection of the pelvis. Some forms of stomach upset and bowel inflammation may also imitate appendicitis.

The treatment for acute (sudden, severe) appendicitis is an appendectomy, a surgical procedure to remove the appendix. Since a ruptured appendix can be life-threatening, people suspected of having appendicitis may be taken to surgery before the diagnosis is certain.

WORDS TO KNOW

Appendectomy: Surgical removal of the appendix.

Appendix: The worm-shaped pouch near the beginning of the large intestine.

Computed tomography (CT) scan: A procedure by which X rays are directed at a patient's body from various angles and the set of photographs thus obtained assembled by a computer program.

Computerized axial tomography (CAT) scan: Another name for a computed tomography (CT) scan.

Laparoscopy: A procedure in which a tube with a small light and viewing device is inserted through a small incision near the navel, allowing a surgeon to look directly into the patient's abdomen.

Laparotomy: A surgical procedure that allows a surgeon to view the inside of the abdominal cavity.

Peritonitis: Inflammation of the membranes that line the abdominal wall.

CAUSES

The causes of appendicitis are not well understood. A number of factors are thought to be responsible for the disease. One is an obstruction (blocking) within the appendix. Another is the development of an ulceration (a sore) within the appendix. A third factor is a bacterial infection.

Under any one of these conditions, disease-causing bacteria may begin to multiply within the appendix. The appendix becomes swollen and filled with pus. Pus is a fluid formed in infected tissue consisting of white blood cells and dead cells. When this happens, the appendix may rupture.

SYMPTOMS

An indication that the appendix is ready to rupture is the presence of certain symptoms that last more than twenty-four hours. These symptoms include a fever, an abnormally high white blood count, and a rapid heart rate.

The characteristic symptom of appendicitis is pain that begins around or above the navel. The pain may be severe or relatively mild. It eventually moves to the lower right-hand corner of the abdomen. There, it becomes more steady and more severe. Movement or coughing makes the pain worse. The abdomen becomes rigid (hard) and tender to the touch. An increase in these symptoms indicates an increased likelihood of perforation and peritonitis.

Loss of appetite is a common symptom of appendicitis. Nausea and vomiting occur in about half of the cases, and constipation or diarrhea may also occur. Body temperature may be slightly elevated, but a fever suggests that the appendix may already have ruptured.

DIAGNOSIS

Many abdominal problems have symptoms like those of appendicitis. The task of the doctor is to rule out other problems before diagnosing appendicitis. The first step in diagnosis usually involves a series of questions about the patient's pain: where did the pain begin; has it moved, and where is the pain now? The doctor also presses on the abdomen to find out where the soreness is and how rigid the abdomen has become.

The sequence of symptoms described occurs in about half of all patients with appendicitis. In certain cases those symptoms may be harder to detect. For example, abdominal pain is common in pregnant women and can be the result of any number of factors relating to a pregnancy. Elderly people are likely to have less pain and tenderness than younger patients. The absence of these symptoms can make diagnosis more difficult. In

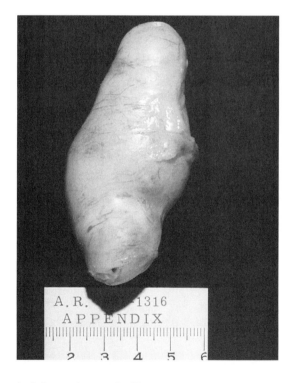

An inflammed appendix. (Photograph by Lester V. Bergman. Reproduced by permission of the Corbis Corporation [Bellevue].)

about 30 percent of cases involving the elderly, the appendix ruptures before a diagnosis has been made. Infants and young children often have diarrhea, vomiting, and fever in addition to pain.

Laboratory tests cannot totally determine appendicitis, but do help in the diagnosis. A blood test that shows a high white blood count may be an indication of the infection. Urine tests can rule out other possible causes of abdominal pain, such as an infection of the urinary tract.

People who are diagnosed with appendicitis are usually taken directly to surgery. The doctor then performs a laparotomy (pronounced lap-uh-ROT-uh-mee), an operation on the abdomen. The laparotomy usually confirms a diagnosis of appendicitis.

In some cases, additional tests may still be necessary. For example, an ultrasound test may help identify appendicitis or other conditions that may have the same symptoms. A computed tomography (CT) scan may also be performed to avoid surgery. A CT scan is a procedure by which X rays are directed at a patient's body from various angles and the set of photographs thus obtained assembled by a computer program. This procedure is sometimes called a computerized axial tomography (CAT) scan.

Often, a diagnosis of appendicitis is not certain until an operation is done. To avoid a ruptured appendix, surgery may be recommended without delay if the symptoms point clearly to appendicitis.

Additional procedures may be used for women of child-bearing age. Women in this age group may have problems with their reproductive organs that produce symptoms similar to those of appendicitis. In these cases, a doctor may perform a laparoscopy (pronounced lap-uh-ROS-kuh-pee). In this procedure, a small incision (cut) is made near the navel. A tube containing a light and viewing device is then inserted through the incision. This allows a surgeon to look directly into the patient's abdomen. He or she can usually determine whether the patient has appendicitis or some other condition.

A normal appendix is found in about 10 to 20 percent of all patients who have a laparotomy. Sometimes the surgeon removes a normal appendix anyway to safeguard against appendicitis in the future. In about 30 percent of these cases, surgeons find other medical problems that have caused the appendicitis-like symptoms.

TREATMENT

The treatment for appendicitis is an immediate appendectomy. This procedure can be carried out as a standard open appendectomy technique or through laparoscopy. Laparoscopy is sometimes preferred because it produces a smaller scar. It does not seem to have other advantages over an open appendectomy. In the case of a ruptured appendix, an open appendectomy must be performed. If the ruptured appendix is left untreated, the condition is fatal.

PROGNOSIS

Appendicitis is usually treated successfully with an appendectomy. Unless there are complications, patients recover without further problems. Less than 0.1 percent of patients die as a result of a standard appendectomy. In cases where the appendix has ruptured or infection has occurred, there is a higher possibility of complications and recovery occurs more slowly. Children and the elderly are more prone to such complications.

PREVENTION

Appendicitis is probably not preventable. But some authorities think the condition can be avoided with a diet rich in green vegetables and tomatoes.

FOR MORE INFORMATION

Periodicals

Van der Meer, Antonia. "Do You Know the Warning Signs of Appendicitis?" *Parents Magazine* (April 1997): p. 49.

Web sites

"Acute Appendicitis." *HealthAnswers.com* [Online] http://www.healthanswers.com/centers/body/overview.asp?id=digestive+system&filename=000256.htm# (accessed on October 16, 1999).

ARTHRITIS

DEFINITION

Arthritis means inflammation of a joint. There are more than one hundred different forms of arthritis. They are similar to each other in the symptoms they produce, which includes sore, stiff, inflamed, and painful joints. Beyond these common symptoms, the various forms of arthritis are quite different from each other. Most forms of arthritis can be subdivided into three major categories: rheumatoid (pronounced ROO-muh-toid) arthritis, osteoarthritis (pronounced OSS-tee-o-ar-THRIE-tis), and gout.

DESCRIPTION

A joint is a part of the body where two bones connect with each other. A joint consists of many structures. In the simplest form, there are two bones separated from each other by a slight gap called the joint cavity. The end of each bone is covered with cartilage, a tough, elastic material.

The space between bones is covered with a thin membrane called the synovial (pronounced si-NO-vee-uhl) membrane. The synovial membrane secretes (releases) a thin fluid called synovial fluid. The synovial fluid acts like a lubricant in the joint, helping the bones move smoothly against each other.

Arthritis usually involves some form of damage to or destruction of joint parts. In the case of rheumatoid arthritis, the synovial membrane becomes inflamed. The membrane becomes thick and stiff. It is also attacked by white blood cells, which can damage or kill tissue in the joint.

In the case of osteoarthritis, cartilage begins to break down and wear away. It is no longer able to cushion the contact of bones with each other. One bone rubs directly on the other bone. It becomes very painful to move the joint.

Rheumatoid arthritis (RA) and osteoarthritis (OA) are both common disorders. They affect both men and women of all races and ethnic background. In the United States alone, about two million people are thought to have RA. Women are three times more likely to have the condition than men. About 80 percent of patients with RA are diagnosed between the ages of thirty-five and fifty. The condition appears to run in families.

OA is one of the most common causes of disability because of limited joint movement. The condition is much more common among older people than among younger people. Somewhere between 65 and 85 percent of Americans over the age of sixty-five have the condition. Some doctors believe that everyone over the age of sixty is affected to some extent by OA. By contrast, only about 2 percent of Americans under the age of forty-five have OA.

CAUSES

The causes of both rheumatoid arthritis and osteoarthritis are not known. At one time, doctors believed that OA was simply a part of grow-

WORDS TO KNOW

Autoimmune disorder: A condition in which the body's immune system attacks some part of the body and treats it as if it were a foreign invader.

Cartilage: Tough, elastic tissue that covers and protects the ends of bones.

Immune system: A network of organs, tissues, cells, and chemicals that protects the body from foreign invaders, such as bacteria and viruses.

Joint: A structure holding two or more bones together.

Synovial fluid: A fluid produced by the synovial membranes in a joint that lubricates the movement of the bones in the joint.

Synovial membrane: A thin tissue that covers the inside surface of a joint.

ing old. They thought that the body's joints just wore out over time. Today, researchers are beginning to explore specific causes for both disorders.

Rheumatoid Arthritis

Current theories suggest that RA is caused by genetic factors. That is, a person is born with the tendency to develop or not develop the condition. Then something in the environment actually sets off the disorder itself. One theory is that an infectious agent, such as a bacterium or virus, initiates the onset (beginning) of RA.

Whatever the cause, RA is an autoimmune disorder. An autoimmune disorder is a condition in which the body's immune system begins to act abnormally. The immune system is a network of organs, tissues, cells, and chemicals whose job it is to protect the body from foreign invaders, like bacteria and viruses.

At times, the immune system may become confused. It may respond to some part of the body as if it were a foreign invader. It releases its whole arsenal of weapons against that part of the body. When the immune system acts against some part of the joint, RA occurs.

Osteoarthritis

Scientists recognize two forms of OA: primary and secondary osteoarthritis. Primary OA is caused by abnormal stresses on healthy joints or by normal stresses on weakened joints. The joints most commonly affected by primary OA include the finger joints, hips and knees, the lower joints of the spine, and the big toe.

There is some evidence that primary OA is caused by genetic factors. Obesity is often a contributing factor. The heavier a person is, the greater the pressure on his or her joints. Finally, some researchers believe that primary OA may be caused by bone disease, liver problems, or other abnormal conditions in the body.

Secondary OA is caused by a chronic (long-term) or sudden injury to a joint. Some factors that may contribute to the development of OA include:

- Physical trauma (shock), including sports injuries
- Repetitive stress associated with certain occupations, such as construction, assembly line work, computer keyboard operation, and hair-cutting

DISEASE OF KINGS

Throughout history, gout has been called the "disease of kings." The reason for this name is that gout can be caused by the over consumption of rich foods. Today, we know that gout is caused by the accumulation of uric (pronounced YER-ik) acid crystals in a joint, most often the joint of the big toe.

Uric acid is produced in the body when proteins are broken down. Proteins are a class of chemicals with many important functions in the body. Uric acid is water soluble. It usually dissolves in urine and is then excreted from the body.

Some people, however, produce an unusually large amount of uric acid. Such a tendency is thought to be caused by genetic factors. When that happens, uric acid remains in the body, circulating through the bloodstream. Eventually, it is deposited as needle-like crystals in joints. These crystals cause friction when the joint is moved. The friction causes severe pain known as gout.

• Repeated episodes of gout or other forms of arthritis
• Poor posture or bone alignment caused by abnormal body development

SYMPTOMS

All forms of arthritis share certain symptoms in common. These symptoms include pain, swelling, and stiffness in the joint. These symptoms may develop slowly over time or they may begin quite suddenly. After a period of time, joints may actually become deformed. Patients may find it difficult to straighten their fingers and toes, or their hands and feet may curve outward in an abnormal way. Eventually, a patient may lose the use of a joint entirely.

Patients with RA often report other symptoms also. These symptoms include increased fatigue, loss of appetite and weight loss, and, sometimes, fever. RA may also be accompanied by the development of rheumatoid nodules. Rheumatoid nodules are bumps that appear under the skin, in tissue covering the lungs and chest, or in the brain and spinal cord. These nodules can cause serious complications, including shortness of breath, poor blood circulation, gangrene (tissue decay), and damage to nerves.

DIAGNOSIS

Rheumatoid arthritis and osteoarthritis are usually both diagnosed based on a patient's history. This history typically includes an increasing occurrence of pain and stiffness in joints. The doctor can also examine the patient's affected joint for swelling, limitations on movement, pain, and a cracking sound that is sometimes heard with a damaged joint.

There are no blood tests that strongly confirm the presence of arthritis. Many tests that can be used for RA are also positive for other disorders. One test measures the amount of a chemical known as rheumatic factor in a patient's blood. Rheumatic factor is produced by the immune system when it attacks a joint. It is found in about 66 percent of patients with RA. But it is also found in 10 to 20 percent of healthy people over the age of sixty.

A good diagnosis for OA can sometimes be obtained from X rays or other imaging techniques. An X-ray photograph may show changes in the space between bones in a joint, indicating the presence of OA.

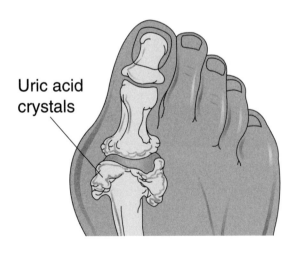

Uric acid crystals

Gout is one form of arthritis caused by the buildup of uric acid crystals in a joint, most often the joint of the big toe. (Reproduced by permission of Electronic Illustrators Group)

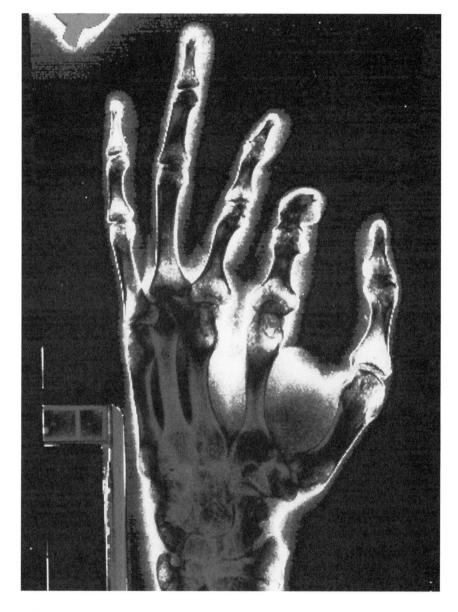

A digitally enhanced X ray of the left hand showing rheumatoid arthritis. (© 1994 Michael English, M.D. Reproduced by permission of Custom Medical Stock Photo.)

TREATMENT

The first line of treatment for most forms of arthritis is medication to reduce inflammation, swelling, and pain. Aspirin, acetaminophen (pronounced uh-see-tuh-MIN-uh-fuhn, trade name Tylenol), and ibuprofen (pronounced i-byoo-PRO-fuhn, trade names Advil, Motrin) are all effective in this regard.

In fact, people with mild cases of arthritis can often control their condition satisfactorily simply with one of these drugs.

In more severe cases of arthritis, stronger medications may be required. The most common of these is one of the corticosteroids (pronounced KOR-ti-ko-steer-oids). The corticosteroids are very effective in the treatment of pain, swelling, and inflammation. However, they have some serious long-term side effects and should be used only when milder medications are not effective.

A variety of other medications have been used against arthritis also. These drugs include gold compounds, D-penicillamine (pronounced pen-i-SIL-uh-meen), and sulfasalazine (pronounced SULL-fuh-SAL-uh-zeen). Medications used to treat malaria can also be helpful. These drugs have potentially dangerous side effects and should be used with caution.

Rest and supportive devices may also be important in the treatment of arthritis. When the pain becomes too great, patients may be advised to take to their bed and stay there until they experience relief. They may also be provided with various protective measures, such as neck braces and collars, crutches, canes, hip braces, and knee supports.

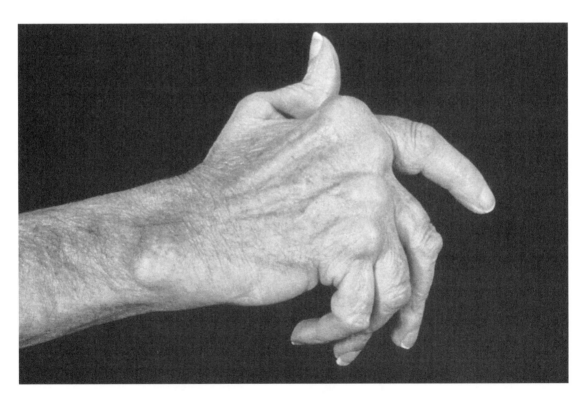

Hand deformed by rheumatoid arthritis. (© 1988 SIU. Reproduced by permission of Custom Medical Stock Photo.)

Physical therapy can also be an important component of treatment programs. Physical therapists can teach patients how to exercise their affected joints. Exercise may reduce the rate at which the joints are worsening. It may increase the patient's balance, flexibility, and range of motion. Physical therapy can also consist of massage, moist hot packs, and soaking in a hot tub.

In the most severe cases, surgery may be required. Some surgical techniques that can be used include:

- Replacement of a damaged joint
- Fusion (joining together) of spinal bones
- Scraping or removing damaged bone from a joint
- Removal of a bone chip to allow realignment of a joint

Alternative Treatment

Some types of food intolerance may contribute to both RA and OA. Patients should try to find out the foods to which they are allergic and eliminate those foods from their diets. In general, nutritionists recommend a diet high in fiber and complex carbohydrates (starches) and low in fats and refined foods.

Some food supplements have been found to be effective in treating arthritis. One substance that is commonly recommended is a combination of glucosamine (pronounced gloo-KO-suh-meen) and chondroitin (pronounced kon-DRO-i-tin) sulfate. This product is thought to help repair cartilage. Other nutritional supplements that have been suggested include vitamins A, B, C, and E, and the minerals selenium and zinc.

Traditional Chinese medicine emphasizes the use of various herbs for the treatment of arthritis. These herbs include turmeric, ginger, feverfew, devil's claw, Chinese thoroughwax, licorice, lobelia, and cramp bark.

Naturopathic treatment may include hydrotherapy (water therapy), diathermy (deep-heat therapy), nutritional supplements, and various herbs.

PROGNOSIS

About 15 percent of patients with RA experience their symptoms for only a short period of time. The symptoms then disappear with no long-term effects. For other patients, however, the symptoms never disappear and become progressively worse over time. In general, patients with RA have a shorter life-span by three to seven years than individuals without the disorder.

Osteoarthritis is a progressive disorder without a permanent cure. The rate of progression can sometimes be slowed. Factors that may help in reducing the disorder's progress include weight loss, exercise, surgical treatment, and some alternative therapies.

PREVENTION

There is no known way to prevent arthritis. The most that can be hoped for is to slow or prevent its progress.

FOR MORE INFORMATION

Books

Aaseng, Nathan. *Autoimmune Diseases.* New York: Franklin Watts, 1995.

Schlotzhauer, M. *Living with Rheumatoid Arthritis.* Baltimore: Johns Hopkins University Press, 1993.

Shenkman, John. *Living with Arthritis.* New York: Franklin Watts, 1990.

Theodosakis, Jason, et al. *The Arthritis Cure.* New York: St. Martin's Press, 1997.

Organizations

American College of Rheumatology. 60 Executive Park South, Suite 150, Atlanta, GA 30329. (404) 633 1870. http://www.rheumatology.org

Arthritis Foundation. 1330 West Peachtree Street, Atlanta, GA 30309. (404) 872–7100. http://www.arthritis.org.

National Institute of Arthritis and Musculoskeletal and Skin Diseases. http://www.nih.gov/niams.

Web sites

"Arthritis." [Online] http://arthritis.miningco.com (accessed on June 20, 1999).

ASTHMA

DEFINITION

Asthma (pronounced AZ-muh) is a chronic (long-lasting) inflammatory disease of the airways in the human body. The inflammation causes the airways to narrow from time to time. This narrowing can produce wheezing and breathlessness. In extreme cases, the asthma patient may need to gasp to get enough air to breathe. Occasionally, a severe asthma attack can be fatal.

This condition sometimes improves on its own. In other cases, medication is needed to reopen airways. When inflammation occurs over and over again, the airways become especially sensitive to certain environmental conditions, such as cold air, dust mites, and pollen in the air. Exercise, stress, and anxiety can produce similar effects.

DESCRIPTION

About ten million Americans have asthma, and the number seems to be increasing. Between 1982 and 1992, the rate rose by 42 percent. Asthma is also becoming a more serious disease. In the same 10-year period, the death rate from asthma in the United States increased by 35 percent. These changes have come about in spite of new and improved drugs for the treatment of asthma.

An asthma attack affects the bronchi (pronounced BRONG-ki) and bronchioles (pronounced BRONG-kee-olz) in the lungs. The bronchi and bronchioles are tiny tubes through which air passes in and out of the body. In people with asthma, certain materials, such as dust and pollen, can irritate these tubes. By contrast, people without asthma are unaffected by these materials.

ABOUT TEN MILLION AMERICANS HAVE ASTHMA, AND THE NUMBER SEEMS TO BE INCREASING.

As these tubes become irritated, they swell and give off mucus, a sticky liquid. The liquid fills air spaces in the bronchi and bronchioles. Both swelling and mucus narrow the tubes, making it more difficult for air to get in and out of the lungs. As a result, an asthmatic person has to make a much greater effort to breathe in air and to expel it.

Asthma usually begins in childhood or adolescence, however it may first appear during the adult years. While the symptoms may be similar for these two cases, certain aspects of asthma are different in children and adults.

Child-onset Asthma

Some children are thought to develop asthma for genetic reasons. Their bodies are especially sensitive to materials in the environment that have little or no effect on other people. These materials are known as allergens (pronounced AL-er-jins) because they produce an allergic response.

When children with this condition are exposed to dust mites, fungi, and other allergens, their bodies produce chemicals known as antibodies. The function of these antibodies is to fight off the invasion of materials from the environment. However, the release of antibodies also inflames the bronchi and bronchioles. The more often an asthmatic child is exposed to allergens,

WORDS TO KNOW

Allergen: A foreign substance which, when inhaled, causes the airways to narrow and produces the symptoms of asthma.

Atopy: A condition in which people are more likely to develop allergic reactions, often because of the inflammation and airway narrowing typical of asthma.

Spirometer: An instrument that shows how much air a patient is able to exhale and hold in his or her lungs as a test to see how serious a person's asthma is and how well he or she is responding to treatment.

the more serious the response becomes. This condition, known as atopy (pronounced A-tuh-pee), is thought to occur in anywhere from 30 to 50 percent of the general population.

Adult-onset Asthma

Some individuals do not exhibit the symptoms of asthma until their adult years. In some cases, the cause of the disease may be the same as they are for children. In other cases, asthma is thought to be a result of exposure to wood dust, metals, certain forms of plastic, or other materials that get into the air in the workplace or at home.

CAUSES

In most cases, asthma is caused by inhaling an allergen. That allergen then sets off a series of reactions in the body that cause inflammation of bronchi and bronchioles. The most common inhaled allergens that lead to asthma attacks are:

- Animal dander (dry skin that is shed)
- Chemicals, fumes, or tiny particles that occur in the air in workplaces
- Fungi (molds) that grow indoors
- Mites found in house dust
- Pollen

Tobacco smoke is another cause of asthma attacks. The smoke irritates bronchi and bronchioles, setting off an asthma reaction. The same effect is caused whether an individual himself is smoking or is inhaling smoke second-hand (from someone else). Air pollutants can have a similar effect.

Three other factors can produce asthma attacks. They are:

- Exercise (exercise-related asthma)
- Inhaling cold air (cold-induced asthma)
- Stress or anxiety

Other factors that can cause an asthma attack or make it worse are rhinitis (pronounced ri-NIE-tuss; inflammation of the nose), sinusitis (pronounced sie-nuh-SIE-tis; inflammation of the sinuses), acid reflux (known as acid stomach), and viral infections of the respiratory (breathing) system.

SYMPTOMS

Wheezing is the most obvious symptom of an asthma attack. In most cases, the wheezing is loud and easy to observe. In other cases, it may be soft and hard to hear. A doctor may be able to hear the wheezing only by listening to the patient's chest with a stethoscope. Coughing and tightness in

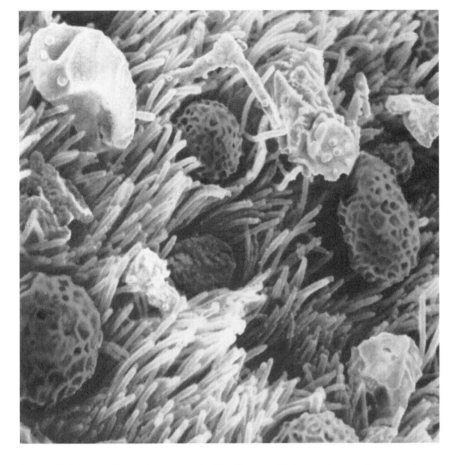

A magnified image of a trachea covered with allergens. Stringy parts are cilia and spheres are pollen. (Reproduced by permission of Custom Medical Stock Photo)

the chest are other symptoms of asthma. Children sometimes complain of an itchiness on their back or neck at the start of an asthma attack.

A number of other outward signs are associated with an asthma attack. An attack may cause a person to become very anxious. He or she may sit upright, lean forward, or take some other position to make breathing easier. The person may be able to say only a few words before stopping to take a breath.

An attack may cause a person to become confused or may cause his or her skin to turn blue. Confusion and a blue skin color are signs that the person's body is not getting enough oxygen. The person should be given emergency treatment immediately. In the most severe cases, air sacs in the lungs may rupture. This causes air to collect in the chest, making it even more difficult for the person to breathe.

Some asthmatics may be free of symptoms most of the time. They may experience shortness of breath only on rare occasions and for short periods. Other asthmatics are in discomfort much of the time, coughing, wheezing, and trying to breathe normally. In some cases, crying or laughing can bring on an asthma attack.

The most serious attack can occur when a person already has an infection of the respiratory tract. High doses of an allergen can also trigger major attacks. Asthmatic attacks vary in their length as well as seriousness. Some attacks last only a few minutes. Others go on for hours or even days. Except in the most severe cases, patients recover from even the most serious asthma attacks.

DIAGNOSIS

A first step in diagnosis often involves taking a personal and family medical history. These histories can help a doctor determine whether asthma is a likely cause of a patient's problems.

Visual signs can also be used to diagnose asthma. Hunched shoulders and tightened neck muscles indicate that a patient is trying to get more air into his or her lungs. Increased amounts of nasal (nose) secretions are another sign of asthma. Eczema (pronounced EK-suh-muh) and other skin disorders (see skin disorders entry) are a sign that a person may have allergic reactions associated with asthma.

A number of tests can be used to diagnose asthma. A spirometer, for example, measures the rate at which air is exhaled from the lungs and how much air remains in the lungs. The device is used before and after a patient inhales a drug that widens the air passages. It tells whether airway narrowing is reversible, a typical finding with asthma. Patients can be given a similar instrument called a peak flow meter to use at home. The instrument helps them to determine how serious an asthma attack is.

Tests can also be used to determine the conditions that trigger an asthma attack. Skin tests may show any allergens to which a person is sensitive. That allergen may or may not, however, also be the cause of asthma attacks. Blood tests for the presence of antibodies can also be performed. Any antibodies found in the blood may indicate the allergens to which a person is sensitive.

Patients can also be asked to inhale specific allergens to see what effects they have. A spirometer is used to determine whether airways have become narrowed by the allergen. The spirometer is also used after a patient has exercised to see whether exercise-induced asthma is a possibility. A chest X ray can be taken to rule out conditions that produce symptoms similar to those of asthma.

TREATMENT

There are three primary goals of an asthma treatment program. First, troublesome symptoms should be prevented to the greatest extent possible. Second, lung function should be kept as close to normal as possible. Third, patients should be able to carry out their normal activities, including those requiring special effort, such as vigorous exercise. Patients should be examined on a regular basis to make sure treatment goals are being met. Spirometer tests are an essential part of these examinations.

Drugs

The goal of drug therapy is to find medications that control the symptoms of asthma with few or no side effects.

METHYLXANTHINES. The most commonly used methylxanthine (pronounced meth-uhl-ZAN-theen) is theophylline (pronounced thee-OFF-uh-

Bronchodilators are drugs that open up bronchi and bronchioles. Taken with an inhaler, they are a common treatment for asthma. (© 1993 B.S.I.P. Reproduced by permission of Custom Medical Stock Photo.)

lin). Theophylline is used to reduce inflammation of the airways. It is especially helpful in controlling nighttime symptoms of asthma. Blood levels of the drug must be measured on a regular basis, however. If levels get too high, they can cause an abnormal heart rhythm or convulsions.

BETA-RECEPTOR AGONISTS. Beta-receptor agonists are bronchodilators (pronounced brong-ko-die-LATE-urs), drugs that open up bronchi and bronchiole. They make it easier for air to get into and out of airways. They are best used for the relief of sudden asthma attacks and to prevent exercise-induced asthma. These drugs generally start acting within minutes and last for up to six hours. They are taken by mouth, by injection, or with an inhaler.

STEROIDS. Steroids are related to natural body hormones. They reduce or prevent inflammation and are very effective in relieving the symptoms of asthma. When taken over a long period of time by inhalation, steroids can reduce the frequency of asthma attacks. They can also make airways less sensitive to allergens. For these reasons, they are the strongest and most effective methods for treating asthma. They can control even the most severe cases of the disease and maintain good lung function.

On the other hand, steroids have a number of side effects, some of which are serious. They can cause stomach bleeding, loss of calcium from bones, cataracts in the eyes, and a diabetes-like condition. Long-term use of steroids can also result in weight gain, loss of some mental function, and problems with wound healing. In children, growth may be slowed. Steroids can be taken by mouth, by injection, or by inhalation.

LEUKOTRIENE MODIFIERS. Leukotriene (pronounced lyoo-kuh-TRI-een) modifiers are drugs that interfere with changes in the bronchi and bronchioles that occur during an asthma attack. They prevent airways from narrowing and the release of mucus. They are recommended in place of steroids for older children and adults who have mild, long-lasting cases of asthma.

OTHER DRUGS. Anti-inflammatory drugs are sometimes used to prevent asthma attacks over the long term in children. Cromolyn (pronounced KRO-muh-lun) and nedocromil are two such drugs. They can also be taken before exercise or when exposure to an allergen cannot be avoided. These drugs are safe but expensive. They must be taken on a regular basis, even if the patient has no symptoms.

A class of drugs known as anti-cholinergics (pronounced ko-luh-NER-jiks) can also be used in the case of severe asthma attacks. Atropine is an example of this class of drugs. Anti-cholinergics are usually taken in combination with beta-receptor agonists. The combination helps widen airways and reduce the production of mucus.

Immunotherapy is used when a person cannot avoid exposure to an allergen. Immunotherapy is a procedure that involves a series of injections of the allergen. The series must be continued over a very long period of time, usually three to five years. During this period, the amount of allergen given in a shot is gradually increased. As more and more allergen is given, the patient's body slowly builds up an immunity (resistance) to the allergen.

Immunotherapy also has its risks. Injecting an allergen can itself cause an asthmatic attack. Studies seem to indicate, however, that the procedure can be effective against certain types of allergens, such as house-dust mites, ragweed pollen, and cat dander.

Managing Asthma Attacks

A severe asthma attack requires immediate treatment. Patients usually require supplemental (extra) oxygen. In rare cases, a mechanical ventilator may be needed to help a patient breathe. Inhalation of a beta-receptor is often effective in treating serious asthma attacks. If the patient does not respond to a beta-receptor, an injection of steroids may be necessary. Follow-up treatments with steroids make a recurrence of the attack less likely.

Maintaining Control

Long-term control over asthma is based on the use of beta-receptor drugs. These drugs are taken with inhalers that monitor the dose. Patients are instructed how to properly use an inhaler to make sure they receive the amount of drug needed to keep their disease under control. Once that goal is achieved, the amount of beta-receptor taken can be reduced. Patients should be seen by a doctor on a regular basis, however (such as once every one to six months).

As early on as possible, asthma patients should be trained in the treatment and control of their disease. They should be taught how to monitor their symptoms so they will know when an attack is starting. Using a flow meter is essential to this process. Over-the-counter medications should be avoided. Patients should also have an action plan to follow if their symptoms become worse. This plan includes how to adjust their medication and when to seek medical help.

Calling an asthma specialist should be considered when:

- There has been a life-threatening asthma attack or the disease has become severe and persistent (long-lasting).
- Treatment for three to six months has not met its goals.
- Some other condition, such as chronic lung disease, is complicating asthma.
- Special tests, such as allergy skin testing, are needed.
- Intensive steroid therapy has been necessary.

Hospitalization can sometimes be necessary for an asthma patient. That decision depends on a number of factors, such as the past history of serious attacks, severity of symptoms, current medication, and the availability of support at home.

PROGNOSIS

Most patients with asthma respond well when the best drug or combination of drugs is found. They are then able to lead relatively normal lives. More than half of all children diagnosed with asthma stop having attacks by the time they reach the age of twenty-one. Many others have less frequent and less severe attacks as they grow older.

MORE THAN HALF OF ALL CHILDREN DIAGNOSED WITH ASTHMA STOP HAVING ATTACKS BY THE TIME THEY REACH THE AGE OF TWENTY-ONE.

A small minority of patients have progressively more trouble breathing as they grow older. These people run the risk of going into respiratory failure (loss of ability to breathe). They require immediate and intensive treatment.

PREVENTION

A number of steps can be taken to minimize or eliminate exposure to allergens and other factors that bring on an asthma attack. These steps include:

- As much as possible, avoid contact between an asthma patient and family pets to which he or she is allergic. Keep the pet out of the bedroom and away from carpets and upholstered furniture. Remove all feathers from the house.
- Avoid exposure to dust mites by removing wall-to-wall carpeting, reducing the humidity, and using special pillows and mattress covers. Remove stuffed toys or wash them each week in hot water.
- Cockroach allergens can be eliminated by killing the insects with poison, traps, or boric acid. Do not use synthetic chemicals. Prevent cockroaches from returning by making sure that food and garbage are not left out.
- Keep indoor air clean by vacuuming carpets once or twice a week while the patient is not present. Do use air conditioners during warm weather, but do not use humidifiers.
- Avoid exposure to tobacco smoke.
- Avoid outdoor exercise when air pollution levels are high.
- Exposure to workplace allergens can be avoided by following simple precautions. Always wear a mask and, if possible, arrange to work in a safer area.

FOR MORE INFORMATION

Books

Adams, Francis V. *The Asthma Sourcebook: Everything You Need to Know.* 2nd edition. Los Angeles, CA: Lowell House, 1998.

Gershwin, M. Eric, and E. L. Klinglhofer. *Asthma: Stop Suffering, Start Living,* 2nd edition. Reading, MA: Addison-Wesley Publishing Co., 1992.

Hyde, Margaret O. *Living With Asthma*. New York: Walker & Company, 1995.

Weiss, Jonathan H. *Breathe Easy: Young People's Guide to Asthma*. Washington, DC: Magination Press, 1994.

Organizations

Asthma and Allergy Foundation of America. 1233 Twentieth Street NW, Suite 402, Washington, DC 20036. 800–7ASTHMA. http://www.aafa.org.

National Asthma Education Program. 4733 Bethesda Avenue, Suite 350, Bethesda, MD 20814. (301) 495–4484.

Web sites

"Ask NOAH About: Asthma." *NOAH: New York Online Access to Health*. [Online] http://www.noah.cuny.edu (accessed on June 15, 1999).

"Asthma Information Center." [Online] http://www.mdnet.de/asthma/home.cfm (accessed on October 5, 1999).

ATHEROSCLEROSIS

DEFINITION

Atherosclerosis (pronounced ath-uh-ro-skluh-RO-siss) is the build-up of a waxy deposit on the inside of blood vessels. Atherosclerosis is a form of arteriosclerosis (pronounced ar-tir-ee-o-skluh-RO-siss). Arteriosclerosis refers to any condition in which the arteries become hard and less flexible. The two terms are often used interchangeably, although it is not really correct to do so.

DESCRIPTION

The arteries are blood vessels that carry blood from the heart to all parts of the body. Arteries are made up of several layers of tissue that are normally soft and pliable. The layers must be able to expand and contract as blood passes through them.

Arteries often become leathery and rigid. When that happens, blood may flow less easily through the arteries. The hardening of arteries is called arteriosclerosis. Many factors can cause arteriosclerosis. Normal aging, high blood pressure, and certain diseases, such as diabetes (see diabetes mellitus entry), are common causes of arteriosclerosis.

Atherosclerosis is a special form of arteriosclerosis. In atherosclerosis, only the inner lining of the artery is affected. Fatty materials deposit on the lining of the artery, forming a larger and larger mass. The mass is usually called a plaque (pronounced PLAK). It becomes more and more difficult for blood to flow through the artery. Eventually the artery may close completely.

The formation of a plaque in an artery can lead to a number of cardio-vascular (heart and blood vessel) problems. If the plaque forms in an artery that leads to the heart, it may block the flow of blood to the heart, and a heart attack may occur. If the plaque occurs in an artery that leads from the heart, it may prevent the brain from getting the blood and oxygen it needs. The result is a stroke (see stroke entry).

The plaque may also break off from the artery wall and travel through the bloodstream. It may then block an artery somewhere else in the body, a process known as thrombosis. A thrombosis that blocks an artery in the heart produces a condition known as a coronary thrombosis.

Atherosclerosis can occur anywhere in the body. It can affect arteries of the neck, kidneys, thighs, and arms. In such cases, the interruption of blood flow can produce many medical conditions, such as kidney failure and gan-grene (death of tissue).

CAUSES

The exact cause of atherosclerosis is not known. Some researchers consider it to be a natural consequence of aging. But that theory does not ex-

WORDS TO KNOW

Angiography: A method for studying the structure of blood vessels by inserting a catheter into a vein or artery, injecting a dye in the blood vessel, and taking X-ray photographs of the structure.

Arteriosclerosis: Hardening of the arteries that can be caused by a variety of factors.

Artery: A blood vessel that carries blood from the heart to other parts of the body.

Cardiovascular: A term that applies to the heart and blood system.

Catheter: A long, narrow tube that can be threaded into a patient's vein or artery.

Cholesterol: A waxy substance produced by the body and used in a variety of ways.

Echocardiogram: A test that uses sound waves to produce an image of the structure of the heart.

Electrocardiogram: A test that measures the electrical activity of the heart.

Gangrene: The death of tissue.

Plaque: A deposit of fatty materials that forms on the lining of an artery wall.

Radioactive isotope: A substance that gives off some form of radiation.

Stress test: An electrocardiogram taken while a patient is exercising vigorously, such as riding a stationary bicycle.

Thrombosis: The formation of a blood clot.

Triglyceride: A type of fat.

plain the actual process of the disease. What is known is that people with certain risk factors are much more likely to develop atherosclerosis than people without those risk factors. Some risk factors are beyond a person's control. For example, some people seem to be genetically more inclined to develop atherosclerosis than other people. Also, the disorder is more common among older than younger people. A person is not able to do much about his or her heredity or the aging process.

Some risk factors, however, are under a person's control. These factors include:

- **Cigarette/tobacco smoking.** Smoking increases the risk of developing atherosclerosis. It also increases the risk of dying from heart disease. Second-hand smoke may also increase risk.
- **High blood cholesterol.** Cholesterol is a soft, waxy substance produced naturally by the body. It also occurs in many foods, such as meat, eggs, and other animal products. A certain amount of cholesterol is needed to keep the body healthy. But high levels of cholesterol can increase the risk of atherosclerosis.
- **High triglycerides.** Triglycerides (pronounced tri-GLIS-uh-ride) are a form of fat. High levels of trigylcerides have been linked with various kinds of artery disease.
- **High blood pressure.** Blood pressure higher than normal (normal is measured 140 over 90) can make the heart work hard. Both the heart and arteries may become weak (see hypertension entry).
- **Physical inactivity.** Lack of exercise increases the risk of atherosclerosis.
- **Obesity.** Excess weight strains the heart. Both heart and arteries may be damaged (see obesity entry).

Some risk factors for atherosclerosis that cannot be changed include:

- **Heredity.** People whose family members have had atherosclerosis are at risk for the disorder.
- **Gender.** Before age sixty men are more likely to have atherosclerosis than women. After sixty, the risk is equal for men and women.
- **Age.** The risk for atherosclerosis increases with age.

- **Diabetes mellitus.** Many diabetics die from heart attacks caused by atherosclerosis.

SYMPTOMS

The symptoms of atherosclerosis vary somewhat depending on the location of a plaque. If the plaque occurs in the arteries of the heart, the patient may experience chest pain, heart attack, or sudden death. A plaque in the brain may lead to sudden dizziness, weakness, loss of speech, or blindness. In arteries of the leg, plaques can lead to cramping and fatigue in the legs when walking. A plaque in the kidneys can cause high blood pressure that is difficult to treat.

DIAGNOSIS

A doctor may be led to suspect atherosclerosis based on any of the symptoms discussed. A variety of tests is available to confirm the diagnosis. For example, an electrocardiogram (pronounced ih-LEK-tro-KAR-dee-o-gram) measures electrical activity of the heart. An abnormal flow of blood to the heart can change this activity. Electrocardiograms are sometimes performed while a patient is taking part in vigorous activity, such as riding a stationary bicycle. Such tests are known as stress tests.

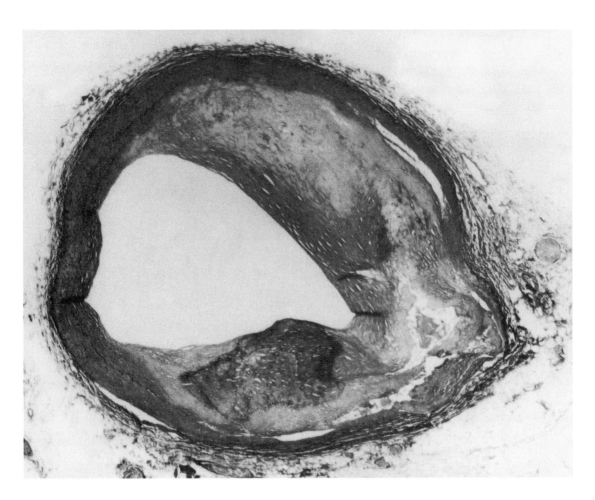

A coronary artery with atherosclerosis, buildup of waxy deposits inside the blood vessels. (Photograph by Martin M. Rotker. Reproduced by permission of Phototake NYC.)

An echocardiogram (pronounced ekko-KAR-dee-o-gram) uses sound waves to study the heart. The sound waves produce a pattern (an echo) as they pass through the heart. The echoes provide information about the heart's structure. Blockages in arteries can sometimes be detected by this method.

Radioactive isotopes can also be used to produce pictures of the heart. A radioactive isotope is a material that gives off some form of radiation. The radioactive isotope is first injected into the patient's bloodstream. It travels through the patient's body, giving off radiation. The radiation can be used to form a picture on a screen, somewhat like an X-ray photograph.

Coronary angiography (pronounced an-gee-AH-graffie) is the most accurate way to diagnose atherosclerosis. In this procedure, a catheter is inserted into a blood vessel in the patient's arm. A catheter is a long, narrow tube that can be pushed through the vein into the patient's heart. A dye is pumped through the catheter into the heart. Then, X-ray pictures are taken of the heart. The dye makes it possible to see structures of the heart in great detail. The presence of plaques can easily be seen.

TREATMENT

Mild cases of atherosclerosis can often be treated with changes in lifestyle. Patients can reduce the amount of fats and cholesterol in their diet, quit smoking, lose weight, and become more physically active. For more serious forms of atherosclerosis, other treatments may be necessary. These include the use of drugs and various forms of surgery.

A class of drugs that is used with atherosclerosis are designed to lower cholesterol. If the amount of cholesterol in the blood is reduced, the chance that plaques will form is also reduced. Aspirin may also be recommended because it tends to cause blood to become thinner.

One form of surgery used with atherosclerosis is angioplasty (pronounced AN-jee-o-PLAS-tee). In angioplasty a catheter tipped with a balloon is inserted into a blood vessel in the patient's thigh or arm. The catheter is then pushed upwards into the artery where a plaque exists. At that point, the balloon is inflated. The balloon pushes on the plaque. It may squeeze the plaque enough to open the artery to its normal size. Blood is then able to again flow through the artery.

Bypass surgery may also be used to treat atherosclerosis. In bypass surgery, the portion of an artery that is blocked by plaque is clamped off. A blood vessel is taken from some other part of the patient's body and inserted just before and just after the section of artery that has been blocked off. Blood is given a new pathway to flow through the body, bypassing the damaged artery. Bypass surgery is completely successful in about 70 percent of all cases and partially successful in another 20 percent.

Alternative Treatment

One focus of alternative treatments for atherosclerosis is diet. Practitioners recommend many of the changes suggested by traditional medicine including reducing the amount of cholesterol and fats eaten. Alternative practitioners also suggest that patients eat more raw and cooked

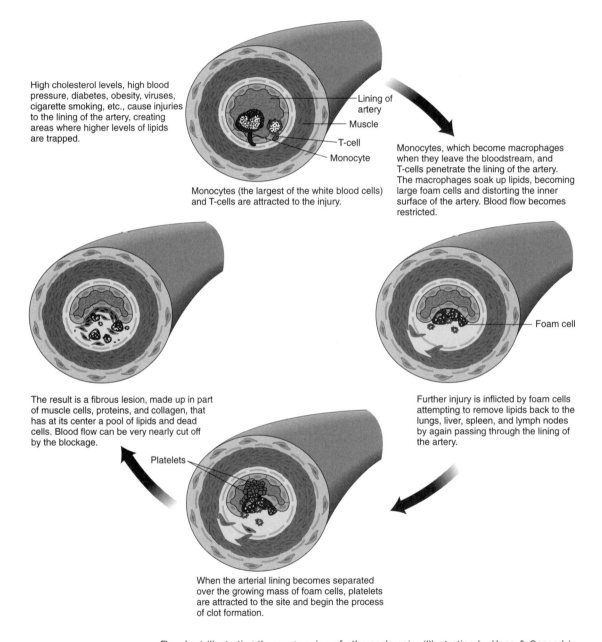

High cholesterol levels, high blood pressure, diabetes, obesity, viruses, cigarette smoking, etc., cause injuries to the lining of the artery, creating areas where higher levels of lipids are trapped.

—Lining of artery
— Muscle
—T-cell
— Monocyte

Monocytes (the largest of the white blood cells) and T-cells are attracted to the injury.

Monocytes, which become macrophages when they leave the bloodstream, and T-cells penetrate the lining of the artery. The macrophages soak up lipids, becoming large foam cells and distorting the inner surface of the artery. Blood flow becomes restricted.

— Foam cell

The result is a fibrous lesion, made up in part of muscle cells, proteins, and collagen, that has at its center a pool of lipids and dead cells. Blood flow can be very nearly cut off by the blockage.

Platelets —

Further injury is inflicted by foam cells attempting to remove lipids back to the lungs, liver, spleen, and lymph nodes by again passing through the lining of the artery.

When the arterial lining becomes separated over the growing mass of foam cells, platelets are attracted to the site and begin the process of clot formation.

Flowchart illustrating the progression of atherosclerosis. (Illustration by Hans & Cassady)

fish and fresh fruits and vegetables. Onion and garlic are particularly recommended.

A variety of herbs is also recommended to improve the patient's overall health. These herbs include hawthorn, ginger, hot red or chili peppers, yarrow, and alfalfa. Another focus of alternative treatments is helping patients to become more relaxed. In this way, they may feel less stress and experience a reduced blood pressure. Yoga, meditation, and massage are methods for improving relaxation.

ONE FOCUS OF ALTERNATIVE TREATMENTS FOR ATHEROSCLEROSIS IS DIET.

PROGNOSIS

Atherosclerosis cannot be cured, but it can be delayed, stopped, and even reversed. One of the most critical steps that a patient can take is to control cholesterol levels. Doctors are now able to detect atherosclerosis in its early stages. That development allows earlier treatment to prevent the most serious complications of the disorder.

PREVENTION

The key to reducing the risk for atherosclerosis is to reduce the risk factors an individual has control over, which includes:

- Eating a healthy diet low in cholesterol and triglycerides. The diet should be high in fruits and vegetables.
- Exercising regularly. Physical activity can lower blood pressure and help control weight.
- Maintaining a desirable body weight.
- Stopping—or never starting—to use tobacco. Even people who smoke can reduce their risk of atherosclerosis by giving up the habit.
- Seeking treatment for hypertension. Hypertension is another name for high blood pressure. High blood pressure is probably a hereditary condition, but it can be brought under control by certain changes in lifestyle. These changes include reducing the amount of sodium and fat in the diet, exercising, learning how to manage stress, giving up smoking, and drinking alcohol in moderation.

FOR MORE INFORMATION

Books

American Heart Association. *Guide to Heart Attack Treatment, Recovery, and Prevention.* New York: Time Books, 1996.

American Heart Association. *Living Well, Staying Well.* New York: American Heart Association and American Cancer Association, 1996.

Arnold, Caroline. *Heart Disease.* New York: Franklin Watts, 1990.

DeBakey, Michael E., and Antonio M. Gotto, Jr. *The New Living Heart.* Holbrook, MA: Adams Media Corporation, 1997.

Parker, Steve. *Heart Disease.* New York: Franklin Watts, 1989.

Periodicals

"Landmark Study Shows Heart Disease Prevention Must Start Early." *The Nation's Health* (March 1997): p. 13.

Morgan, Peggy. "What Your Heart Wishes You Knew about Cholesterol." *Prevention* (September 1997): p. 96.

Organizations

American Heart Association. National Center. 7272 Greenville Avenue, Dallas, TX 75231–4596. (214) 373–6300. http://www.amhrt.org.

National Heart, Lung, and Blood Institute. P.O. Box 30105, Bethesda, MD 20824–0105. (301) 496–4236. http://www.nhlbi.nih.gov.

ATHLETE'S FOOT

DEFINITION

Athlete's foot is a common fungus infection that occurs between the toes. The skin becomes itchy and sore and cracks and peels away. Athlete's foot is also known as tinea pedis (pronounced TIN-ee-uh PED-uhs) or foot ringworm (see ringworm entry). The disease can be treated, but it can be persistent and difficult to clear up completely.

DESCRIPTION

Athlete's foot is characterized by itchy, peeling skin on the feet. It is a very common condition. Most people have the condition at least once in their lives. It occurs less often in women and in children under the age of twelve. Young children may have the symptoms of athlete's foot, but those symptoms are usually caused by other skin conditions.

The fungi that cause athlete's foot grow well in warm, damp areas. For that reason, they often occur in and around swimming pools, showers, and locker rooms. That explains why tinea pedis is called athletes foot: it occurs frequently among athletes who use these facilities.

CAUSES

Athlete's foot is caused by a fungal infection that occurs most frequently between the fourth and fifth toes. The fungi that cause the disease are unusual in that they live exclusively on dead body tissue, such as dead skin and nails. These fungi grow best in moist, damp, dark places with poor ventilation. For that reason, athlete's foot is less common among people who go barefoot.

Many people carry the fungus that causes athlete's foot on their skin. The fungus becomes active, however, only when conditions are right. Many people believe that the fungus is very contagious. But that does not seem to be the case. Research shows that it is difficult to pick up the infection by simply walking barefoot on a damp floor that contains the fungus. Scientists do not know exactly why some people develop the disease and others do not.

THE FUNGI THAT CAUSE ATHLETE'S FOOT ARE UNUSUAL IN THAT THEY LIVE EXCLUSIVELY ON DEAD BODY TISSUE

Other factors can contribute to the growth of the athlete's foot fungus. These include sweaty feet, tight shoes, socks that do not absorb moisture, a warm climate, and inadequate drying of the feet after swimming or bathing.

SYMPTOMS

Symptoms of athlete's foot include itchy, sore skin on the toes, with scaling, cracking, inflammation, and blisters. Blisters that break can expose raw patches of tissue. These patches can also cause pain and swelling. As the infection spreads, itching and burning may get worse.

If left untreated, athlete's foot can spread to the bottom of the feet and toenails. Toenail infections may be accompanied by crumbling, scaling, and thickened nails, and nail loss. The infection can also be spread if the patient scratches him or herself and then touches another part of the body. The fungus also grows well in the groin area and under the arms. The infection can also be spread to other body parts by bed sheets and clothing that carry the fungus.

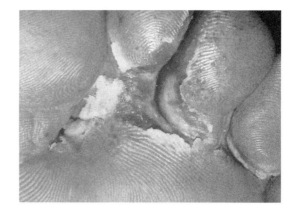

Athete's foot infection. (Reproduced by permission of Custom Medical Stock Photo)

DIAGNOSIS

Patients may be tempted to treat their rash with nonprescription drugs. However, if the condition is not properly diagnosed, such drugs could make the rash worse. It is better to see a doctor about the rash. A dermatologist (skin specialist) can diagnosis athlete's foot by conducting a physical examination and studying skin scrapings from the foot under a microscope. When treated with potassium hydroxide, the scrapings show the presence of fungi.

TREATMENT

Athlete's foot may be resistant to medication and should not be ignored. Simple cases can usually be cured with antifungal (fungus-killing) creams or sprays. If creams do not work, the doctor may prescribe antifungal drugs to be taken by mouth. Untreated athlete's foot may lead to a bacterial infection in the skin cracks.

Alternative Treatment

A footbath containing cinnamon can slow down the growth of certain fungi and can be effective in clearing up athlete's foot. The bath is made by adding eight to ten cinnamon sticks to four cups of boiling water. The mixture is allowed to simmer for five minutes and then to steep for forty-five minutes. When the mixture is lukewarm, it can be used to soak the feet.

Other herbal remedies include a foot soak or powder made with goldenseal or tea tree oil. A cream made with calendula (pronounced KUH-len-juh-luh) can also help heal cracked skin.

PROGNOSIS

Athlete's foot usually responds well to treatment. Patients should be sure to use all the medication given to them by a doctor. The disease may seem to be gone, but some fungus might still remain on the skin. In that case, the disease will reappear. Toenail infections that sometimes occur with athlete's foot can be very difficult to treat.

PREVENTION

Athlete's foot can be prevented by following some simple rules of good hygiene, including:

- Wash feet daily
- Dry feet thoroughly, especially between the toes
- Avoid tight shoes, especially in summer
- Wear sandals during warm weather
- Wear cotton socks and change them often if they get damp
- Do not wear socks made of synthetic materials
- Go barefoot outdoors when possible

- Wear bathing shoes in public bathing or showering areas
- Use a good quality foot powder
- Do not wear sneakers without socks
- Wash towels, contaminated floors, and shower stalls well with hot soapy water if anyone in the family has athlete's foot

FOR MORE INFORMATION

Books

Donahue, Peggy Jo. *Relief from Chronic Skin Problems.* New York: Dell Publishing, 1992.

Stoffman, Phyllis. *The Family Guide to Preventing and Treating 100 Infectious Illnesses.* New York: John Wiley & Sons, 1995.

Organizations

American Academy of Dermatology. 930 North Meachum Road, P.O. Box 4014, Schaumburg, IL 60168–4014. http://www.aad.org.

American Podiatric Medical Association. 9312 Old Georgetown Road, Bethesda, MD 20814. (301) 571–9200. http://www.apma.org.

ATTENTION-DEFICIT/HYPERACTIVITY DISORDER

DEFINITION

Attention-deficit/hyperactivity disorder (ADHD) is a condition that shows up most commonly in boys and girls after puberty begins. Puberty is the period in life when a person's sex hormones become active. ADHD is characterized by an inability to concentrate on tasks, hyperactivity (an abnormally high level of physical activity), and unpredictable behavior. ADHD is known as hyperkinetic disorder (HKD) outside of the United States.

DESCRIPTION

ADHD is thought to affect 3 to 9 percent of all children and is more common in boys than in girls. The signs of ADHD may first appear as early as the age of two or three. In most cases, however, the disorder is not diagnosed until adolescence. Some symptoms of ADHD, such as hyperactivity, tend to disappear in early adulthood. But others, such as inattention to details, remain with up to half of all ADHD individuals throughout their lives.

Children with ADHD have short attention spans. They may become bored or frustrated with tasks. They may be intelligent, but they receive poor grades in school because they do not focus on their work. They tend to be overly active, constantly moving, running, climbing, squirming, and fidgeting. They often have trouble controlling their muscles, which makes them clumsy and physically awkward. Such problems can cause social difficulties as well. Other children may avoid youngsters with ADHD because they may be noisy or bothersome.

CAUSES

The causes of ADHD are not known. Some people believe that an imbalance in neurotransmitters causes the disorder. Neurotransmitters are chemicals that carry messages from one part of the brain to another. Damage to neurotransmitters can be caused by a number of factors. For example, a head injury can damage the brain cells that produce neurotransmitters. Children who are exposed to toxins (poisons) early in life may experience similar brain cell damage.

Heredity also seems to play a role in ADHD. Studies show that children born to people who have the disorder tend to inherit the disorder.

Some medical authorities have suggested that diet may be a factor in causing ADHD. For example, a high intake of sugar was once thought to be a possible cause of the disorder. Today, that explanation for ADHD is no longer accepted. Dietary factors do not seem to be responsible for ADHD.

SYMPTOMS

WORDS TO KNOW

Conduct disorder: A behavioral and emotional disorder of childhood and adolescence. Children with a conduct disorder act inappropriately, infringe on the rights of others, and violate social rules.

Nervous tic: An involuntary action, continually repeated, such as the twitching of a muscle or repeated blinking.

Doctors use a standard reference book called the *Diagnostic and Statistical Manual of Mental Disorders, Fourth Edition* (DSM-IV) to diagnose ADHD. A patient must show some combination of the following symptoms to be diagnosed with ADHD.

- Fails to pay close attention to detail or makes careless mistakes in schoolwork and other activities
- Has difficulty paying attention to tasks or activities

- Does not seem to listen when spoken to
- Does not follow through on instruction and does not finish tasks
- Has difficulty in organizing tasks and activities
- Avoids or dislikes tasks that require sustained mental effort, such as homework
- Is easily distracted
- Is forgetful in daily activities
- Fidgets with hands or feet or squirms in seat
- Does not remain seated when expected to
- Runs or climbs when inappropriate
- Has difficulty playing quietly
- Is constantly on the move
- Talks excessively
- Blurts out answers before questions have been completed
- Has difficulty waiting for his or her turn
- Interrupts and/or intrudes on others

Doctors also make use of other information in diagnosing ADHD. For example, some symptoms have to show up before the age of seven. In addition, there must be evidence that a child cannot function normally in at least two settings, such as home and school.

DIAGNOSIS

The first step in diagnosing ADHD is to have the child see a pediatrician. A pediatrician is a medical doctor who specializes in the diseases and disorders of children. Because many of the symptoms of ADHD are normal and common in all children, the pediatrician is careful to determine whether the child is behaving normally compared with other children of the same age. The pediatrician may also conduct a physical examination to make sure that there is nothing physically wrong with the patient, which may be causing the inadequate behaviors.

If the pediatrician finds no problems during the physical examination, the child may be referred to someone who works with mental disorders, such as a psychologist or a psychiatrist. The specialist then conducts his or her own examination, which may include a medical, family, educational, social, and psychological history. The specialist is likely to hold interviews with the child and to have the child take certain standard tests. The Achenbach Child Behavior Rating Scales, for example, attempts to provide information about a child's behavior in different settings.

Diagnosis of ADHD can be difficult because its symptoms are similar to those of other disorders. For example, depression (see depressive disorders entry) and anxiety disorders can cause symptoms similar to those of ADHD.

Federal law now requires all public schools to offer free ADHD testing upon request.

TREATMENT

ADHD is usually treated with one of two approaches: drugs or behavior modification. Drugs tend to be the more popular therapy because they are easy to use and seem to have more dependable results. Prescribing drugs for children, however, is not without controversy.

One group of drugs used to treat ADHD is psychostimulants. These drugs work by stimulating the production of neurotransmitters. One of the best known of these drugs is methylphenidate (pronounced meth-uhl-FEN-uh-date, trade name Ritalin). For children who do not respond to psychostimulants, a variety of other drugs are available. These include desipramine (pronounced dez-uh-PRAM-uhn, trade names Norpramin, Pertofane) and fluoxetine (pronounced floo-AHK-suh-teen, trade name Prozac), which are antidepressants, and carbamazepine, (pronounced KAHR-buh-MAZ-uh-peen, trade names Tegretol, Atretol), an anticonvulsant. The most effective drug for any one child may change as that child grows and becomes more mature.

All drugs used to treat ADHD have side effects, some of which can be serious. For example, methylphenidate may cause insomnia, nervousness, and loss of appetite; desipramine can cause dry mouth, disorientation, and irregular heartbeat.

ARE WE "DRUGGING" PROBLEM CHILDREN?

Not all experts agree that ADHD is a disease or a disorder. According to some, many children have a lot of energy when they are growing up. A normal, healthy child is naturally curious and full of activity, so should parents and teachers really be surprised when some students have trouble sitting still in classes for six or more hours a day? Some experts think this behavior is perfectly normal.

These experts argue that giving children drugs is the wrong answer to a perceived problem. They agree that the drugs work in the short-term: drugs help children settle down and focus on their school work. But they argue that parents and doctors should also deal with the emotional or psychological problems that may have contributed to the child's behavior. Some re-searchers are concerned over whether children are being helped in the long-term.

Another issue has arisen about the use of drugs to control ADHD. Some young men and women have now been taking Ritalin for more then ten years. They started taking the drug during elementary or high school and continue to take the drug in college. They find that Ritalin helps them to concentrate on their class assignments. Some students report that they take up to twenty-five pills a day to get the effect they need. Such doses can have harmful effects on users. These effects include sleeplessness, loss of appetite, and fatigue.

Most authorities agree that drugs can solve ADHD problems for some children. How frequently drugs are prescribed and just how to properly diagnosis ADHD is still being debated.

Behavior modification therapy is a set of techniques designed to change the way people behave. Rewards are provided for good or correct behavior, while punishment may be given for bad or inappropriate behavior. For example, a child may be given a token each time he or she behaves in an approved manner. When the child has collected enough tokens, he or she may redeem the tokens for some kind of prize or reward.

One form of behavior modification is called cognitive-behavioral therapy. In this form of therapy, the child is taught to recognize the connection between thought and action. He or she is then shown how to change behavior by changing his or her negative thoughts.

Individual and family counseling can also help ADHD patients. Patients and their families can be helped to understand possible causes for the inappropriate behavior and how to deal with and eventually change that behavior.

Alternative Treatment

A number of alternative treatments for ADHD exist. In many cases, there is little or no scientific evidence that these treatments are effective. Many people believe strongly in them, however, and recommend their use with ADHD children. These treatments include:

- **EEG biofeedback.** During EEG (electroencephalograph; pronounced ih-LEK-tro-in-SEH-fuh-lo-graf) biofeedback, an ADHD child watches the brain waves produced when he or she is behaving correctly or incorrectly. The child is then trained to adjust that behavior to produce correct brain waves.
- **Dietary therapy.** This therapy is based on the theory that ADHD is caused by incorrect diet. Patients are taught to eat foods high in protein and complex carbohydrates (such as starches like potatoes and pasta), and to avoid white sugar and other types of foods.
- **Herbal therapy.** Herbal therapy uses a variety of natural products to relieve the symptoms of ADHD. Some examples include ginkgo, to improve memory and mental sharpness, and chamomile, to help calm the patient. Although herbs like these are popular with some doctors, their effectiveness and safety have not been proved scientifically.
- **Homeopathic medicine.** This approach has perhaps the best chance of success of all alternative treatments. It treats the person as a whole, seeking to discover the fundamental problems that have led to ADHD in the first place.

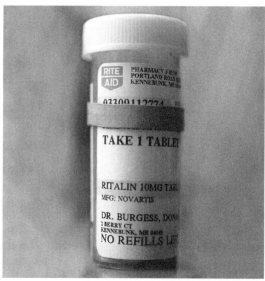

Ritalin is a drug commonly given to children with ADHD. (Reproduced by permission of AP/Wide World Photos)

Children who have been properly diagnosed with ADHD and who do not receive treatment may experience serious problems. They tend to develop low self-esteem and often have problems relating to other children. Their education may also suffer because of teachers who think of them as slow learners or troublemakers. Parents and siblings (brothers and sisters) may also develop negative feelings toward the ADHD child. Over time, ADHD children are also likely to develop learning disorders or emotional problems, such as depression or anxiety disorders.

ADHD can also lead to an even more serous problem known as conduct disorder. Among adolescents diagnosed with both ADHD and conduct disorder, up to 25 percent go on to become criminals, drug abusers, or suicide victims.

Approximately 70 to 80 percent of ADHD patients who receive drug treatment experience significant improvement in their condition, at least on a short-term basis. About half of all ADHD children seem to outgrow the disorder by the end of adolescence. The other half seem to retain some or all symptoms of ADHD as adults.

PREVENTION

Researchers have not yet determined if ADHD is preventable.

FOR MORE INFORMATION

Books

Alexander-Roberts, Colleen. *The ADHD Parenting Handbook: Practical Advice for Parents from Parents.* Dallas: Taylor Publishing Co., 1994.

Barkley, Russell A. *Taking Charge of ADHD: The Complete, Authoritative Guide for Parents.* New York: Guilford Press, 1995.

Hallowell, Edward M., and John J. Ratey. *Driven to Distraction.* New York: Pantheon Books, 1994.

Kennedy, Patricia, Leif Terdal, and Lydia Fusetti. *The Hyperactive Child Book.* New York: St.Martin's Press, 1993.

Osman, Betty B. *Learning Disabilities and ADHD: A Family Guide to Living and Learning Together.* New York: John Wiley & Sons, 1997.

Stein, David B. *Ritalin Is Not the Answer: A Drug-Free, Practical Program for Children Diagnosed with ADD or ADHD.* New York: Jossey-Bass, Inc., 1999.

Periodicals

Hallowell, Edward M. "What I've Learned from A.D.D." *Psychology Today* (May–June 1997): pp. 40–46.

Organizations

American Academy of Child and Adolescent Psychiatry (AACAP). 3615 Wisconsin Avenue NW, Washington, DC 20016. (202) 966–7300. http://www.aacap.org.

Children and Adults with Attention Deficit Disorder (CHADD). 499 Northwest 70th Avenue, Suite 101. Plantation, FL 33317. (800) 233–4050. http://www.chadd.org.

The National Attention Deficit Disorder Association. (ADDA). 9930 Johnnycake Ridge Road, Suite 3E, Mentor, OH 44060. (800) 487–2282. http://www.add.org.

AUTISM

DEFINITION

Autism is a severe disorder of brain function. It is marked by problems with social contact, intelligence, and use of language. People who suffer from autism usually exhibit behaviors that are repeated over and over again in very standard patterns.

DESCRIPTION

Autism is a lifelong disorder. It interferes with a person's ability to understand what he or she sees, hears, and touches. For this reason, a person with autism has very difficult problems knowing how to behave properly and how to interact with other people. The person has to be taught behaviors that develop normally in most people. Autism varies in its degree of severity among individuals. The disease has a full range of symptoms, ranging from mild to severe.

Autism occurs in about 1 out of every 1,000 children. It is found four times more often in boys than in girls. It occurs everywhere in the world among all races and social backgrounds. Autism is usually evident in the first three years of life. In some children, the disease is difficult to detect. It may not be diagnosed until the child enters school.

Some children with autism have an unusual form of the disease. They show a unique talent in one specific area, such as mathematics, memory, music, or art. These children are known as autistic savants (pronounced sa-VAHNT), or intellectual autistics.

CAUSES

Autism is a brain disorder that affects the way the brain uses or transmits information. This disorder almost certainly develops before the child is born. The problem may be located in parts of the brain that process information that comes from the senses, such as the eyes and ears.

Autism appears to be a genetic disorder. Identical twins are more likely to both have the disease than are fraternal twins. Identical twins have exactly the same genetic make-up. Fraternal twins do not. In a family with one autistic child, the chance of having a second autistic child is about one in twenty. That rate is fifty times greater than in the general population.

Relatives of autistic children sometimes display autistic-like behaviors. For example, they may have problems communicating with other people, or they may repeat certain behaviors over and over again. They may also have certain emotional disorders.

In a few cases, autistic behavior is caused by a disease, such as rubella (German measles; see rubella entry) in a pregnant woman, encephalitis (pronounced in-seh-fuh-LIE-tess; brain fever; see encephalitis entry), or phenylketonuria (pronounced fen-uhl-keet-n-YOOR-ee-uh, PKU) left untreated.

SYMPTOMS

The severity of autism varies among individuals. Some children have severe symptoms. They may act aggressively against other people and even try to harm themselves. Other children have mild symptoms. They may have problems getting along with others and have mild learning disorders.

The most common symptom of autism is a serious inability to relate to other people. Infants with the disorder refuse to cuddle and avoid eye

WORDS TO KNOW

Antidepressants: Medications that treat depression and that can also be used to treat autism.

Asperger syndrome: A type of autism that involves no problems with language.

Encephalitis: An inflammation of the brain caused by a viral infection.

Fragile X syndrome: A genetic condition involving the X chromosome that results in mental, physical, and sensory problems.

Opiate blockers: Drugs that interfere with the action of natural opiates, substances that cause sleepiness and numbness.

Phenylketonuria (PKU): A genetic disorder in which a person's body is unable to break down the amino acid phenylalanine, causing damage to the brain.

Stimulants: A class of drugs that tends to arouse the body but that seem to calm down children with autism.

Tranquilizers: Drugs that help a person to calm down.

contact. They do not seem to want or need physical contact or affection. They become stiff or totally relaxed when held and begin to cry when picked up. Autistic babies form no attachment to their parents and are frightened by strangers. They do not learn typical childhood games, such as peek-a-boo.

INFANTS WITH AUTISM DO NOT SEEM TO WANT OR NEED PHYSICAL CONTACT OR AFFECTION.

Language Problems

Autistic children may not speak at all. If they do, it is often in single words. They may repeat words or phrases over and over again. Pronouns may get reversed, as in "You go sleep" instead of "I want to go to sleep."

Restricted Interests and Activity

Autistic children usually do not play normally. They do not act out adult roles, such as pretending to be a doctor or parent. Nor do they use their imaginations to create fantasy worlds. Instead, they repeat simple behaviors of the people around them.

These behaviors may become complex and ritualistic. That is, they are repeated over and over again in a very precise way. Autistic children are also prone to strange behavior patterns such as screaming fits, rocking back and forth, arm flapping, and finger twiddling. Austic children may play with their own saliva, feces, or urine. They may be self-destructive, biting their own hands, gouging at their eyes, pulling their hair, or banging their heads.

Sensory Problems

The world of sight and sound poses a real problem to many autistic children. They may ignore objects or become obsessed by them. Or they may watch those objects very carefully or act as if they are not even there. Sounds can also be a problem. Autistic children may react to sounds by banging their heads or flapping their fingers.

Some adults who have overcome autism have written books about their childhood experiences. They report that sounds were often terribly painful to them. They were forced to withdraw into their own world to avoid dealing with the sounds of the real world.

Intellectual Problems

Most autistic children appear to be somewhat mentally challenged. They may giggle or cry for no reason. They may be very frightened of harmless objects, but have no fear of real danger.

DIAGNOSIS

There is no medical test for autism. It is diagnosed by observing a child's behavior, communication skills, and interactions with other people. The problem is that the symptoms of autism are varied, so the disease may not be recognized for a long time. It is easily confused with other diseases with similar symptoms, such as fragile X syndrome and untreated phenylketonuria.

The first step in diagnosing autism is a series of medical tests to rule out other diseases. Then mental health experts use various signs to diagnose the disease. These include:

- Problems in developing friendships
- Problems with make-believe or social play
- Endlessly repeated words or phrases
- Difficulty in carrying on a conversation
- Obsessions with rituals
- Fascination with parts of objects

Some children have some, but not all, of the symptoms of autism. For example, some children exhibit autistic behaviors, but have no problems with language. This condition is known as Asperger syndrome. Some children seem normal at first, but develop autism as they grow older. This condition is known as childhood disintegrative disorder (CDD).

TREATMENT

There is no cure for autism. Treatments are aimed at reducing specific symptoms. Since symptoms differ from person to person, no single treatment program works for every patient. Some of the treatments used include training in music, listening, vision, speech, and language. Special diets and medication may also be prescribed.

THE HUG BOX

Some behavioral treatments for autism are quite simple. An example is the hug box, which was invented by Temple Grandin. Grandin is an adult with autism who has written two books about her life, *Emergence: Labeled Autistic* and *Thinking in Pictures*.

Grandin remembers what her childhood years as an autistic were like. One memory she has was the need to feel somebody or something close around her. Sometimes she would crawl under sofa cushions or wrap herself in a blanket. As she grew older Grandin realized that the feeling of pressure all around her helped her to relax.

As an adult, she decided to develop a treatment for other autistic children based on her own experience. So, she invented the hug box.

The hug box consists of two boards covered with padding, which are hinged along one edge to form a V-shaped device. The device is big enough for a child to comfortably crawl in. The two boards can be pushed closer together simply by pushing on a lever. This allows a child to get a short hug or a long hug, a tight hug or a loose hug.

The hug box seems to be successful in helping some autistic children to feel better and relax. They are now being used in many hospitals and care centers around the United States.

People with autism can improve significantly with proper treatment. A child with autism learns best in a well organized environment with a single specially trained teacher. The two treatments used most often include educational or behavior treatment and medication.

Educational or Behavioral Treatment

In this form of treatment, autistic children are rewarded for correct (good) behaviors. A child who speaks correctly, for example, might be given a piece of candy or other favorite food. Over time, correct behaviors become more common and incorrect behaviors less common. This form of treatment should be started as early as possible. It seems to affect the way the child's brain develops, making autistic behavior less likely.

Educational and behavioral treatments seem to work best when carried out at home. In many cases, however, these treatments occur in specialized schools, at day care, or in psychiatric hospitals.

Medication

No single medication has been found to work with all features of autism. A combination of drugs can be used, however, to treat the most serious symp-

Autistic children sometimes respond to behavioral and educational treatments in schools such as this one in Salt Lake City, Utah, that offer teachers specially trained to work with autistic children. (Reproduced by permission of AP/Wide World Photos.)

toms. These symptoms include aggressiveness and the tendency to injure one-self. Drugs can also be used to control epilepsy (see epilepsy entry), which affects about 20 percent of patients with autism.

Five types of drugs are used to treat autism:

- Stimulants, such as methylphenidate (pronounced meth-uhl-FEN-uh-date, trade name Ritalin)
- Antidepressants, such as fluroxamine (trade name Luvox)
- Opiate blockers, such as naltrexone (pronounced nal-TREK-sone, trade name ReVia)
- Antipsychotics
- Tranquilizers

Most experts recommend a combination of drug therapies that begins early and continues through the teenage years. Behavioral treatments are used in combination with medications.

Alternative Treatments

Many parents report success with megavitamin therapy. Megavitamin therapy involves the use of very large doses of vitamins. Vitamin B_6 seems to improve eye contact and speech. It may also reduce tantrums. Vitamin B_6 has few side effects and is considered safe to use. However, many health practitioners are not convinced by parent reports or scientific studies reported thus far.

Dimethylglycine (DMG)

DMG is chemically similar to glycine, a naturally occurring amino acid. It is available in many health food stores. Some people believe that it improves speech in autistic children. Those who respond to DMG usually do so within a week. Again, many doctors are not convinced about the effectiveness of this compound.

Exercise

One research study has found that vigorous exercise decreases some of the symptoms of autism. Additional research is needed to confirm this finding.

PROGNOSIS

People with autism have a normal life expectancy, but there is no available cure. However, many of its symptoms can be relieved by treatment. At one time, autistic children were placed in institutions, from which they might never be released. Today, most autistic children can be treated at home, in special schools, and in other more comfortable and familiar settings. Some eventually come to understand the world better and to learn how to interact with other people. They can go on to lead nearly normal lives. Some may be able to handle a job. The best work settings for autistic people are those with structure in which the same task is repeated over and over again.

PREVENTION

There is currently no known way of preventing autism.

FOR MORE INFORMATION

Books

Barron, Sean, and Judy Barron. *There's a Boy in Here*. New York: Simon & Schuster, 1992.

Bratt, Berneen. *No Time for Jello*. Cambridge, MA: Brookline Books, 1989.

Cohen, Shirley. *Targeting Autism: What We Know, Don't Know, and Can Do to Help Young Children with Autism and Related Disorders*. Berkeley: University of California Press, 1998.

Grandin, Temple, and Oliver Sacks. *Thinking in Pictures: And Other Reports from My Life With Autism*. New York: Vintage Books, 1996.

Grandin, Temple, and Margaret M. Scariano. *Emergence: Labeled Autistic*. New York: Warner Books, 1996.

Greenfield, Josh. *A Child Named Noah*. New York: Holt, Rinehart and Winston, 1971.

Hart, Charles. *A Parent's Guide to Autism: Answers to the Most Common Questions*. New York: Pocket Books, 1993.

Kaufman, Barry Neil. *Son-Rise*. New York: Harper & Row, 1976.

Williams, Donna. *Nobody Knows*. New York: Times Books, 1992.

Periodicals

Roeder, Jason, "Can Medication Change Behavior in Autism?" *The Exceptional Parent* (November 1995): pp. 50–54.

Shapiro, Joseph, "Beyond the Rain Main: A Singular Woman Changes the Cattle Industry and Our Image of Autism." *U.S. News & World Report* (May 27, 1996): pp. 78–79.

Organizations

Autism Network International. PO Box 448, Syracuse, NY 13210.

Autism Research Institute. 4182 Adams Avenue, San Diego, CA 92116. (619) 281–7165.

Autism Society of America. 7910 Woodmont Avenue, Suite 650, Bethesda, MD 20814. (301) 657–0881; (800) 3AUTISM. http://www.autism-society.org.

Center for the Study of Autism. P.O. Box 4538, Salem, OR 97302. http://www.autism.org

National Autism Hotline. c/o Autism Services Center, PO Box 507, 605 Ninth Street, Huntington, WV 25710. (304) 525–8014.

Web sites

National Alliance for Autism Research. http://www.naar.org (accessed on October 18, 1999).

National Information Center for Children and Youth with Disabilities. http://www.nichcy.org (accessed on October 18, 1999).

"Autism." *Drkoop.com Medical Encyclopedia.* [Online] http://www.drkoop.com/conditions/encyclopedia/articles/025000a/autism.html?id=avkey.autism.lk (accessed on October 18, 1999).

AUTOIMMUNE DISORDERS

DEFINITION

Autoimmune disorders are conditions in which a person's immune system (the network of organs, tissues, cells, and chemicals whose job it is to protect the body from foreign invaders, like bacteria and viruses) attacks the body's own cells. As cells are killed, tissues begin to die off.

DESCRIPTION

Many forms of autoimmune disorders are now recognized. These disorders are classified as general or organ specific. A general autoimmune disorder is one that attacks a number of tissues throughout the body. An organ specific disorder attacks only one type of organ at a time.

Some examples of autoimmune disorders include:

• Systemic lupus erythematosus (pronounced LOO-puhs er-uh-THEM-uh-tuhs; see lupus entry) is a general autoimmune disorder. The condition occurs primarily in young and middle-aged women.

• Rheumatoid (pronounced ROO-muh-toid) arthritis (see arthritis entry) is inflammation of joints. It occurs when the immune system attacks and destroys tissue that lines the bone joints and cartilage.

• Goodpasture's syndrome is an inflammation of the lungs and kidneys. It occurs primarily in young males.

- Grave's disease affects the thyroid gland. The diseases causes the gland to make an excessive amount of thyroid hormone.
- Hashimoto's thyroiditis also affects the thyroid gland. But it causes a reduction in the amount of thyroid hormone produced by the gland.
- Pemphigus vulgaris (pronounced PEM-fi-guhs vuhl-GARE-uhs) is a group of autoimmune disorders that affects the skin.
- Myasthenia (pronounced MY-uhs-THEE-nee-uh) gravis is caused when messages from nerve cells to muscles are disrupted. Muscles become weakened.
- Scleroderma (pronounced SKLEER-uh-DIR-muh) causes a toughening and hardening of connective tissue.
- Autoimmune hemolytic anemia is a condition that causes damage to red blood cells (see anemia entry).
- Autoimmune thrombocytopenic purpura (pronounced THROM-buh-SI-tuh-PEE-nick PIR-puh-ruh) results in destruction to blood platelets, cells that help blood to clot.
- Pernicious anemia develops when the body can no longer make use of vitamin B_{12}, resulting in a decreased production of red blood cells (see anemia entry).
- Sjögren's (pronounced SHO-grenz) syndrome occurs when glands are damaged, increasing the loss of water by the body and causing excessive dryness.
- Ankylosing spondylitis (pronounced ANG-kuh-lozing spon-duh-LIE-tis) results in the destruction of joints and soft tissue in the spine.
- Vasculitis is a group of disorders in which blood vessels are destroyed.
- Type I diabetes mellitus (see diabetes mellitus entry) is caused when the islet cells of the pancreas are damaged, preventing the release of insulin to the body.

CAUSES

Autoimmune disorders occur when the body's immune system becomes confused. Because the immune system is used to fight foreign invaders, under normal circumstances, the immune system is able to tell if a group of cells is part of the body or not. For example, it generally has no problem recognizing that bacteria and viruses do not belong to the body. In such cases, the immune system takes a number of actions to fight off and kill the foreign cells.

An important component of the immune system is the production of antibodies. Anti-

WORDS TO KNOW

Anemia: A medical condition caused by a reduced number of red blood cells, characterized by general weakness, paleness, irregular heart beat, and fatigue.

Antibody: A chemical made by the immune system to destroy foreign invaders.

General autoimmune disorder: An autoimmune disorder that involves a number of tissues throughout the body.

Immune system: A network of organs, tissues, cells, and chemicals designed to fight off foreign invaders, such as bacteria and viruses.

Organ specific disorder: An autoimmune disorder in which only one type of organ is affected.

Steroids: A group of naturally occurring substances that are very effective in reducing pain and swelling in tissues.

bodies are chemicals made by the immune system to destroy foreign invaders. Antibodies are very specific. The immune system makes only one type of antibody for each different foreign invader. For example, there is a very specific antibody for each different virus that gets into the body.

But the immune system sometimes makes mistakes. It may somehow regard cells from its own body as being foreign. In such cases, it takes the same actions against those cells as it does against bacteria, viruses, and other truly foreign organisms. It actually begins to destroy healthy, normal cells in the body. When this happens, an autoimmune disorder results.

SYMPTOMS

Each type of autoimmune disorder has its characteristic symptoms. Some of these symptoms include:

- Systemic lupus erythematosus: Fever, chills, fatigue, weight loss, skin rashes, patchy hair loss, sores in the mouth or nose, problems with the digestive system, vision problems and, in women, irregular periods. Lupus can also affect the central nervous system, causing seizures, depression, and mental disorders.
- Rheumatoid arthritis: Mild fever, loss of appetite, weight loss, and, most important, pain in the joints. In advanced stages, rheumatoid arthritis can lead to deformities of the body.
- Goodpasture's syndrome: Fatigue and paleness. Bleeding may occur in the lungs or the urinary system.
- Grave's disease: An enlarged thyroid gland, weight loss, sweating, irregular heart beat, nervousness, and an inability to tolerate heat.

ORGAN TRANSPLANTATION

An organ transplantation may be necessary when a person's heart, kidney, lungs, liver, or some other vital organ becomes diseased. In such cases, a second person may offer to donate his or her organ to replace the diseased or damaged organ. Autoimmune disorders can often occur when organs are transplanted from one person to another. The problem is that the patient's immune system may reject the donated organ because it thinks the donated organ is a foreign body. It begins to attack the new organ as it would bacteria, viruses, fungi, or other disease-causing organisms.

Patients who receive transplanted organs are also given immunosuppressant drugs. An immunosuppressant drug is a chemical that reduces the body's natural defenses against foreign bodies. It gives the donated organ a chance to become implanted in the new body and start functioning again.

However, immunosuppressant drugs can cause a different set of problems: they prevent the immune system from doing its normal jobs; a patient becomes much more sensitive to diseases that the immune system is usually able to fight; and patients may become ill very easily. For most patients, though, the tradeoff is well worth it. Without the new, healthy organ and the immunosuppressant drugs to sustain it, they might not live.

- Hashimoto's thyroiditis: Generally no symptoms.
- Pemphigus vulgaris: Blisters and deep, open sores on the skin.
- Myasthenia gravis: General muscle weakness that may develop into paralysis. Chewing, swallowing, and breathing may be difficult.
- Scleroderma: Pain, swelling, and stiffness of the joints. The skin takes on a tight, shiny appearance. Digestive problems may develop, leading to weight loss, loss of appetite, diarrhea, constipation, and swelling of the abdomen.
- Autoimmune hemolytic anemia: Fatigue and tenderness in the abdomen.
- Autoimmune thrombocytopenic purpura: Tiny, red dots on the skin, unexplained bruises, bleeding from the nose and gums, and blood in the stool.

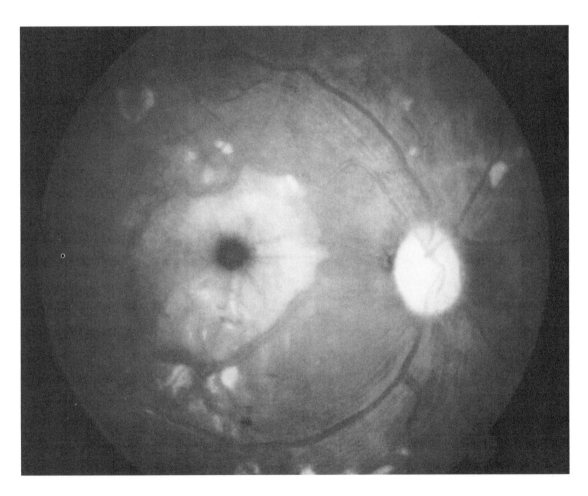

A view of the retina showing symptoms of lupus erythmatosis, a type of autoimmune disorder. (© 1997 SPL, Sue Ford/Science Photo Library. Reproduced by permission of Custom Medical Stock Photo.)

- Pernicious anemia: General weakness, sore tongue, bleeding gums, and tingling in the arms and legs. A deficiency of vitamin B_{12} can also cause a number of nervous disorders, including weakness, lack of coordination, blurred vision, loss of the sense of taste, ringing in the ears, and loss of bladder control.
- Sjögren's syndrome: Excessive dryness of the mouth and eyes.
- Ankylosing spondylitis: Lower back pain that usually moves up the spine.
- Vasculitis: Symptoms range widely depending on the part of the body affected.
- Type I diabetes mellitus: Fatigue and an abnormally high level of sugar in the blood.

DIAGNOSIS

The first step in diagnosing any autoimmune disorder is usually a review of symptoms. An additional step involves ruling out other medical conditions that might produce similar symptoms.

The final diagnosis for an autoimmune disorder, however, usually involves a blood test. The purpose of the blood test is to look for antibodies. If ankylosing spondylitis is present in the body, for example, very specific antibodies for that disorder will be present. If no such antibodies are found in the patient's blood, the disorder is not present.

TREATMENT

Treatments differ for each type of autoimmune disorder. However, there is one treatment that is common to many forms of autoimmune disorders. That treatment is the use of drugs to reduce the inflammation, swelling, and pain that accompanies most autoimmune disorders. Inflammation occurs when antibodies attack and irritate tissues. Some common drugs, such as aspirin and ibuprofen (pronounced i-byoo-PRO-fuhn), help reduce inflammation and pain. Aspirin should not be given to children due to the danger of contracting Reye's syndrome (see Reye's syndrome entry). A more powerful medication is one of the many steroid medications. But steroids have some serious long-term side effects, and they are generally used only in severe cases or in situations where milder drugs are ineffective.

PROGNOSIS

Prognosis differs for each type of autoimmune disorder.

PREVENTION

There is currently no way to prevent any of the autoimmune disorders.

See also: Anemias, arthritis, diabetes, and lupus.

FOR MORE INFORMATION

Books

Aaseng, Nathan. *Autoimmune Diseases.* New York: Franklin Watts, 1995.

Organizations

American Autoimmune Related Diseases Association, Inc. 15475 Gratiot Avenue, Detroit, MI 48205. (313) 371–8600. http://www.aarda.org.

BIPOLAR DISORDER

DEFINITION

Bipolar disorder is a mental condition that usually involves extreme mood swings. A person with the condition may feel happy and excited at one moment and depressed the next. The disorder was once called manic-depression. Mania is a mental disorder characterized by great excitement and sometimes uncontrolled, violent behavior. Depression (see depressive disorders entry) is characterized by persistent and long-term sadness or despair.

DESCRIPTION

Bipolar disorder affects about two million Americans. The average age at which the disorder first appears is between adolescence and the mid-twenties. Sometimes a correct diagnosis of the disorder is not made for years. It is complex and difficult to identify. In one study of bipolar disorder patients, half said that they saw three or more doctors before receiving a correct diagnosis. Over one third waited more than ten years before their condition was recognized.

BIPOLAR DISORDER AFFECTS ABOUT TWO MILLION AMERICANS.

Psychiatrists list four types of bipolar disorder. The four types differ largely on three factors. One factor is whether mania (the highs) or depression (the lows) is more common in the patient. The second factor is how serious each condition is. The third factor is how fast the patient alternates between stages.

Patients with bipolar I disorder, for example, have extreme high periods with relatively moderate periods of depression. By contrast, those with bipolar II disorder are more likely to have severe depression, separated by relatively modest periods of mania.

A third type of bipolar disorder is called cyclothymia (pronounced sie-kluh-THIE-mee-uh). Patients with this condition have relatively moderate periods of both mania and depression. They may almost appear to be without either symptom for long periods of time. The fourth type of bipolar disorder is called rapid cycling. In this condition, a patient changes from periods of great energy to periods of depression fairly often, usually at least four times in a single year.

CAUSES

The cause of bipolar disorder has not yet been discovered. Many researchers believe that heredity is an important factor. Two-thirds of bipolar patients have a family history of mental disorders. Some research studies claim to have found a genetic link for bipolar disorder. Genes are the chemical units present in all cells that tell cells what functions to perform. Genes are passed down from parents to children.

Some researchers also believe that abnormal levels of certain chemicals in the body can cause bipolar disorder. For example, some studies have shown that people with bipolar disorder have abnormal levels of dopamine in their brains. Dopamine is a neurotransmitter, a chemical that carries messages in the brain.

Drug abuse may be associated with bipolar disorder also. Up to 30 percent of those who abuse cocaine also have bipolar disorder. Researchers are not sure about this connection, however. It may be that bipolar disorder leads to drug abuse, or that drug abuse leads to bipolar disorder. Or it may be that both conditions are caused by some abnormal condition in a person's body.

Bipolar disorder has also been shown to be associated with the seasons. Some patients experience mania during the summer months and depression during the winter months.

WORDS TO KNOW

Anticonvulsant medication: A drug used to prevent convulsions or seizures that is sometimes also effective in the treatment of bipolar disorder.

Benzodiazepines: A group of tranquilizing drugs that have a calming influence on a person.

DSM-IV: The *Diagnostic and Statistical Manual of Mental Disorders,* Fourth Edition, the standard reference book used for diagnosing and treating mental disorders.

ECT: Electroconvulsive shock therapy, a method for using electric shocks to treat patients with mental disorders, such as bipolar disorder.

Mania: A mental condition in which a person feels unusually excited, irritated, or happy.

Neurotransmitter: A chemical found in the brain that carries electrical signals from one nerve cell to another nerve cell.

SYMPTOMS

The symptoms of bipolar disorder vary depending on the part of the cycle a patient is experiencing. During a low period, the patient has low energy levels, feelings of despair, difficulty concentrating, extreme fatigue, and slower mental and physical functions.

The manic, or high, part of a cycle is characterized by feelings of happiness and well-being, lack of restraint, talkativeness, racing thoughts, reduced need for sleep, and irritability. In extreme cases, mania can be expressed in the form of hallucinations and other mental fantasies.

DIAGNOSIS

Bipolar disorder is usually diagnosed by a psychiatrist, a doctor who specializes in mental conditions. One set of tools that is often used is a series of tests of a person's mental condition. Some examples of these tests include the Millon Clinical Multiaxial Inventory III (MCMI-III), the Minnesota Multiphasic Personality Inventory II (MMPI-2), the Internal State Scale (ISS), and the Self-Report Manic Inventory (SRMI). These tests may be either verbal or written and are conducted in a hospital or a doctor's office.

Psychiatrists rely on a book called the *Diagnostic and Statistical Manual of Mental Disorders,* Fourth Edition (DSM-IV), in diagnosing bipolar disorder. DSM-IV is the standard reference manual for all kinds of mental disorders. It describes the conditions for which a psychiatrist should look in diagnosing a condition. The guidelines set down in DSM-IV are very clear and specific for each condition.

For example, DSM-IV defines mania as a period of abnormally intense excitement that lasts for a period of at least one week. The patient must also demonstrate at least three specific symptoms from the following list:

- Inflated self-esteem
- Decreased need for sleep
- Talkativeness
- Racing thoughts
- Becoming distracted easily
- Increase in desire to get specific jobs done
- Unusual interest in activities that can lead to painful results

The symptoms of bipolar disorder are often different in children and adolescents. For example, their symptoms may be considerably more severe than in adults. A psychiatrist may diagnose schizophrenia (pronounced skit-suh-FREE-nee-uh, see schizophrenia entry), a severe and disabling mental disorder, rather than bipolar disorder. The symptoms of bipolar disorder in those under the age of twenty lead to many incorrect diagnoses, including attention-deficit/hyperactivity (ADHD; see attention-deficit/hyperactivity disorder entry) or conduct disorder.

Other conditions can also produce symptoms similar to those of bipolar disorder. Drug abuse is one such condition. A drug abuser cannot be examined for possible bipolar disorder until he or she has stopped using drugs. Disorders of the thyroid gland and the use of prescribed and over-the-counter medication can also produce bipolar-like symptoms.

TREATMENT

Bipolar disorder is usually treated with some form of medication. Some drugs help to elevate a person's moods during the low part of a bipolar cycle. Others help to calm the person down during the high part of a cycle. Some examples of commonly used drugs include:

- **Lithium.** The common name for a group of chemicals that contain the chemical element lithium. These chemicals are among the oldest and most frequently prescribed of all drugs for the treatment of bipolar disorder. While they do not work equally well for all forms of the disorder, they can be very effective for many patients when taken according to the schedule prescribed by a doctor. Some side effects of lithium drugs include weight gain, thirst,

While counseling cannot cure bipolar disorder, patients can sometimes better understand the nature of their condition and learn to adjust to it. (© 1995 Peter Berndt, M.D., P.A. Reproduced by permission of Custom Medical Stock Photo.)

nausea, and hand tremors (shaking). Long-term use sometimes leads to hyperthyroidism. Hyperthyroidism is a condition caused by an overactive thyroid gland. It can result in a variety of symptoms, both mild and serious.

- **Carbamazepine.** Carbamazepine (pronounced KAHR-buh-MAZ-uh-peen) is an anticonvulsant drug used to prevent convulsions (spasms). It is often prescribed to patients for whom lithium treatment is ineffective. Blurred vision and other eye problems are possible side effects of carbamazepine use.
- **Valproate.** Used primarily for the treatment of patients with rapid cycling bipolar disorder. These patients often do not respond to treatment with lithium. Side effects of valproate use include stomach cramps, indigestion, diarrhea, hair loss, appetite loss, nausea, and unusual weight loss or gain.
- **Antidepressants.** Sometimes used to treat bipolar disorder on a short-term basis. An antidepressant is a drug that tends to overcome a person's depression and lift his or her spirits. Antidepressants are not used on a long-term basis because they may intensify the manic period in a person's bipolar cycle. That is, the person may not be depressed, but he or she may become more manic. Some examples of antidepressants used to treat bipolar disorder are the drugs known as selective serotonin (pronounced sihr-uh-TOE-nun) reuptake inhibitors (SSRIs), monoamine (pronounced mon-oh-AM-een) oxidase inhibitors (MAO inhibitors), and tricyclic antidepressants.

Electroconvulsive Shock Therapy

Bipolar disorder is sometimes treated with electroconvulsive shock therapy, or ECT. ECT is a procedure in which intense electrical shocks are administered through electrodes attached to the patient's head. The patient is first given anaesthesia (pronounced an-is-THEE-zhuh) and a muscle relaxant. The muscle relaxant prevents the patient from going into convulsions that would cause broken bones and strained muscles.

No one knows how electric shocks affects the patient's brain. In some cases, however, the treatment is able to relieve the conditions of bipolar disorder. The side effects of ECT include headaches, muscle soreness, nausea, confusion, and memory loss.

Some doctors are reluctant to use ECT unless all other treatments fail. The procedure has many critics who regard it as inhumane. Most cases of bipolar disorder now respond to some form of drug treatment, making ECT unnecessary.

Other Drugs

A variety of drugs are available for treating other aspects of bipolar disorder. For example, some patients have very severe episodes of mania or depression. They may need to have drugs to get them through the worst parts of these episodes. One group of drugs, known as benzodiazepines (pronounced ben-zo-die-A-zuh-peenz), can be used to calm a patient who is having a severe attack of mania. The drug known as clozapine (pronounced KLO-zuh-peen) can also be used to help prevent manic episodes and to treat patients who do not respond to other drugs designed to stabilize their moods.

Counseling

Counseling can also be of some help with bipolar disorder. While it cannot cure the disorder because mania and depression are caused by biological factors, patients can sometimes better understand the nature of their condition and learn to adjust to it. Perhaps most important, counseling can help patients and their families to understand the need for a person to stay on a strict schedule of drug therapy.

Alternative Treatment

Bipolar patients can often benefit from some simple suggestions, such as maintaining a calm environment, avoiding over-simulation, getting plenty of rest and regular exercise, and eating a proper diet. Some practitioners believe that Chinese herbs can soften mood swings. Biofeedback can sometimes help patients control their symptoms, such as irritability, poor self-control, racing thoughts, and sleep problems. During biofeedback a patient watches the brain waves produced when he or she is behaving a certain way. The patient than learns to adjust that behavior to produce correct brain waves. A diet high in vitamin C is thought by some to help reduce depression.

PROGNOSIS

Most patients benefit to some extent from treatment, however responses vary widely from complete recovery to no improvement at all with any form of treatment. One of the most difficult problems is to find the right drug, the right combination of drugs, and the right dosage for any one patient. Bipolar disorder is a chronic condition. That is, most patients experience the condition throughout their lives and require lifelong treatment and observation.

Suicide is common among people with severe bipolar disorder who do not receive prompt or adequate treatment. The suicide rate is 15 to 25 percent among these individuals. With proper and early diagnosis and treatment, however, it is possible for bipolar patients to live normal lives.

PREVENTION

There is currently no known way to prevent bipolar disorder, but the chances of stabilizing the condition improves considerably with proper treatment. Educating the patient about the disorder is also important. He or she

can learn to recognize the signs of mania and depression and be taught how
to respond to those signs.

FOR MORE INFORMATION

Books

Mondimore, Francks Mark. *Bipolar Disorder: A Guide for Parents and Families.*
Baltimore: Johns Hopkins Press, 1999.

Whybrow, Peter C. *A Mood Apart.* New York: Harper Collins, 1997.

Organizations

American Psychiatric Association. Office of Public Affairs. 1400 K Street NW,
Washington, DC 20005. (202) 682–6119. http://www.psych.org.

National Alliance for the Mentally Ill. 200 North Glebe Road, Suite 1015, Arlington, VA 22203–3754. (800) 950–6264. http://www.nami.org.

National Depressive and Manic-Depressive Association. 730 North Franklin
Street, Suite 501, Chicago, IL 60610. (800) 826–3632. http://www
.ndmda.org.

National Institute of Mental Health. 5600 Fishers Lane, Room 7C–02,
Bethesda, MD 20857. (301) 443–4513. http://www.nimh.nih.gov.

Web sites

"Ask NOAH About: Bipolar Disorders." *NOAH: New York Online Access to Health*
[Online]. http://www.noah.cuny.edu/mentalhealth/mental.html#Bipolar
Disorder (accessed on October 7, 1999).

Bowden, Charles L. "Choosing the Appropriate Therapy for Bipolar Disorder." *Medscape Mental Health.* [Online] http://www.medscape.com (accessed on October 7, 1999).

Bowden, Charles L. "Update on Bipolar Disorder: Epidemiology, Etiology,
Diagnosis, and Prognosis." [Online] *Medscape Mental Health,* http://www
.medscape.com (accessed on October 7, 1999).

BREAST CANCER

DEFINITION

Breast cancer is cancer of the breast. Cancer (see cancer entry) is a disease in which cells begin to grow rapidly and out of control. Cancer cells can
travel through the body by way of blood or lymph nodes. They can then
come to rest and start growing in other parts of the body.

DESCRIPTION

breast cancer

Every woman is at risk for breast cancer. The risk varies with age. At age twenty-five, a woman's risk is about 1 in 20,000. At age forty-five, it is 1 in about 100. At age eighty-five, it is more than 1 in 10. About 80 percent of all breast cancers are found in women over the age of fifty.

CAUSES

Researchers do not know how normal cells suddenly become cancerous. Thus, the fundamental cause or causes of breast cancer are still a puzzle. Scientists do know that certain risk factors are related to the development of breast cancer. These factors include:

- Family history of breast cancer occurring in mother or sister.
- Early onset (beginning) of menstruation and late menopause. Menopause is the end of menstruation.
- Reproductive history. Women who have no children or have children late in life have increased risk. Women who have never breast-fed also have increased risk.
- History of abnormal breast biopsies. A biopsy is a medical procedure in which a small sample of tissue is removed for study under a microscope.

The acknowledged risk factors are of limited value, however. More than 70 percent of women who develop breast cancer have no known risk factors.

SYMPTOMS

The primary method of discovering the symptoms of breast cancer is self-examination. Doctors recommend that women learn how to properly exam-

WORDS TO KNOW

Benign: Not harmful or cancerous.

Biopsy: A medical procedure in which a small sample of tissue is removed so that it can be studied under a microscope.

Lumpectomy: A procedure in which the cancerous lump is removed from the breast.

Mammogram: An X-ray photograph of the breast.

Mastectomy: Surgical removal of a breast.

Menopause: The end of menstruation.

Metastasis: The process by which cancer cells spread to other parts of the body.

Radical mastectomy: Surgical removal of an entire breast along with the chest muscles around the breast and all the lymph nodes under the arm.

Reconstructive surgery: A medical procedure in which an artificial breast is created to replace the breast removed during a mastectomy.

Systemic treatment: A form of treatment that affects the whole body.

Tamoxifen: A naturally occurring substance that has shown promise in preventing the return of breast cancer.

ine their breasts and to do so on a regular basis. The purpose is to look for any changes in the breasts. One warning sign of breast cancer may be a lump in the breast or armpit area. The presence of a lump suggests that medical advice should be sought. A lump does not necessarily indicate breast cancer. In many cases, lumps are benign (not cancerous) and can be removed without any lasting harm to the patient.

Other symptoms that may be detected during a self-examination include:

- Thickening in the breast or armpit
- Change in the size, shape, or color of a nipple
- Dimples or redness of the skin on the breast
- Change in size or shape of the breast

DIAGNOSIS

The primary medical tool in diagnosing breast cancer is a mammogram. A mammogram is an X-ray photograph of the breast. The American Cancer Society currently recommends that women between the ages of forty and fifty have a mammogram every year or two. The society suggests a yearly mammogram for women over the age of fifty.

The purpose of a mammogram is to find any lumps or other changes in the breast. If such changes are found, additional tests may be necessary. One test is a breast biopsy. The tissue removed during a biopsy can be studied under a microscope, which allows a doctor to determine whether cells in the sample are cancerous or not.

If cancer is found, tests can also be used to determine if the cancer has metastasized (pronounced muh-TASS-tuh-sized). Metastasis (pronounced muh-TASS-tuh-sis) is the process by which cancer cells spread to other parts of the body. Testing for metastasis involves removal of lymph nodes from the armpit. The presence of cancer cells in the lymph nodes suggests that the cancer has begun to spread.

TREATMENT

The treatment used for breast cancer depends on how serious a patient's condition is.

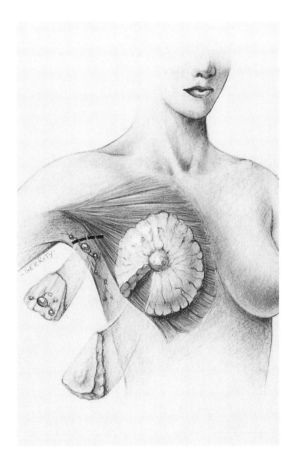

The simplest treatment for breast cancer is a lumpectomy, a procedure in which the cancerous lump is removed from the breast. (Illustration by Peg Gerrity. Reproduced by permission of Custom Medical Stock Photo.)

Under the best circumstances, the cancer is found at an early stage. It may consist of nothing more than a small lump in the breast. In other cases, it may have developed into a larger lump or begun to metastasize.

The simplest treatment is a lumpectomy, a procedure in which the cancerous lump is removed from the breast. The surgeon also removes some tissue around the lump and some of the lymph nodes under the arm. Removing healthy tissue around the lump ensures that all of the cancer has been removed. Removing the lymph nodes allows the doctor to test for metastasis.

A more serious form of treatment is a mastectomy (pronounced mas-TEK-tuh-mee). A mastectomy may be required if a lump has become quite large or the cancer has spread to the chest muscles. In a mastectomy, the patient's entire breast is removed. In the most extreme conditions, the surgeon may also remove the chest muscles around the breast and all the lymph nodes under the arm. This procedure is called a radical mastectomy. Radical mastectomies are rarely done.

Some women also choose to have reconstructive surgery. In reconstructive surgery, an artificial breast is created to replace the breast removed during a mastectomy. The artificial breast may provide a women with a better sense of self-esteem by restoring her natural shape.

If cancer cells are found in the lymph nodes, more aggressive treatment may be necessary. The presence of these cells suggests that the cancer has begun to spread to other parts of the body. Additional treatments are then needed to kill cancer cells in all parts of the body. Such forms of treatment are known as systemic (for "system") treatments.

Three common forms of systemic treatment include radiation, chemotherapy, and hormone therapy. In radiation treatments, some form of radiation is used to kill any remaining cancer cells in the breast or other parts of the body. The radiation used is similar to X rays, but much more powerful.

Chemotherapy involves the use of certain chemicals known to kill cancer cells. These chemicals are given to the patient either by injection or by mouth. They travel through the body and kill cancer cells wherever they are found. Both radiation and chemotherapy have some serious side effects, including nausea and vomiting, temporary hair loss, mouth or vaginal sores, fatigue, and infertility.

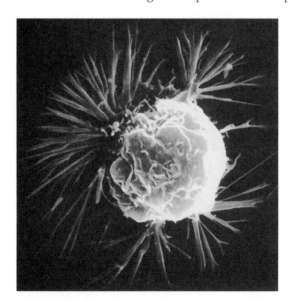

Breast cancer cell. (Reproduced by permission of Kunkel/Phototake NYC)

Hormone therapy is a special type of chemotherapy. In one form, it makes use of a natural product known as tamoxifen (pronounced tuh-MOK-sih-fen) to kill cancer cells. Patients take one pill a day for at least two years and sometimes as long as five. Studies show that the use of tamoxifen can lower the chance that breast cancer can return by between 25 and 35 percent.

STUDIES SHOW THAT THE USE OF TAMOXIFEN CAN LOWER THE CHANCE THAT BREAST CANCER WILL RETURN BY BETWEEN 25 AND 35 PERCENT.

PROGNOSIS

Survival rates for breast cancer depend very much on the type of cancer found and how early it was diagnosed. In general, cancers that are found earlier are more likely to be treated successfully. Patients who have surgery often return to a normal lifestyle within about a month. Exercises help patients regain strength and flexibility of the arms, shoulders, and chest.

Patients who receive treatment for breast cancer often experience emotional problems. They may become moody or depressed, lose their appetite, or feel unworthy or uninterested in sexual activities. Support groups are available to help women get through the most difficult period after diagnosis and treatment. Support groups consist of other individuals who have experienced the same medical problem and, sometimes, professional counselors.

PREVENTION

There is no way to prevent breast cancer. The best way to deal with the disease is to perform regular self-examinations and have regular mammograms. For women who have had breast cancer, tamoxifen treatments appear to be a promising factor in preventing reoccurrence of the disease.

FOR MORE INFORMATION

Books

Hirshaut, Yashar, and Peter Pressman. *Breast Cancer: The Complete Handbook.* New York: Bantam Books, 1996.

Kneece, Judy C. *Finding a Lump in Your Breast: Where to Go, What to Do.* Columbia, SC: Educate Publishing, 1996.

Lauersen, Niels, and Eileen Stukane. *The Complete Book of Breast Care.* New York: Fawcett Columbine, 1996

Love, Susan, and Karen Lindsey. *Dr. Susan Love's Breast Book.* Reading, MA: Addison-Wesley, 1995.

Mayer, Musa. *Holding Tight, Letting Go: Living with Metastatic Breast Cancer.* Sebastopol, CA: O'Reilly & Associates, 1997.

Porter, Margit Esser. *Hope Is Contagious: The Breast Cancer Treatment Survival Handbook.* New York: Simon & Schuster, 1997.

Stoppard, Miriam. *The Breast Book.* New York: DK Publishing, 1996.

Periodicals

"Early Detection: The Best Defense." *Family Circle* (October 31, 1992): p. 107.

Fackelmann, Kathy. "Refiguring the Odds." *Science News* (July 31, 1993): pp. 76–77.

Organizations

American Cancer Society. 1599 Clifton Road NE, Atlanta, GA 30329. (800) ACS–2345. http://www.cancer.org.

Cancer Care, Inc. 1180 Avenue of the Americas. New York, NY 10036. (800) 813–HOPE. http://www.cancercareinc.org.

National Alliance of Breast Cancer Organizations. 9 East 37th Street, 10th Floor, New York, NY 10016. (888) 80–NABCO.

National Cancer Institute. 31 Center Drive, Bethesda, MD 20892–2580. (800) 4–CANCER. http://www.nci.nih.gov.

National Coalition for Cancer Survivorship. 1010 Wayne Avenue, 5th Floor, Silver Springs, MD 20910. (301) 650–8868.

National Women's Health Resource Center. 2425 L Street NW, 3rd Floor, Washington, DC 20037. (202) 293–6045.

Web sites

Community Breast Health Project at Stanford. [Online] http://www.med.Stanford.EDU:80/CBHP (accessed on October 18, 1999).

BRONCHITIS

DEFINITION

Bronchitis (pronounced brong-KIE-tis) is an inflammation of the air passages between the nose and the lungs. It affects the trachea (pronounced TRAY-kee-uh), or windpipe, and the bronchi. The bronchi (pronounced BRON-kee) are air tubes through which air flows into and out of the lungs.

Bronchitis can be either acute (of brief duration) or chronic (long-lasting). Acute bronchitis is usually caused by a viral or bacterial infection.

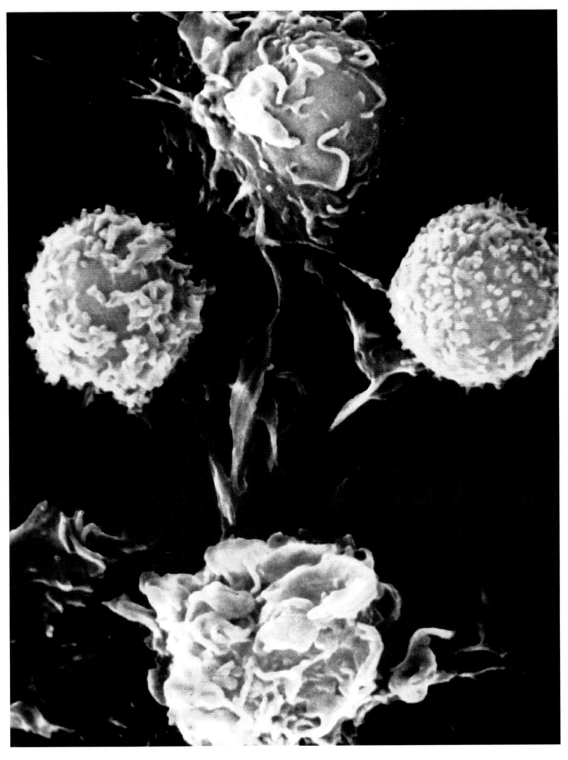

Color enhanced, magnified image of dividing cancer cells. (Photograph by Nina Lampen. Reproduced by permission of Science Source/Photo Researchers, Inc.)

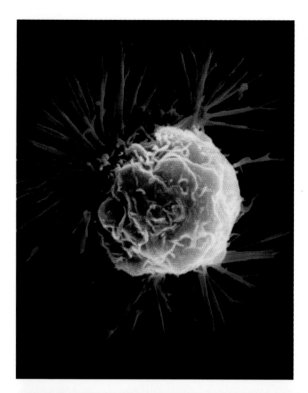

Color enhanced, magnified image of a breast cancer cell. (Reproduced by permission of Kunkel/Phototake NYC.)

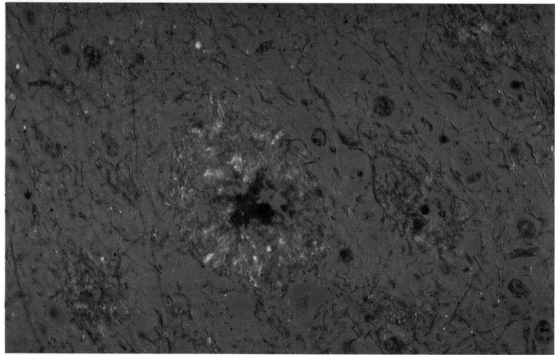

Diseased brain tissue from an Alzheimer's patient showing senile plaques, seen as darker spots surrounded by lighter halos. (Photograph by Cecil Fox/Science Source. Reproduced by permission of the National Audubon Society Collection/Photo Researchers, Inc.)

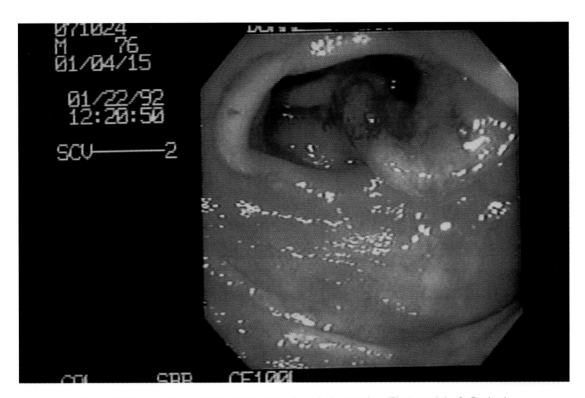

Endoscopic view of colorectal cancer. Tumors can be seen through the opening. (Photograph by S. Benjamin. Reproduced by permission of Custom Medical Stock Photo.)

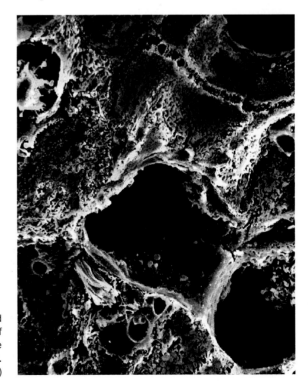

A magnified image of liver cirrhosis, a disease caused by drinking too much alcohol. (© Prof. P. Motta/Dept of Anatomy/University of "La Sapienza," Rome/Science Photo Library, National Audubon Society Collection. Reproduced by permission of Photo Researchers, Inc.)

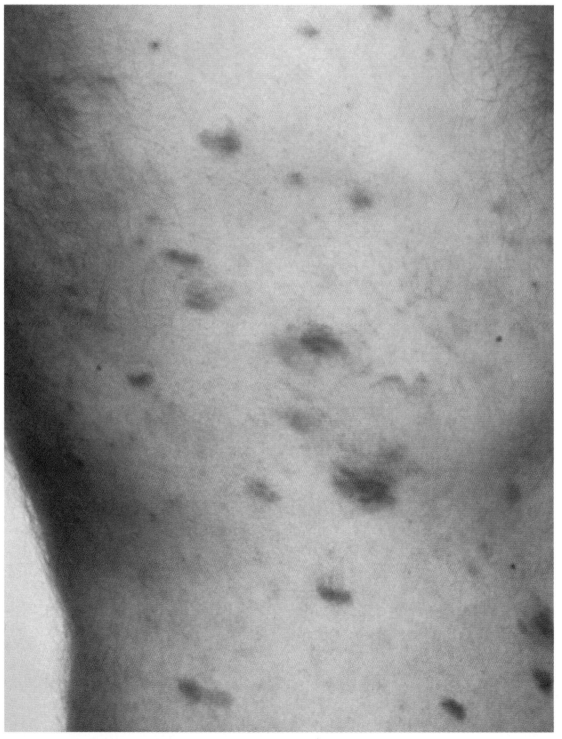

Patients with late-stage AIDS may develop a form of cancer known as Kaposi's sarcoma (KS), a skin cancer characterized by reddish-purple blotches or patches. KS is one of the most common causes of death in AIDS patients.
(Reproduced by permission of Custom Medical Stock Photo.)

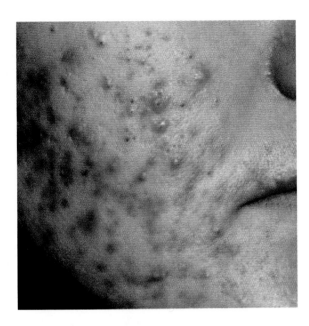

Acne is the most common of all skin diseases, affecting about seventeen million Americans. (© 1991 National Medical Slide. Reproduced by permission of Custom Medical Stock Photo.)

Athlete's foot is a common fungus infection that occurs between the toes. The skin becomes itchy and sore and cracks and peels away. (Reproduced by permission of Custom Medical Stock Photo.)

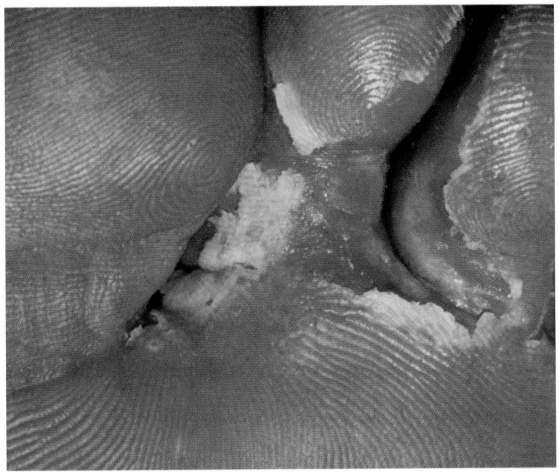

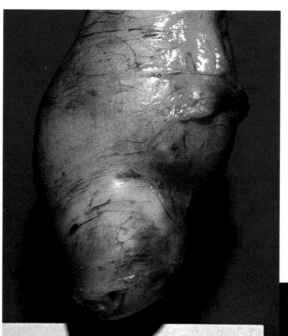

Often, a diagnosis of appendicitis is not certain until an operation is done. To avoid a ruptured appendix, surgery may be recommended without delay if the symptoms point clearly to appendicitis. (Photograph by Lester V. Bergman. Reproduced by permission of the Corbis Corporation [Bellevue].)

A. R.   1316
APPENDIX

An allergy scratch test can be carried out to discover the allergens to which a patient might be sensitive. Small amounts of many different allergens are placed directly on a person's skin. Any reaction that occurs to an allergen indicates that the person is allergic to that allergen. (Reproduced by permission of Custom Medical Stock Photo.)

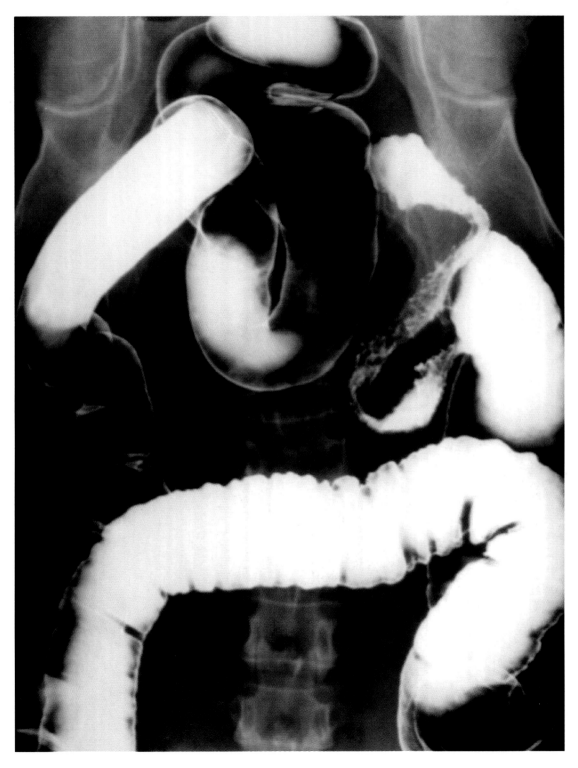

A barium X ray showing the colon of a patient with Crohn's disease where the large and small intestines join at the bottom left. (Photo by CNRI/Science Photo Library. Reproduced by permission of Custom Medical Stock Photo.)

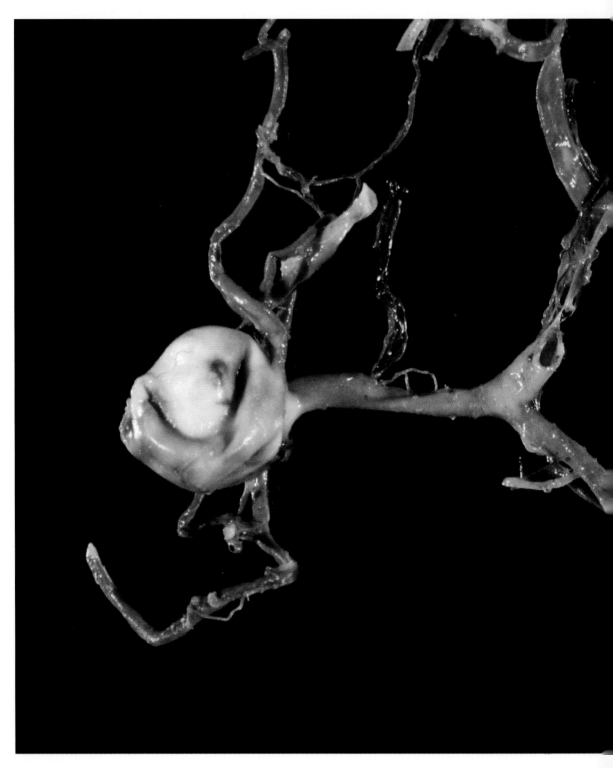

Three pre-burst aneurysms in the cerebral arteries of a human brain. (© Martin Rotker. Reproduced by permission of Phototake NYC.)

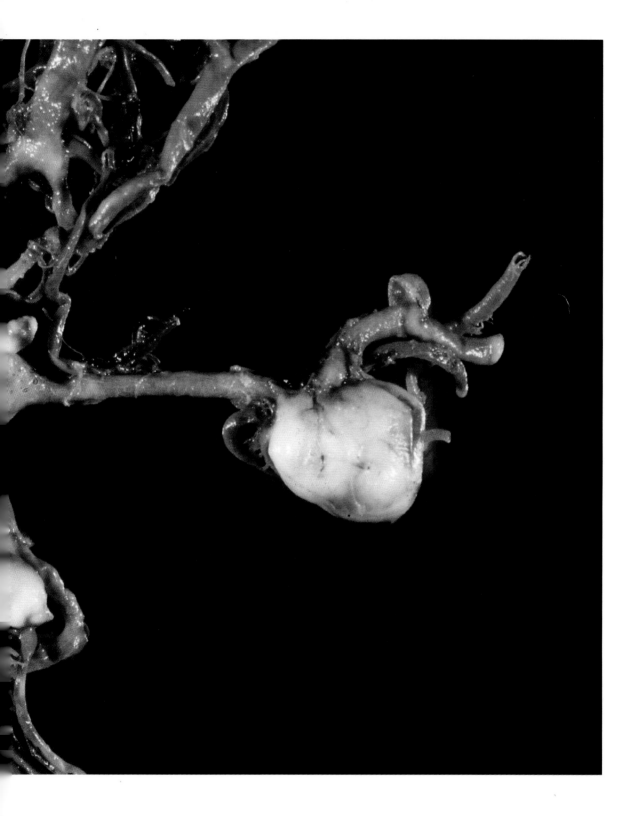

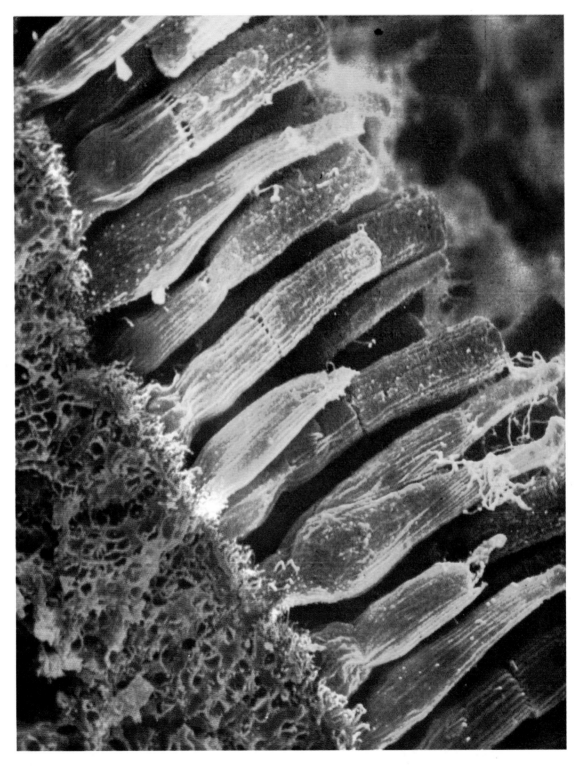

A color-enhanced scanning electron micrograph showing the rods and cones of the human eye. (© Omikron. Reproduced by permission of Photo Researchers, Inc.)

Traffic light as seen by a person with normal color vision. (© Ralph C. Eagle, Jr., M.D. Reproduced by permission of Photo Researchers, Inc.)

Traffic light as seen by a person with red color-blindness. (© Ralph C. Eagle, Jr., M.D. Reproduced by permission of Photo Researchers, Inc.)

Common symptoms of conjunctivitis include redness of the eye, swelling of the eyelid, and a discharge from the eye. (Photograph by SPL. Reproduced by permission of Custom Medical Stock Photo.)

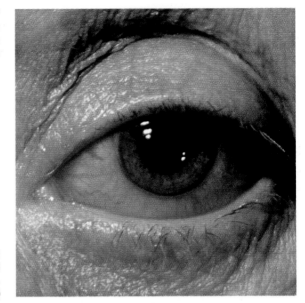

The success rate for cataract surgery is very high; more than 90 percent of patients experience improved vision. (Photograph by David Sutton/Zuma Image. Reproduced by permission of The Stock Market.)

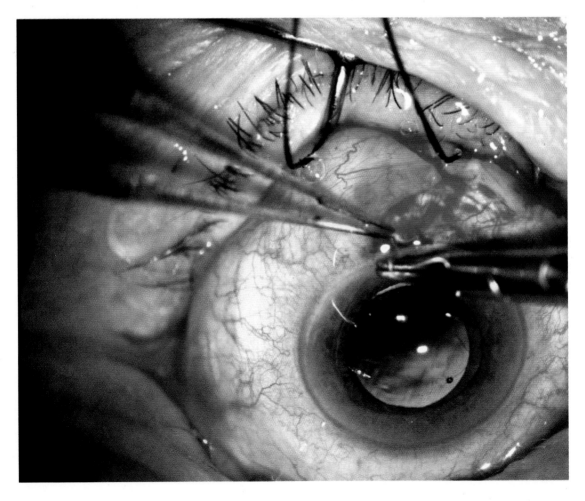

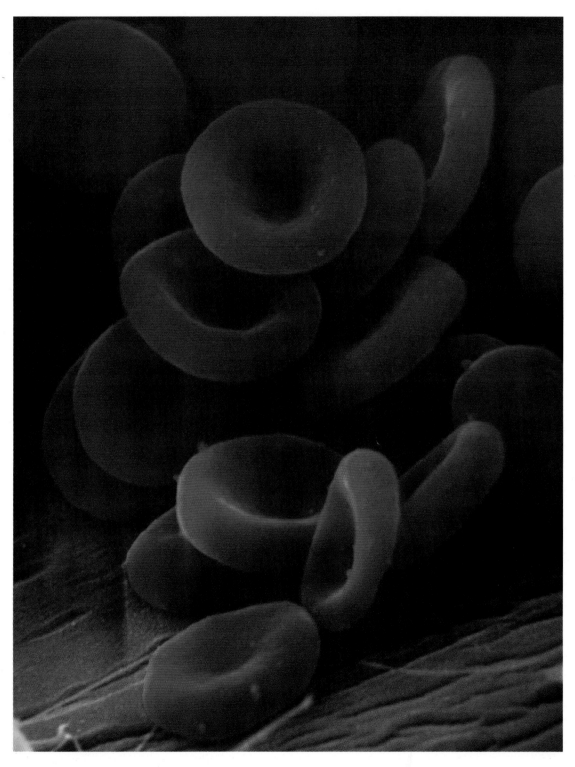

Magnified red blood cells floating inside a blood vessel. Anemia is a condition characterized by abnormally low levels of red blood cells. (Photograph by Dennis Kunkel. Reproduced by permission of Phototake NYC.)

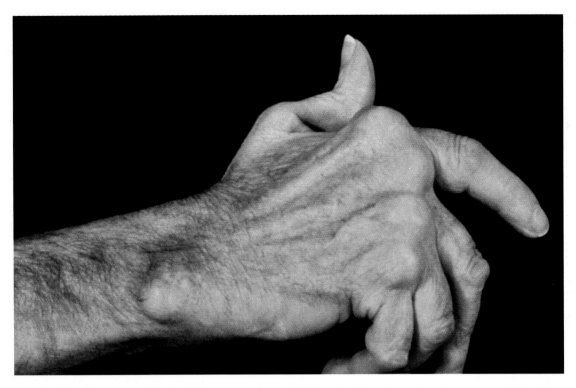

Rheumatoid arthritis can cause joints to become permanently deformed. (© 1988 SIU. Reproduced by permission of Custom Medical Stock Photo.)

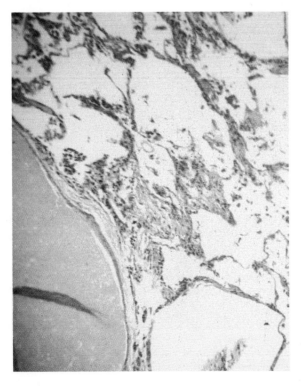

Cystic fibrosis lung tissue, with thick mucus, as seen through a microscope. (Reproduced by permission of Custom Medical Stock Photo.)

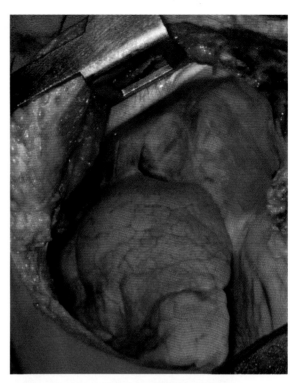

Lung transplantation for cystic fibrosis is a treatment of last resort. (© 1992 Michael English, M.D. Reproduced by permission of Custom Medical Stock Photo.)

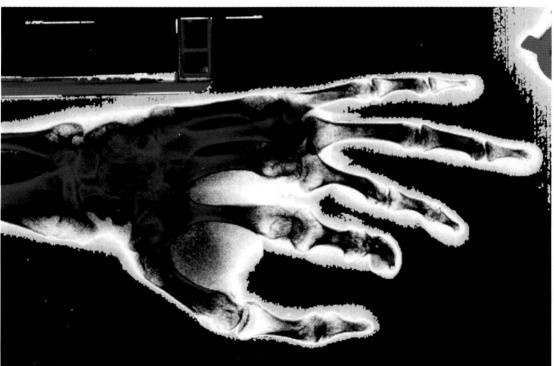

A digitally enhanced X ray of a hand showing symptoms of rheumatoid arthritis. (© 1994 Michael English, M.D. Reproduced by permission of Custom Medical Stock Photo.)

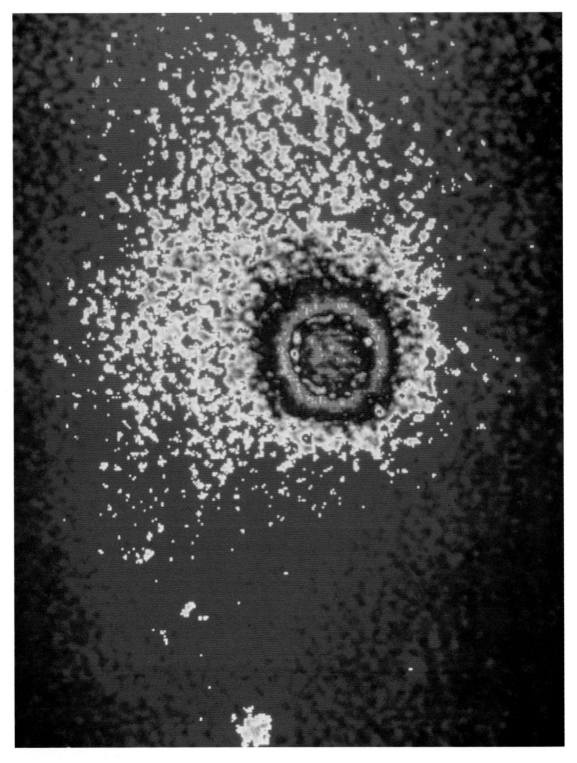

The rhinovirus (shown magnified 100,000 times) causes between 30 and 50 percent of all colds. (© 1991 CMSP. Reproduced by permission of Custom Medical Stock Photo.)

It usually heals fairly quickly without complications. Chronic bronchitis is a sign of more serious lung disease. It can often be slowed, but it cannot be cured.

DESCRIPTION

Acute and chronic bronchitis are both inflammations of the air passages. However, their causes and treatments are different. Acute bronchitis occurs most frequently during the winter. It often follows a viral infection, such as a cold (see common cold entry) or the flu (see influenza entry), and may accompany a bacterial infection.

A person who has acute bronchitis is usually better within two weeks. The cough that accompanies the disease may last longer, however. As with similar infections of the airways, pneumonia (see pneumonia entry) may also develop.

Anyone can get acute bronchitis. However, people with weak immune systems, such as infants and the elderly, are more prone to the disease. Smokers and people with heart or lung disease are also at higher risk for acute bronchitis, as are people who are exposed to chemical fumes or high levels of air pollution.

Chronic bronchitis is a major cause of disability and death. The American Lung Association estimates that about fourteen million Americans suffer from the disease. Like acute bronchitis, chronic bronchitis is accompanied by severe coughing and spitting up of phlegm (pronounced FLEM). Chronic bronchitis is characterized by the presence of these symptoms for a period of at least three months in each of two consecutive years. Chronic bronchitis develops slowly. As a result, the disease is seen more often among older people than among the young and middle-aged.

CAUSES

Chronic bronchitis is caused by inhaling substances that irritate the trachea and bronchi. The most common substance is cigarette smoke. The American Lung Association estimates that 80 to 90 percent of all cases of chronic bronchitis are caused by smoking. Until recently, chronic bronchitis occurred more frequently among men than women because traditionally more men smoked than women. That trend is changing and the number of women suffering from chronic bronchitis is also increasing. Other substances

WORDS TO KNOW

Bronchi: The larger air tubes of the lung that bring air in from the trachea.

Cilia: Fine, hair-like projections that line the trachea and bronchi. Cilia wave back and forth, carrying mucus through the airways.

Emphysema: A serious and usually fatal disease of the lungs.

Trachea: The windpipe, a tube that brings air from the back of the throat to the bronchi.

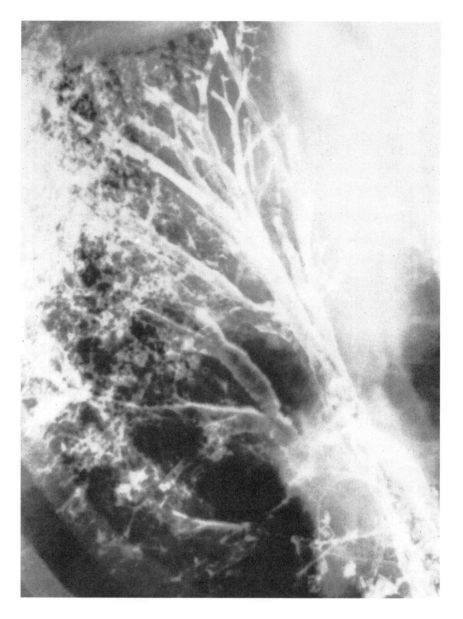

X ray of lungs with chronic bronchitis. (Reproduced by permission of Custom Medical Stock Photo)

that can irritate the trachea and bronchi include chemical fumes, air pollution, and other materials in the air, such as mold and dust.

Chronic bronchitis develops slowly over time. It is caused by changes in the cilia (pronounced SIL-ee-uh) that line the trachea and bronchi. Cilia are fine, hair-like projections that wave back and forth, carrying mucus through the airways. Smoke and other irritants can damage cilia, causing them to lose their ability to move mucus normally. The airways become narrow and clogged with mucus. The patient has difficulty breathing because he or she cannot get enough air into the lungs. Eventually chronic bronchitis leads to an even more serious and life-threatening disease, emphysema (pronounced em-fi-SEE-muh; see emphysema entry).

SYMPTOMS

Acute bronchitis usually begins with cold-like symptoms, such as a runny nose, sneezing, and dry cough. However, the cough soon becomes deep and painful. Coughing produces a greenish-yellow phlegm or sputum (pronounced SPYOO-tum). Phlegm and sputum are substances coughed up from the inflamed airways. They include blood, mucus, dead cells, and other materials. A fever with temperatures of up to 102°F (39°C) are common. The coughing may also be accompanied by wheezing.

In simple cases of acute bronchitis, most symptoms disappear in three to five days. The cough remains and may continue for several weeks. Acute bronchitis is often accompanied by a bacterial infection that causes its own symptoms, including fever and a general feeling of illness. The bacterial infection can be treated with antibiotics. Drugs are usually not effective against the original viral infection, however.

The first sign of chronic bronchitis is often a mild cough, sometimes called smokers' cough. This coughing may bring up small or greater amounts of phlegm. Wheezing and shortness of breath may accompany the cough. As the disease develops, breathing becomes more difficult. The patient finds it necessary to become less active. The body no longer gets enough oxygen, leading to changes in the composition of the blood.

THE FIRST SIGN OF CHRONIC BRONCHITIS IS OFTEN A MILD COUGH, SOMETIMES CALLED SMOKERS' COUGH.

DIAGNOSIS

To diagnose bronchitis, the doctor first takes the patient's health history and observes his or her symptoms. The doctor then listens to the patient's chest with a stethoscope. Certain sounds indicate narrowing of the airways. These sounds include moist rales, crackling, and wheezing. Moist rales is a bubbling sound caused when fluids are present in the bronchial tubes.

A sputum culture may be performed, especially if the sputum is green or has blood in it. The culture allows the doctor to determine what kinds of bacteria are present in the sputum. He or she can then decide what kind of drugs to use in killing the bacteria.

The first step in taking a sputum culture is to have the patient cough up a small amount of sputum (material from the lungs). The sample is then placed in a warm environment for two to three days. Under these conditions, bacteria grow rapidly and are easy to identify. Sputum can also be collected by means of a bronchoscopy. In this procedure, the patient is first given a local anesthetic. A tube is then passed down the airway to collect a sputum sample.

Another step in diagnosing bronchitis is a lung function test. This step requires the use of a spirometer, which is a device that measures the amount of air entering and leaving the lungs. The test is performed by having the patient breathe into the spirometer, first normally and then with force. The test is quick, easy, and painless. It is usually done in the doctor's office. A lung

The American Lung Association estimates that 80 to 90 percent of all cases of chronic bronchitis are caused by smoking. (Reproduced by permission of AP/Wide World Photos)

function of less than 80 percent can be the sign of bronchitis or a related lung disease.

Many lung diseases have similar symptoms. To tell them apart, a doctor may order other tests, such as a chest X ray, electrocardiogram (ECG; pronounced ih-LEK-tro-KAR-dee-o-gram), or blood tests. An ECG measures electrical activity in the heart. Other tests may be used to measure how effectively oxygen and carbon dioxide are being exchanged in the lungs.

TREATMENT

Simple cases of acute bronchitis are treated like a common cold. The patient is told to drink plenty of fluids, to rest, and to avoid smoking. An air humidifier should be used to increase moisture in the air. Acetaminophen (pronounced uh-see-tuh-MIN-uh-fuhn, trade names Datril, Tylenol, Panadol) should be taken for fever and pain. Aspirin should not be given to children because it may cause the serious illness Reye's syndrome (see Reye's syndrome entry).

Coughing that brings up phlegm should not be treated because it helps remove mucus and other harmful materials from the lungs. If not removed, they collect in the lungs and block airways. Cough suppressants can be used with dry coughs, however.

People with bronchitis may get some relief from expectorant cough medicines. While these medicines do not reduce coughing, they do thin mucus in the lungs, which makes the mucus easier to cough up.

Bacterial infections may accompany acute bronchitis. These infections can be treated with antibiotics. The most important rule about antibiotics is to take the full amount prescribed. Failure to do so can cause the infection to return. A variety of antibiotics is available for use with adults, including trimethoprim/sulfamethoxazole (pronounced tri-METH-o-prim/SULL-fuh-meth-OCK-suh-zole, trade names Bactrim or Septra), azithromycin (pronounced uh-zith-ro-MISE-uhn, trade name Zithromax), and clarithromycin (pronounced kluh-rith-ruh-MISE-uhn, trade name Biaxin). Children under the age of eight are usually given amoxicillin (pronounced uh-MOK-sih-SIL-in, trade names Amoxil, Pentamox, Sumox, Trimox).

Chronic Bronchitis

The treatment of chronic bronchitis is complex. It depends on the stage of the disease and whether other health problems are present. An important first step is giving up smoking and avoiding second-hand smoke (smoke from other people's cigarettes) and air pollutants. A regular program of controlled exercise is also important.

Drug therapy begins with bronchodilators (pronounced brong-ko-die-LATE-urs). These drugs relax the muscles of the bronchial tubes and allow air to flow more freely. Common bronchodilators include albuterol (pronounced al-BYOO-tuh-rol, trade names Ventolin, Proventil, Apo-Salvent) and metaproterenol (pronounced met-uh-pro-TER-uh-nol, trade names Alupent, Orciprenaline, Metaprel, Dey-Dose). They can be taken by mouth or inhaled with a nebulizer. A nebulizer is a device that delivers a carefully measured amount of medication to the airways.

Anti-inflammatory medications are used to reduce swelling of airway tissues. Corticosteroids (pronounced kor-tih-ko-STIHR-oids), such as prednisone (pronounced PRED-nih-zone), can be taken by mouth or by injection. Other steroids are inhaled. Long-term steroid use can have serious side effects and should be avoided.

Drugs are available to reduce the amount of mucus produced. Ipratropium (pronounced ip-ruh-TRO-pee-uhm, trade name Atrovent) is one such drug. In the late stages of the disease, patients may need extra oxygen supplied from an oxygen tank through a mask. Hospitalization may also be required to provide the medical care needed in the last stages of the disease.

Alternative Treatment

The focus of alternative treatments is a healthy diet that strengthens the immune system. A number of herbal medicines have also been recommended for the treatment of bronchitis. These treatments include the inhaling of eucalyptus (pronounced yoo-kuh-LIP-tus) or certain other oils in warm steam and drinking a tea made of mullein, coltsfoot, and anise seed. Hydrotherapy, the use of water and water vapors, may also help clean out the chest and stimulate the immune system.

PROGNOSIS

With treatment, acute bronchitis usually clears up in one to two weeks. The cough that accompanies the disease may last for several more weeks, however. By contrast, chronic bronchitis is a progressive disease. Brief improvements may be seen, but in the long term, no cure is available. The disease often develops into emphysema or other lung diseases, all of which are eventually fatal.

PREVENTION

The best way to prevent bronchitis is not to begin smoking or to stop smoking. Smokers are ten times more likely to die of bronchitis and other lung disorders than are nonsmokers. Other irritants in the environment, such as chemicals and air pollutants, should also be avoided. Immunizations (shots) can also help protect against certain diseases of the lungs, such as pneumonia and the flu.

FOR MORE INFORMATION

Books

Adams, Francis V. *The Breathing Disorders Sourcebook.* Los Angeles, CA: Lowell House, 1998.

Haas, Francois, and Sheila Sperber Haas. *The Chronic Bronchitis and Emphysema Handbook.* New York: John Wiley & Sons, 1990.

Shayevits, Myra, Berton Shayevits, and the editors of Consumer Reports Books. *Living Well with Chronic Asthma, Bronchitis, and Emphysema.* Yonkers, NY: Consumer Report Books, 1991.

Smolley, Laurence A., Debra Fulghum Bruce, and Rob Muzzio. *Breathe Right Now : A Comprehensive Guide to Understanding and Treating the Most Common Breathing Disorders.* New York: W. W. Norton & Company, 1998.

Organizations

American Lung Association. 1740 Broadway, New York, NY. (800) LUNGUSA. http://www.lungusa.org

National Heart, Lung, and Blood Institute Information Center. PO Box 30105, Bethesda, MD 20824–0105. (301) 251–1221.

National Jewish Center for Immunology and Respiratory Medicine. 1400 Jackson Street, Denver, CO 80206. (800) 222–5864.

BULIMIA NERVOSA

DEFINITION

Bulimia (pronounced bu-LIM-ee-uh) nervosa is a serious and sometimes life-threatening eating disorder that affects primarily young women. Bulimics (people who have bulimia) go through cycles of binging and purging. Binging is the consumption of abnormally large amounts of food in a very short period of time, and purging is the elimination of food by some unusual activity. Bulimics use fasting (not eating), excessive exercise, vomiting, or laxatives to purge themselves of food. Bulimia is partly caused by excessive concern about weight control and self-image. It is considered to be a psychiatric (mental) disorder.

DESCRIPTION

Bulimia nervosa is a serious health problem for over two million adolescent girls and young women in the United States. In the most extreme cases, bulimia can cause severe bodily damage or even death. For example, in rare cases, binging can cause the stomach to break open. Purging can be dangerous because the body loses nutrients it needs to function properly. The loss of potassium, for example, can cause heart failure.

Vomiting is a common source of problems. When a person vomits, he or she brings up partially digested food and stomach acid. The acid is very strong and can burn the digestive tract, the mouth, and the lips. It can also damage the teeth. Binging and purging also disrupts the menstrual cycle.

Most bulimics know that their eating patterns are not normal, but they feel unable to change their behavior. Their binging and purging is done in secrecy so that family and friends often do not even know about their disorder. Some bulimics may turn to other ways of solving their problems, such as drugs and alcohol. Many develop other mental disorders, such as depression (see depressive disorders) and anxiety. In many cases, a physician or mental health professional must be consulted.

Most bulimics are females in their teens or early twenties; males of the same age range make up about 5 to 10 percent of bulimics. People of all races develop the disorder. The majority of bulimics who receive treatment, however, are white.

CAUSES

The cause of bulimia nervosa is unknown. Both genetic and social factors are probably responsible. Bulimia does appear to run in families, so a child is at risk for bulimia if another family member already has the disorder.

An important factor contributing to bulimia is the social pressure for women to be thin. Advertisements, television programs, and motion pictures are full of images depicting beautiful, successful women who are very thin. Young women often feel that they, too, need to be slender in order to be attractive and ultimately accepted in society. For young women with these feelings, bulimia may be the only way to achieve such standards.

For some young women, the social pressure to maintain thinness may come from family, friends, or the social activities in which they participate. For instance, modeling, dancing, and gymnastics tend to emphasize an importance on body size and shape.

WORDS TO KNOW

Binge: To consume large amounts of food without control in a short period of time.

Purge: To rid the body of food by vomiting, the use of laxatives, or some other method.

SYMPTOMS

The following are typical symptoms of bulimia nervosa:

- Eating large amounts of food uncontrollably (binging)
- Vomiting, using laxatives, or using other methods to eliminate food (purging)
- Excessive concern about body weight
- Depression or changes in mood
- Irregular menstrual periods
- Unusual dental problems, swollen cheeks or glands, heartburn, or bloating (swelling of the stomach)

DIAGNOSIS

Bulimia is often difficult to diagnose because patients often try to hide their condition and may deny they have a problem. Early diagnosis, however, is important. The sooner the condition is diagnosed, the better the chance it can be treated. One step in diagnosis is a physical examination. Because the symptoms of bulimia are similar to those of other diseases, a doctor needs to make sure that a patient is not suffering from some other physical problem.

IS IT BARBIE'S FAULT?

The causes of bulimia are many and complex. Could the Barbie doll be one of those causes? Some researchers think so. They point out that Barbie dolls have been one of the most popular toys ever developed and that an untold number of young girls have grown up playing with Barbie. So, in some ways, Barbie may have become a role model for young girls.

But how realistic is Barbie? For years critics have complained that Barbie's measurements are exaggerated. They argue that Barbie's waist was so small and breasts so large that a woman with the same measurements would not be able to stand. The fear is that young girls may begin to think that they should look like Barbie. And if their idea of beauty is being molded by a doll who was incredibly thin and unnaturally shaped, the message may lead to dangerous behavior such as anorexia or bulimia.

Scientists are also wondering if toys can affect the way boys view their bodies. For example, GI Joe has long been a very popular action figure among young boys. Unlike Barbie, GI Joe had a relatively realistic design. For example, the size of the doll's biceps (upper arm) was equivalent to 11 and one-half inch biceps on an adult male. This size falls within normal range for the average adult male.

In 1997, however, a new version of GI Joe was introduced called GI Joe Extreme. The new toy's dimensions increased so that the adult equivalent of his biceps would now measure 26 inches around, which is unnaturally exaggerated. It is interesting to note that also in 1997, Mattel, the toy company that produces both Barbie and GI Joe, announced that it was changing the shape of Barbie. In efforts to create a more realistic Barbie, the new and improved doll has smaller breasts and a wider waist.

Excessive concern about body weight along with repeated episodes of binging and purging are symptoms of bulimia nervosa. (Oscan Burriel/Latin Stock/Science Photo Library. Reproduced by permission of Custom Medical Stock Photo.)

According to the American Psychiatric Association, there are four signs that indicate bulimia. They are:

- Repeated episodes of binge eating
- Repeated use of purging devices, such as vomiting
- A feeling of lack of control over binge eating
- An ongoing concern over body shape and weight

TREATMENT

Bulimia nervosa is usually treated with a combination of drugs and counseling. Drugs are used to help the patient deal with his or her mental concerns. For example, anti-depressants may be used to help a person feel better about himself or herself.

Many types of counseling may be needed in the treatment of bulimia. Individual and group therapy can help patients understand the cause of their disorder, which may help patients learn to deal with their problems in ways other than binging and purging. Family counseling is also valuable.

Alternative Treatment

Light therapy may prove helpful in treating bulimia. Some people become depressed when there is an absence of light. The winter months can be especially difficult. Light therapy involves the use of artificial light to improve a patient's mood. Massage and hydrotherapy (water therapy) are also recommended for the treatment of bulimia. These techniques may help a person feel better about the shape and appearance of his or her own body.

PROGNOSIS

Bulimia may become chronic. That is, it can turn into an ongoing problem that lasts for many years. In such cases, it can cause a number of health problems, including seizures, irregular heartbeat, and thin bones. On rare occasions, bulimia can be fatal. Early treatment is the key to a promising prognosis. People who learn to deal with their problems of self-image can often be cured of the condition and can go on to lead normal, productive lives.

PREVENTION

Because bulimia is a psychiatric disorder with many possible causes, it is difficult to identify methods of prevention. Many suggest that the reason for eating disorders comes from society at large and that until the images of women in the media are changed to become more realistic, eating disorders such as bulimia, will continue to exist.

FOR MORE INFORMATION

Books

Cassell, Dana K. *The Encyclopedia of Obesity and Eating Disorders.* New York: Facts on File, 1994.

Jablow, Martha M. *A Parent's Guide to Eating Disorders and Obesity.* New York: Dell Publishing, 1992.

Kubersky, Rachel. *Everything You Need to Know about Eating Disorders.* New York: The Rosen Publishing Group, 1992.

Organizations

American Anorexia/Bulimia Association. 165 West 46th Street, Suite 1108 New York, NY 10036. (212) 575–6200.

Anorexia Nervosa and Related Eating Disorders. PO Box 5102, Eugene, OR 97405. (541) 344–1144.

Center for the Study of Anorexia and Bulimia. 1 W. 91st Street, New York, NY 10024. (212) 595–3449.

Eating Disorder Awareness & Prevention. 603 Steward St., Suite 803, Seattle, WA 98101. (206) 382–3587.

National Association of Anorexia Nervosa and Associated Disorders. Box 7, Highland Park, IL 60035. (708) 831–3438.

National Eating Disorders Organization. 6655 South Yale Avenue, Tulsa, OK 74136. (918) 481–4044.

Web sites

Anorexia Nervosa and Related Eating Disorders, Inc. [Online] http://www.anred.com (accessed on June 15, 1999).

"A Teen Guide to Eating Disorders." [Online] http://kidshealth.org. (accessed on October 5, 1999).

"Understanding Eating Disorders." [Online] http://www.ndmda.org. (accessed on June 15, 1999).

BURNS AND SCALDS

DEFINITION

Burns are injuries to tissues caused by heat, friction, electricity, radiation, or chemicals. Scalds are a type of burn caused by a hot liquid or steam.

DESCRIPTION

Burns are classified according to how seriously tissue has been damaged. The following system is used:

- A first degree burn causes redness and swelling in the outermost layers of the skin.
- A second degree burn involves redness, swelling, and blistering. The damage may extend to deeper layers of the skin.
- A third degree burn destroys the entire depth of the skin. It can also damage fat, muscle, organs, or bone beneath the skin. Significant scarring is common, and death can occur in the most severe cases.

The severity of a burn is also judged by how much area it covers. Health workers express this factor in a unit known as body surface area (BSA). For example, a person with burns on one arm and hand is said to have about a 10 percent BSA burn. A burn covering one leg and foot is classified as about a 20 percent BSA burn.

CAUSES

Burns may be caused in a variety of ways. In every case, the burn results from the death of skin tissue and, in some cases, underlying tissue. Burns caused by hot objects result from the death of cells caused by heat. In many cases, contact with a very hot object can damage tissue extensively. The contact may last for no more than a second or so, but the damage still occurs.

In other cases, cells are killed by heat produced by some physical event. For example, a rope burn is caused by friction between the rope and a person's body. The rope itself is not hot, but the heat produced by friction is sufficient to cause a burn.

Chemicals can also cause burns. The chemicals attack and destroy cells in skin tissue. They produce an effect very similar to that of a heat burn.

SYMPTOMS

The major signs of a burn are redness, swelling, and pain in the affected area. A severe burn will also blister. The skin may also peel, appear white or charred (blackened), or feel numb. A burn may also trigger a headache and fever. The most serious burns may cause shock. The symptoms of shock include faintness, weakness, rapid pulse and breathing, pale and clammy skin, and bluish lips and fingernails.

DIAGNOSIS

Most burn cases are easily diagnosed. Patients know that they have touched a hot object, spilled a chemical on themselves, or been hit by steam. Doctors can confirm that a burn has occurred by conducting a physical examination.

WORDS TO KNOW

BSA: A unit used in the treatment of burns to express the amount of the total body surface area covered by the burn.

Debridement: The surgical removal of dead skin.

Scald: A burn caused by a hot liquid or steam.

Shock: A life-threatening condition that results from low blood volume due to loss of blood or other fluids.

Skin graft: A surgical procedure in which dead skin is removed and replaced by healthy skin, usually taken from the patient's own body.

Thermal burns: Burns caused by hot objects.

burns and scalds

The form of treatment used for a burn depends on how serious it is. Minor burns can usually be treated at home or in a doctor's office. A minor burn is defined as a first or second degree burn that covers less than 15 percent of an adult's body or 10 percent of a child's body.

Moderate burns should be treated in a hospital. Moderate burns are first or second degree burns that cover more of a patient's body or a third degree burn that covers less than 10 percent of BSA.

The most severe burns should be treated in special burn-treatment facilities. These burns are third degree burns that cover more than 10 percent of BSA. Specialized equipment and methods are used to treat these burns.

Thermal Burn Treatment

Thermal burns are burns caused by heat, hot liquids, steam, fire, or other hot objects. The first objective in treating thermal burns is to cool the burned

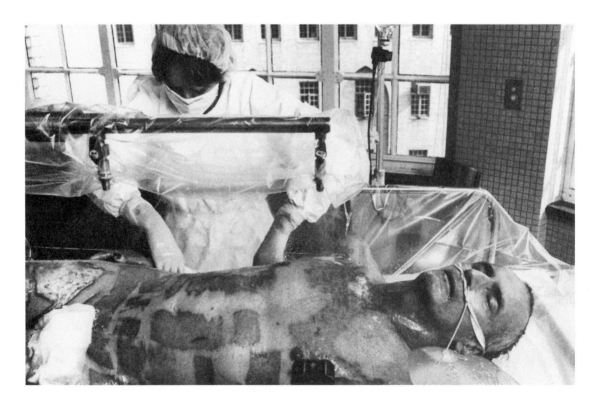

A burn victim receiving debridement treatment, or removal of dead skin, for severe burns. (Photograph by Ann Chawatsky. Reproduced by permission of Phototake NYC.)

area. Cool water, but not very cold water or ice, should be used for the cooling process. Minor burns can also be cleaned with soap and water. Blisters should not be broken. If the skin is broken, the burned area should be covered with an antibacterial ointment and covered with a bandage to prevent infection. Aspirin, acetaminophen (pronounced uh-see-tuh-MIN-uh-fuhn, trade name Tylenol), or ibuprofen (pronounced i-byoo-PRO-fuhn, trade names Advil, Motrin) can be used to ease pain and relieve inflammation. However, children should not take aspirin due to the risk of contracting Reye's syndrome (see Reye's syndrome entry). If signs of infection appear, the patient should see a doctor.

More serious burns may require another approach. A burn may be so severe that it causes life-threatening symptoms. The patient may stop breathing or go into shock. In such cases, the first goal of treatment is to save the patient's life, not treat the burns. The patient may require mouth-to-mouth resuscitation or artificial respiration.

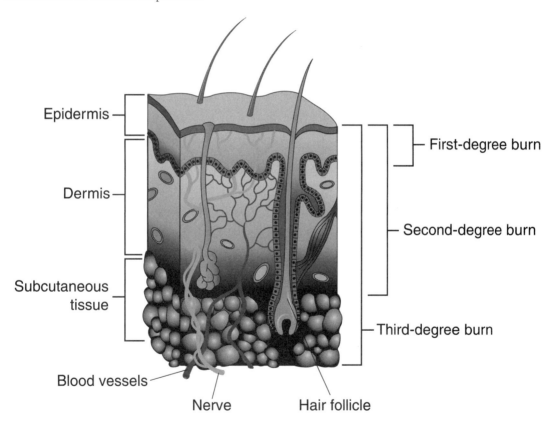

There are three classifications of burns based on how deeply the skin has been damaged: first degree, second degree, and third degree. (Reproduced by permission of Electronic Illustrators Group)

Specialized treatment for severe burn cases may also include:

- Installation of a breathing tube if the patient's airways or lungs have been damaged
- Administration of fluids through an intravenous tube
- Immunization with tetanus vaccine to prevent infection
- Covering the burned area with antibiotic ointments and bandages
- Debridement, or removal of dead tissue
- Removal of scars as healing occurs in order to improve blood flow
- Physical and occupational therapy to keep burn areas flexible and prevent scarring

Sometimes skin tissue is damaged so badly that it cannot heal properly. In that case, a skin graft may be required. In a skin graft, a doctor removes a section of healthy skin from an area of the patient's body that has not been burned. The tissue scarred by the burn is also removed. The healthy tissue is then put into place where the damaged tissue was removed. Over a period of time, the healthy tissue begins to grow and replace the damaged tissue.

Chemical Burn Treatment

The first step in treating a chemical burn is to remove the material causing the burn. If the material is a dry powder, it can be brushed off. If the material is a liquid, it can be flushed away with water. If the chemical that caused the burn is known, it may be neutralized with some other chemical. For example, if the burn is caused by an acid, a weak base can be used to neutralize the acid. The burned area can then be covered with a clean gauze and, if necessary, treated further by a doctor.

Electrical Burn Treatment

As with severe thermal burns, the first step in treating electrical burns usually involves saving the patient's life. An electrical charge large enough to burn the skin may also produce life-threatening symptoms. The source of electricity must be removed and life support treatment provided to the patient. When the patient's condition is stable, the burn can be covered with a clean gauze and medical treatment sought.

Alternative Treatment

Serious burns should always be treated by a medical doctor. Less serious burns may benefit from a variety of alternative treatments. Some herbs that can be used to treat burns include aloe, oil of St. John's wort, calendula (pronounced KUH-len-juh-luh), comfrey, and tea tree oil. Supplementing one's diet with vitamins C and E and the mineral zinc may help a wound to heal faster.

PROGNOSIS

The prognosis for burns depends on many factors. These factors include the degree of the burn, the amount of skin affected by the burn, what parts of the body were affected, and any additional complications that might have developed.

In general, minor burns heal in five to ten days with few or no complications or scarring. Moderate burns heal in ten to fourteen days and may leave scarring. Major burns take more than fourteen days to heal and can leave significant scarring or, in the most severe cases, can be fatal.

PREVENTION

Most thermal burns are caused by fires in the home. Every family member should be aware of basic safety rules that can reduce the risk of such fires. The single most important safety device is a smoke detector. The installation of smoke detectors throughout a house can greatly reduce the chance that injuries will result if a fire breaks out. Children should also be taught not to play with matches, lighters, fireworks, gasoline, cleaning fluids, or other materials that could burn them.

MOST THERMAL BURNS ARE CAUSED BY FIRES IN THE HOME.

Burns from scalding water can be prevented by monitoring the temperature in the home hot water heater. That temperature should never be set higher than about 120°F (49°C). Taking care when working in the kitchen can also prevent scalds. For instance, be cautious when removing the tops from pans of hot foods and when uncovering foods heated in a microwave oven.

Sunburns can be prevented by limiting the time spent in the sun each day. The use of sunscreens can also reduce exposure to the ultraviolet radiation that causes sunburns.

Electrical burns can be prevented by covering unused electrical outlets with safety plugs. Electrical cords should also be kept out of the reach of infants who may chew on them. People should seek shelter indoors during thunderstorms in order to avoid being struck by lightning or coming in contact with fallen electrical wires.

Chemical burns may be prevented by wearing protective clothing, including gloves and eyeshields. Individuals should also be familiar with the chemicals they handle and know which ones are likely to pose a risk for burns.

burns and scalds

Books

Munster, Andrew M., and Glorya Hale. *Severe Burns: A Family Guide to Medical and Emotional Recovery.* Baltimore: Johns Hopkins University Press, 1993.

Organizations

American Burn Association. 625 North Michigan Avenue, Suite 1530, Chicago, IL 60611. http://www.ameriburn.org.

Shriners Hospitals for Children. 2900 Rocky Point Drive, Tampa, FL 33607–1435. (813) 281–0300. http://www.shriners.org.

Web sites

"Cool the Burn: A Site for Children Touched by a Burn." [Online] http://www.cooltheburn.com (accessed on October 11, 1999).

CANCER

DEFINITION

Cancer is not just one disease, but a group of almost one hundred diseases. These diseases have two common characteristics. First, cells begin to grow out of control in the body. Second, those cells have the ability to travel from their original site to other locations in the body. If the spread is not controlled, cancer can result in death.

DESCRIPTION

Cancer is responsible for one out of every four deaths in the United States. It is second only to heart disease as a cause of death in this country. About 1.2 million Americans were diagnosed with cancer in 1998. Of that number, more than 500,000 are expected to die of the disease.

Cancer can attack anyone, but the chances of getting the disease increase with age. The most common forms of cancer are skin cancer, lung cancer, colon cancer, breast cancer (in women; see breast cancer entry), and prostate cancer (in men; see prostate cancer entry). Other major cancers that affect Americans include those of the kidneys, ovaries, uterus, pancreas, bladder, rectum, and blood and lymph nodes (see leukemia entry).

Cancer is a disorder that affects the genes. A gene is a small part of a de-oxyribonucleic (pronounced dee-OK-see-RIE-bo-noo-KLEE-ik) acid (DNA) molecule. DNA molecules carry the master plan in cells that tells them how to behave. Genes carry the directions for making proteins. Proteins are involved in a wide number of functions in the body that make it possible to move, think, breathe, and carry out other activities.

Normally, cells go through a cycle in which they grow, divide, and die. Gene mutations (changes) can interrupt that cycle. Cells forget how to stop growing and reproduce over and over again, forming a lump of cells that gets bigger and bigger. The lump is known as a tumor or neoplasm ("new growth," pronounced NEE-o-plaz-um).

A healthy person's immune system can usually recognize and destroy neoplastic cells. Sometimes, though, mutant cells can escape detection. When they do, they can go on to become tumors. Tumors are of two types: benign ("harmless," pronounced bih-NINE) and malignant (harmful and possibly terminal, pronounced muh-LIG-nent). Benign tumors grow slowly and do not spread in the body. Once removed, they usually do not reappear. Malignant tumors, by contrast, invade surrounding tissue and spread through the body. If removed, a malignant tumor often grows back.

Most gene mutations are caused by environmental factors called carcinogens (pronounced car-SIN-o-genz). Carcinogens are things in our environment that cause cancer. Many kinds of carcinogens are known.

Some kinds of cancer are caused by genetic factors. Faulty genes can be passed from parents to children. When that happens, the children are at risk for cancer. In most such cases, a cancer is caused by some combination of genetic and environmental factors.

WORDS TO KNOW

Benign: A growth that does not spread to other parts of the body, making recovery likely with treatment.

Biopsy: Surgical removal and microscopic examination of tissue for diagnostic purposes.

Bone marrow: Spongy material that fills the center of bones, from which blood cells are produced.

Carcinogen: Any substance capable of causing cancer.

Chemotherapy: Treatment of cancer that uses chemicals or drugs that destroy cancerous cells or tissues.

Epithelium: The layer of cells covering the body's outer and inner surfaces.

Hormone therapy: Treatment of cancer by slowing down the production of certain hormones.

Immunotherapy: Treatment of cancer by stimulating the body's immune system.

Malignant: Cancer cells that have broken loose from a tumor and spread to other parts of the body.

Metastasis: The process by which cancer cells have spread from their original source to other parts of the body.

Radiation therapy: Treatment that uses various forms of radiation to kill cancer cells.

Tumor: An abnormal growth that has developed as cancer cells grow out of control.

X rays: A kind of high-energy radiation that can be used to take pictures of the inside of the body, to diagnose cancer, or to kill cancer cells.

Normal body characteristics can increase the likelihood that a person will develop cancer. For example, people with fair skin are more likely to get skin cancer (see skin cancer entry) than those with darker skin.

Cancers can be classified according to the part of the body in which they occur:

- **Carcinomas.** Carcinomas (pronounced car-sen-O-muhz) are cancers that arise in the epithelium (pronounced eh-peh-THEE-lee-um). The epithelium is the layer of cells that covers the outside (the skin) and the inside of the body. Carcinomas covering the exterior epithelium are called squamous (pronounced SKWAY-muss) cell carcinomas. Those that develop in an organ or gland are called adenocarcinomas (pronounced add-en-o-car-sen-O-muhz).
- **Melanomas.** Melanomas are another form of skin cancer, and usually occur in cells that give skin their color (melanocytes).
- **Sarcomas.** Sarcomas are cancers of the supporting tissues of the body, such as bone, muscle, and blood vessels.
- **Leukemias.** Leukemias are cancers of the blood.
- **Lymphomas.** Lymphomas are cancers of the lymph system.
- **Gliomas.** Gliomas are cancers of nerve tissue.

CAUSES

The major risk factors for cancer are tobacco and alcohol use, diet, sexual and reproductive behavior, infectious agents, family history, occupation, radiation, and pollution.

The American Cancer Society estimates that about 40 percent of all cancer deaths in the United States are caused by tobacco and excessive alcohol use. An additional one-third of the deaths are caused by poor diet and nutrition. The vast majority of deaths from skin cancer are due to overexposure to ultraviolet light in the sun's rays.

THE AMERICAN CANCER SOCIETY ESTIMATES THAT ABOUT 40 PERCENT OF ALL CANCER DEATHS IN THE UNITED STATES ARE CAUSED BY TOBACCO AND EXCESSIVE ALCOHOL USE.

Tobacco

Smoking is responsible for 80 to 90 percent of all cases of lung cancer (see lung cancer entry). Smoking is also a factor in other forms of cancer affecting the upper respiratory (breathing) tract, larynx, bladder, pancreas, and, probably, liver, stomach, and kidney. Secondhand smoke (smoke exhaled by smokers and inhaled by others nearby) can also increase the risk of developing cancer.

Alcohol

People who drink too much alcohol are at risk for certain forms of cancer, such as liver cancer. In combination with smoking, the use of alcohol can also increase the risk of developing cancer of the mouth, pharynx (pronounced FAHR-inks), larynx, and esophagus (pronounced SAH-fuh-guss).

Diet

One in three cancers can be traced to dietary factors. Obesity (see obesity entry) has been connected with cancers of the breast, colon, rectum, pancreas, prostate, gallbladder, ovaries, and uterus.

Sexual and Reproductive Behaviors

Some cancer-causing viruses can be transmitted by sexual activity. People who begin sexual activity early in their lives and have many partners appear to have a higher risk for developing cancer. Women who never have children or have them late in life may be at higher risk for developing ovarian and breast cancer.

Infectious Agents

Scientists believe that about 15 percent of all cancers are caused by viruses, bacteria, or parasites. A list of the most common cancer-causing infectious agents is shown in the table below.

Family History

Certain forms of cancer recur generation after generation in some families. These include breast, colon, ovarian, and uterine cancers.

Occupational Hazards

About 4 percent of all cancers are thought to be connected with one's occupation. For example, people who work with asbestos have an increased chance of developing lung cancer. Asbestos is a naturally occurring mineral that was once used widely as insulation for housing and other buildings. Many other forms of occupational cancer have been identified. These include:

- Bladder cancer, among dye, rubber, and gas workers
- Skin and lung cancer, among those who work in smelters, with arsenic, and in gold mines
- Leukemia, among glue and varnish workers
- Liver cancer, among workers in the PVC (polyvinyl chloride plastics) industry

COMMON PATHOGENS AND THE CANCERS ASSOCIATED WITH THEM

Causative Agent	Type Of Cancer
Viruses	
Papillomaviruses	Cancer of the cervix
Hepatitis B virus	Liver cancer
Hepatitis C virus	Liver cancer
Epstein-Barr virus	Burkitt's lymphoma
Cancers of the upper pharynx	Hodgkin's lymphoma, Non-Hodgkin's lymphoma, Gastric cancers
Human immunodeficiency virus (HIV)	Kaposi's sarcoma Lymphoma
Bacteria	
Helicobacter pylori	Stomach cancer Lymphomas

(Reproduced by permission of Stanley Publishing)

- Lung, bone, and bone marrow cancer, among people who work with X rays and other forms of radiation, or with uranium

Radiation

Ultraviolet radiation is responsible for the majority of deaths from melanoma. Other sources of radiation include X rays, radon gas, and radiation from nuclear materials. These sources combined are thought to be responsible for about 1 to 2 percent of all cancer deaths.

Pollution

Experts think that roughly 1 percent of all cancer deaths are caused by air, land, and water pollution. Industries that release harmful chemicals into the environment are the primary source of these pollutants.

EXPERTS THINK THAT ROUGHLY 1 PERCENT OF ALL CANCER DEATHS ARE CAUSED BY AIR, LAND, AND WATER POLLUTION.

SYMPTOMS

Cancer is a progressive disease. That is, it goes through a series of stages that are progressively worse. The symptoms are different at each stage. One of the earliest symptoms of cancer is pain. As tumors grow, they push on organs, nerves, blood vessels, and other tissues around them, causing pain.

The earlier cancer is detected, the more effectively it can be treated. For this reason, the American Cancer Society has prepared a list of seven warning signs of cancer. They are:

- Change in the size, color, or shape of a wart or mole
- A sore that does not heal
- Persistent cough, hoarseness, or sore throat
- A lump or thickening in the breast or elsewhere
- Unusual bleeding or discharge (release of fluids)
- Chronic indigestion or difficulty in swallowing
- Any change in bowel or bladder habits

Diseases other than cancer can also produce these symptoms, so the symptoms need to be checked as soon as possible. Many forms of cancer have no early warning signs at all. For that reason, regular medical tests may be important. For example, women should check their own breasts regularly and should have regular mammograms (X rays of the breasts).

DIAGNOSIS

The first steps in diagnosing cancer are doing a complete physical examination and getting a medical history. During the physical examination, the doctor looks at, feels, and palpates (applies pressure by touch) various parts of the body. He or she watches for unusual size, feel, or texture of organs or tissues.

Some of the specific symptoms a doctor looks for during such a physical examination are the following:

- Thickening or sores in the lips, tongues, gums, throat, or roof of the mouth
- Tenderness or lumps in the neck
- Swelling or soreness of the lymph nodes in the neck, under the arms, and in the groin
- Sores, itchiness, or bleeding on the skin
- Sores or abnormal discharge from the ovaries, vagina, cervix, or uterus
- Discharge, unevenness, or discoloration of the breasts

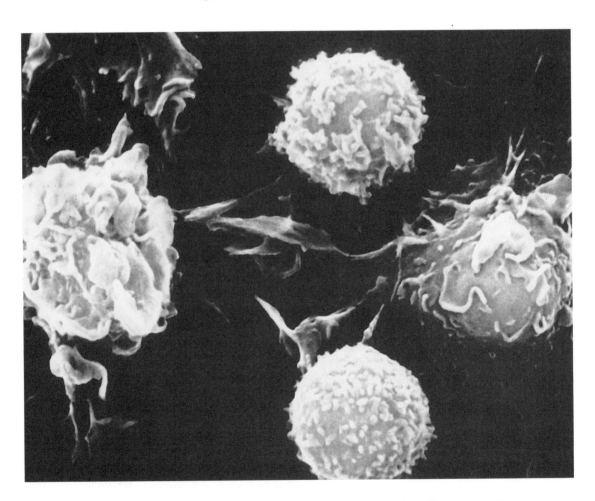

A magnified image of dividing cancer cells. (Photograph by Nina Lampen. Reproduced by permission of Science Source/Photo Researchers, Inc.)

- The presence of lumps or unusual masses in the breasts (in women) or in the rectum or testicles (in men)

If the doctor finds any of these signs, he or she may order tests. Some of the most common tests are the following:

- Sputum (material coughed up from the lungs; pronounced SPYOO-tum) is studied under a microscope to look for lung cancer.
- Blood tests can be used to look for tumor markers. A tumor marker is a special type of protein released by cancer cells. Blood tests are also used to follow the course of cancer and to see how well treatment is working.
- Imaging tests help doctors find tumors deep within the body. Most imaging tests use a form of radiation (such as X rays) to look for abnormal masses inside the body.
- A biopsy is the most reliable test for cancer. In a biopsy, the doctor removes a piece of tissue from an abnormal area of the body. The tissue is then studied under a microscope. A specialist can tell whether the tissue is normal or cancerous.

Screening tests are often helpful in detecting cancer at its earliest stages. A screening test is a relatively simple test that should be done regularly. A routine chest X ray is an example of a screening test. Some of the screening tests used for cancer include sigmoidoscopy (pronounced sig-moy-des-ca-pee; inspection of the colon) for colorectal cancer (see colorectal cancer entry), mammography for breast cancer, and a pap smear for cervical cancer.

Genetic testing is a relatively new form of screening that holds great promise. It can help doctors decide when people may be at risk for certain kinds of cancer because of their genetic makeup.

TREATMENT

Cancer treatment has two goals. First, as much of the original tumor as possible should be removed. Second, the tumor should be prevented from recurring or spreading to other parts of the body. One decision that often has to be made concerns the side effects of cancer treatments. Most cancer treatments are designed to kill cancer cells, but those treatments can also kill healthy cells. A patient undergoing cancer treatment can, therefore, become very ill from the treatments themselves.

A TEAM EFFORT

Cancer treatment often requires the work of a team of doctors. At the head of the team is often an oncologist (pronounced on-KOLL-o-jist), a doctor who specializes in cancer care. Other doctors who may work with the oncologist include the following:

- Radiation oncologists, who specialize in the use of radiation to treat cancer.
- Gynecologist-oncologists who specialize in treatment of women with cancer of the reproductive organs.
- Pediatric-oncologists who specialize in the treatment of children with cancer.
- Radiologists, who use techniques such as X rays, ultrasound, and computed tomography (CT) scans to diagnose cancer.
- Hematologists, who study blood disorders.
- Pathologists, who analyze and identify the abnormal tissues that are present in tumors.

In such cases, patients sometimes choose not to make use of treatments that try to cure the cancer. Instead, they are given other kinds of treatments designed to relieve their symptoms and make them more comfortable.

Many forms of cancer treatment are available. The form used with any one patient depends on many factors, including the patient's age, sex, general health, personal preferences, type and location of the cancer, and extent to which it has already metastasized (spread to other parts of the body, pronounced muh-TASS-tuh-sized). The major types of cancer treatment are surgery, radiation, chemotherapy, immunotherapy, hormone therapy, and bone marrow transplantation.

Surgery

Surgery involves the removal of a visible tumor and is the most common form of cancer treatment. Surgery is most effective when the tumor is small and confined to one area of the body. Surgery can be used for many purposes:

- **Treatment.** When a tumor is removed surgically, a small amount of surrounding tissue is also removed. This ensures that no cancer cells are left in the area. Since cancer cells are often spread by means of the lymphatic system, nearby lymph nodes may also be removed.
- **Cytoreduction.** In some cases, it may be impossible to completely remove all the cancer cells by surgery. Cytoreduction ("cell reduction"; pronounced SITE-o-ree-duk-shun) involves the removal of as much cancerous tissue as possible. Any remaining abnormal tissue is then treated with radiation, chemotherapy, or both.
- **Palliation.** Tumors are sometimes so large that they cannot be removed completely by surgery. In such cases, palliative surgery is used to take out as much of the tumor as possible. This procedure often helps to relieve the symptoms of cancer even if it does not cure the disease itself. For example, a large tumor in the abdomen may press on and block a part of the intestine. The patient may be unable to digest food and feel constant pain and discomfort. Even if the whole tumor cannot be removed, some part of it can probably be taken out. The digestive system can then function normally again.
- **Prevention.** Preventive surgery may be used even if no tumors exist. The presence of abnormal tissue may suggest that tumors could eventually form. To avoid that possibility, the tissue can be removed. Preventive surgery is often used, for example, to prevent ulcerative colitis (see ulcerative colitis entry). About 40 percent of the people with this form of cancer die from the disease. People with the disease may choose to have their colons removed rather than risk dying of ulcerative colitis.
- **Diagnosis.** Whenever possible, biopsies are conducted with a needle. The needle is used to take out a small piece of tissue for study. Sometimes, a

needle biopsy cannot be used. In those cases, surgery may be necessary to get the tissue needed for study.

Radiation

Radiation kills cancer cells. It can be used alone when a tumor cannot be removed surgically. More often, radiation is used in combination with surgery and chemotherapy. Radiation can be performed from either the outside or the inside of the body. An example of outside radiation is the use of X rays to treat a tumor. Inside radiation can be carried out by inserting pellets or liquids in a patient's body. Radiation given off by the pellets or liquid attacks and kills cancer cells.

Chemotherapy

Chemotherapy is the use of chemicals or drugs to kill cancer cells. It is used to destroy cells that have spread from the original tumor and are circulating in the body. The drugs used for chemotherapy can be given orally (by mouth) or by injection. They are used alone or in combination with surgery and radiation.

Chemotherapy is sometimes used before surgery or radiation because drugs are often able to kill cancer cells and reduce the size of a tumor. Surgery and radiation are likely to be more effective when used on smaller tumors. More often, chemotherapy is used after surgery or radiation treatments. In such cases, drugs may be able to destroy cancer cells remaining in the body after the initial treatment.

Immunotherapy

Immunotherapy is a relatively new form of cancer treatment. Its goal is to kill cancer cells by using chemicals that occur naturally in the body. Chemicals known as interferons are an example. Interferon can be given to a cancer patient to stimulate his or her own immune system to fight cancer more effectively.

Research is also being done to develop a cancer vaccine. A cancer vaccine is different from other kinds of vaccines. It is not being designed to prevent cancer. Instead, it will be given to patients who already have the disease. It is intended to help the patient's immune system fight cancer cells.

Hormone Treatment

Some forms of cancer grow faster when certain hormones are present. Examples of such cancers include cancer of the breast, prostate, and uterus. Hormone therapy involves the use of drugs that reduce the amount of hormones produced and their ability to cause changes in the body. These drugs can slow down the rate at which hormone-related cancers develop, extending the patient's life by months or years.

Bone Marrow Transplantation

Bone marrow is tissue found in the center of bones. It produces cells that develop into new blood cells. Radiation and chemotherapy often destroy bone marrow and the patient's body is no longer able to produce the amount of blood it needs to stay healthy.

Bone marrow transplantation involves the removal of some bone marrow from one person so that it can be given to another person. For the procedure to be successful, the two people must be closely related or have similar blood characteristics. Bone marrow transplantation can be important with patients who require very aggressive (serious) forms of treatment that are likely to destroy their own bone marrow.

Alternative Treatment

Many alternative forms of cancer treatment are available, however, patients should always seek the advice of trained health practitioners before trying alternative treatments. Treatment methods from other cultures can sometimes be effective in treating the symptoms of cancer or the side effects of radiation or chemotherapy. Two examples are acupuncture (a Chinese therapy technique where fine needles puncture the body) and Chinese herbal medicines. Body massage can help to ease muscle tension and reduce side effects such as nausea and vomiting.

Experts now believe that certain kinds of food, such as fruits, vegetables, and grains, can help protect against various forms of cancer. For example, a diet rich in fiber, which includes fruits and vegetables, seems to reduce the risk of colon cancer. Exercise and a diet low in fat can help control weight and reduce the risk of breast and colon cancers.

Scientists are not sure what is in foods that prevents cancer. Vitamins A, C, and E and the compound known as beta-carotene are likely prospects. So are two groups of compounds known as the isothiocyanates (pronounced I-so-THI-o-si-uh-nates) and the dithiolthiones (pronounced di-THI-ul-THI-ownz). These compounds are found in broccoli, cauliflower, cabbage, and carrots.

Some drugs used for cancer treatment may also help prevent the disease. Tamoxifen (pronounced tuh-MOK-sih-fen, trade name Nolvadex) is an example. Research is now being conducted to determine its effectiveness in preventing breast cancer. Compounds known as retinoids, obtained from vitamin A, are also being tested for use against head and neck cancers. The mineral selenium may also hold some promise for the prevention of some forms of cancer.

PROGNOSIS

"Lifetime risk" is the term used by cancer researchers to estimate the chance that a person will develop or die from cancer. In the United States, men have a 1 in 2 lifetime risk of developing cancer. For women, the risk is 1 in 3. African Americans have a higher lifetime risk than whites; they are also 30 percent more likely to die of cancer.

Most cancers can be cured if they are discovered and treated at an early stage. Prognosis depends on a number of factors, including the type of cancer, the stage at which it was detected, and how far it has already progressed. Personal factors, such as age, general health status, and treatment effectiveness also determine prognosis.

IN THE UNITED STATES, MEN HAVE A 1 IN 2 LIFETIME RISK OF DEVELOPING CANCER. FOR WOMEN, THE RISK IS 1 IN 3.

PREVENTION

Experts believe that the risk of getting cancer can be reduced by following some simple guidelines:

- Eat plenty of vegetables and fruits.
- Exercise vigorously for at least twenty minutes each day.
- Avoid excessive weight gain.
- Avoid tobacco, including secondhand smoke.
- Decrease or avoid consumption of animal fats and red meat.
- Avoid excessive amounts of alcohol.
- Avoid overexposure to sunlight.
- Avoid risky sexual practices.
- Avoid known carcinogens in the environment and workplace.

See also: Breast cancer, colorectal cancer, Hodgkin's disease, lung cancer, prostate cancer, and skin cancer.

FOR MORE INFORMATION

Books

Buckman, Robert. *What You Really Need to Know about Cancer: A Comprehensive Guide for Patients and Their Families.* Baltimore: Johns Hopkins University Press, 1997.

Dollinger, Malin. *Everyone's Guide to Cancer Therapy.* Toronto: Somerville House Publishing, 1994.

Morra, Marion E. *Choices.* New York: Avon Books, 1994.

Murphy, Gerald P. *Informed Decisions: The Complete Book of Cancer Diagnosis, Treatment and Recovery.* Atlanta, GA: American Cancer Society, 1997.

Periodicals

"What You Need to Know about Cancer." *Scientific American* (September 1996).

Organizations

American Cancer Society. 1599 Clifton Road NE, Atlanta, GA 30329. (800) 227–2345. http://www.cancer.org.

Cancer Care, Inc. 1180 Avenue of the Americas. New York, NY 10036. (800) 813–HOPE. http://www.cancercareinc.org.

Cancer Research Institute. 681 Fifth Avenue, New York, NY 10022. (800) 992–2623. http://www.cancerresearch.org.

National Cancer Institute. 31 Center Drive, Bethesda, MD 20892–2580. (800) 4–CANCER. http://www.nci.nih.gov.

National Coalition for Cancer Survivorship. 1010 Wayne Avenue, 5th Floor, Silver Springs, MD 20910. (301) 650–8868.

Web sites

Oncolink. [Online] University of Pennsylvania Cancer Center. http://cancer .med.upenn.edu. (accessed on October 13, 1999).

CARPAL TUNNEL SYNDROME

DEFINITION

Carpal tunnel syndrome (CTS) is a disorder caused by pressure on the median nerve in the wrist. Numbness and tingling are characteristic symptoms of the disorder.

DESCRIPTION

The carpal (pronounced CAR-pull) tunnel is an area in the wrist formed by bones and ligaments. It provides a protected passageway for the median nerve. The median nerve is responsible for feelings and movement in the hand, especially the thumb and first three fingers. When pressure is applied to the median nerve, the hand feels as if it has gone to sleep.

Carpal tunnel syndrome is most common among women between the ages of thirty and sixty. The disorder is a major cause of missed workdays because of the pain it causes. In 1995 about $270 million was spent for sick days taken as a result of CTS-related problems.

WORDS TO KNOW

Carpal tunnel: A passageway in the wrist, created by bones and ligaments, through which the median nerve passes.

Electromyography: A test used to measure how well a nerve is functioning.

Median nerve: A nerve that runs through the wrist and into the hand, providing feeling and movement to the hand, thumb, and fingers.

CAUSES

The carpal tunnel is a narrow passageway. Any swelling in this area causes pressure on the median nerve. That pressure eventually makes it difficult for a person to use the hand normally. Some conditions that can lead to pressure on the median nerve include pregnancy, obesity (see obesity entry), arthritis (see arthritis entry), diabetes (see diabetes mellitus entry), certain diseases of the thyroid and pituitary glands, and injuries to the arm and wrist.

IN 1995 ABOUT $270 MILLION WAS SPENT FOR SICK DAYS TAKEN AS A RESULT OF CTS-RELATED PROBLEMS.

One of the most common causes of CTS is repetitive motion. Repetitive motion is any activity that a person performs over and over again. Typing, working at a computer keyboard or cash register, playing some kinds of musical instruments, and working at certain types of factory jobs may involve repetitive motion. Repetitive motion forces a person to use the wrist over and over again and can lead to swelling in the carpal tunnel area, subsequent pressure on the media nerve, and thus to CTS.

SYMPTOMS

Symptoms of carpal tunnel syndrome include numbness, burning, tingling, and a prickly pin-like sensation in the palm of the hand, thumb, and fingers. Some individuals notice a shooting pain that starts in the wrist and goes up into the arm or down into the hand and fingers. CTS can also lead to muscle weakness in the hand. A person may have difficulty opening jars and holding objects. In advanced cases, hand and thumb muscles may actually decrease in size. If left untreated, CTS can result in permanent weakness in the hand and fingers, loss of feeling, and even paralysis of the thumb and fingers.

DIAGNOSIS

The first step in diagnosing carpal tunnel syndrome is a simple one. The doctor asks the patient to hold his or her hand in position with the wrist bent for about a minute. The presence of the symptoms described suggests the presence of CTS. The doctor may also perform other simple tests to measure muscle strength and feeling in the hand and arm. Additional tests may be used to rule out other problems. For example, an X ray can show that a tumor is causing pressure on the median nerve.

The doctor may also order an electromyograph (pronounced e-LEK-tro-my-uh-graf) of the affected area. An electromyograph measures the speed with which nerve transmissions move through the median nerve. It indicates the amount of damage that has been done to the nerve.

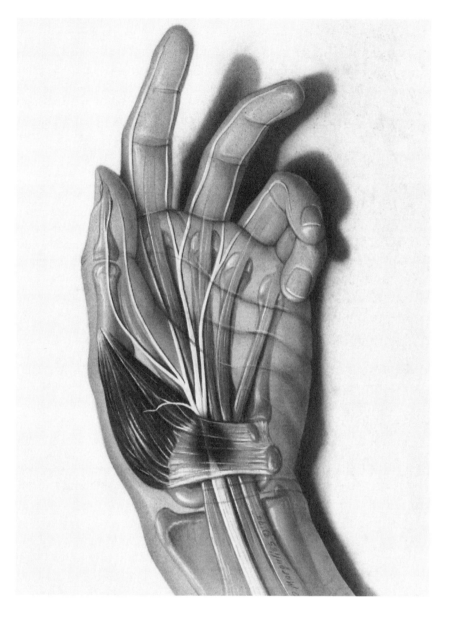

Illustration of the carpal tunnel, tendons, and median nerve (white line running up the wrist). (© R. Margulies. Reproduced by permission of Custom Medical Stock Photo.)

TREATMENT

The first step in treating carpal tunnel syndrome is to immobilize the wrist, that is, prevent it from moving. A splint around the wrist is used for this purpose. Some people get relief from CTS by wearing the splint at night. Others may also need to wear the splint during the day.

Certain drugs may be prescribed to reduce pain and swelling. Non-steroidal anti-inflammatory drugs (NSAIDs), such as ibuprofen (pronounced i-byoo-PRO-fuhn), are commonly used for this purpose. In advanced cases of CTS, injections of steroids may be necessary. Steroids also reduce pain and swelling.

In the most serious cases of CTS, surgery may be necessary. The doctor cuts a ligament in the wrist, increasing the size of the carpal tunnel. This procedure results in decreased pressure on the median nerve and, therefore, less pain for the patient. This procedure is almost always done in a doctor's office. A local anesthetic is used to numb the hand and wrist. The patient usually recovers quickly.

PROGNOSIS

Without proper diagnosis and treatment, carpal tunnel syndrome may lead to permanent damage to the affected hand. In most cases, splints and anti-inflammatory drugs are able to control the symptoms of CTS. For those who require surgery, about 95 percent will get complete relief from the disorder.

PREVENTION

The goal of CTS prevention is to reduce the amount of repetitive motion that places stress on the wrist. Ergonomics (pronounced ur-ga-NAHM-iks) can be a major help in reaching this goal. Ergonomics works with the design of machines and other equipment to make them less stressful for humans. For example, research in ergonomics has led to the development of new computer keyboard designs that are easier and less stressful to use. The early use of splints can also help prevent people at risk for CTS from developing the condition.

FOR MORE INFORMATION

Books

Butler, Sharon J. *Conquering Carpal Tunnel Syndrome and Other Repetitive Strain Injuries.* Oakland, CA: New Harbinger Publications, 1996.

Crouch, Tammy. *Carpal Tunnel Syndrome and Repetitive Stress Injuries: The Comprehensive Guide to Prevention, Treatment and Recovery.* Berkeley: North Atlantic Books, 1996.

Pascarelli, Emil. *Repetitive Strain Injury: A Computer User's Guide.* New York: John Wiley & Sons, 1994.

Periodicals

Brody, Jane E. "Experts on Carpal Tunnel Syndrome Say that Conservative Treatment is the Best First Approach." *New York Times* (February 28, 1996): p. 89+.

Glazer, Sarah. "Repetitive Stress Injury: A Modern Malady." *Washington Post* (March 12, 1996): p. WH12.

CATARACTS

DEFINITION

A cataract is a cloudiness in the lens of the eye, which is normally clear and transparent. The cloudiness caused by a cataract may eventually lead to decreased vision and blindness.

DESCRIPTION

The lens is positioned near the front of the eyeball. It is protected by the cornea, which covers the front of the eyeball. The purpose of the lens is to focus the light waves that enter the eye. Muscles around the lens can change the shape of the lens. In this way, objects both close at hand and far away can be brought into focus.

The lens is made up of about 35 percent protein and 65 percent water. Proteins are chemical compounds found in all cells. As people grow older, the chemicals present in their eyes may change. Proteins may break down, water may seep out of the eye, or other changes may occur. One consequence of such changes is the formation of cataracts.

Cataracts are common in older people. They are so common that they are regarded as a normal part of the aging process. For those between the ages of 50 and 65, the chance of having a cataract is about 50 percent. Beyond the age of 70, the risk rises to about 70 percent.

Cataracts also occur in young people, but are much less common. For example, the lens may be injured by some foreign object, which may

WORDS TO KNOW

Cornea: The transparent outer coating on the front of the eyeball.

Lens: A transparent oval body located near the front of the eye that focuses light waves.

Proteins: Chemicals that are found in every cell in the human body and carry out many essential functions.

Retina: A thin layer of tissue at the back of the eyeball on which light waves are focused and then transmitted to the brain by way of the optic nerve.

Steroids: Naturally occurring chemicals that help reduce inflammation, pain, and swelling.

lead to the formation of a cataract. Cataracts are also caused by certain diseases, such as diabetes mellitus (see diabetes mellitus entry).

Cataracts generally have little or no effect on vision in their early stages. As they develop, they can lead to vision problems and, eventually, blindness may result.

CAUSES

The vast majority of cataracts are thought to have no specific cause. They simply develop as a person grows older. Researchers are exploring a number of theories about possible causes of cataracts. These theories suggest that smoking, alcohol, and high-fat diets may increase a person's risk for cataracts. They also suggest that vitamin supplements may decrease the risk for cataracts.

SYMPTOMS

The most common symptom of cataracts is a gradual, painless change in one's vision. Objects become more blurry, filmy, or fuzzy to a person with cataracts. Some other common symptoms of cataracts include the following:

• Frequent changes in eyeglass prescription
• Changes in color vision
• Increased difficulty in seeing at night
• Poor vision in sunlight
• Presence of a milky white film in the pupil of the eye

DIAGNOSIS

Cataracts are easily diagnosed by any eye specialist. They can often be detected before a patient is aware of vision problems. The most direct diagnosis is made by shining a light into the patient's eyes. Color changes or cloudiness are often visible if a cataract is developing.

TREATMENT

No treatment is needed for mild cases of cataracts. If they do not interfere with a patient's vision, they are not treated. If moderate vision problems develop, a stronger eyeglass prescription may be all that is needed.

In more serious cataract cases, surgery may be necessary. Surgery is the only procedure available for treating advanced cases of cataracts. Cataract surgery is relatively simple. By the late 1990s, it was the most frequently performed surgery in the United States.

Cataract surgery can be performed in a doctor's office and usually lasts about an hour. The cloudy lens is removed. An artificial plastic lens is then inserted into the space formerly occupied by the damaged lens. The patient is given antibiotics and steroids after the surgery. The antibiotics protect against infection by bacteria. The steroids help reduce the pain and inflammation caused by the surgery.

PROGNOSIS

Many cases of cataracts never require treatment other than a change in one's eyeglass prescription. If surgery is required, the success rate is very high. More than 90 percent of patients experience improved vision. Complications occur in a very small fraction (3 to 5 percent) of cataract surgeries. These complications include infections, swelling of the cornea, bleeding, and damage to the retina.

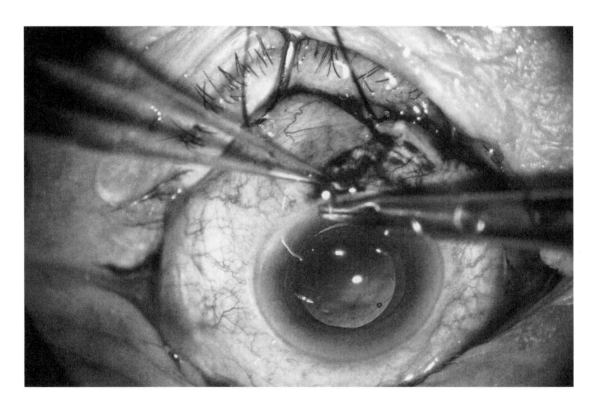

Cataract surgery. More than 90 percent of patients experience improved vision after cataract surgery. (Photograph by David Sutton/Zuma Image. Reproduced by permission of The Stock Market.)

PREVENTION

Since most cases of cataracts are part of the natural aging process, there is not much that can be done to prevent their development. Wearing dark glasses in direct sunlight may be helpful. Radiation from the sun is thought to be one possible cause of changes in proteins in the lens. A healthy diet rich in citrus fruits, sweet potatoes, carrots, and green leafy vegetables, and supplemented by vitamins, may also be helpful in delaying the onset of cataracts.

FOR MORE INFORMATION

Books

Salmans, Sandra. *Your Eyes: Questions You Have . . . Answers You Need.* Allentown: People's Medical Society, 1996.

Shulman, Julius. *Cataracts—from Diagnosis to Recovery: The Complete Guide for Patients and Families.* New York: St. Martin's Press, 1995.

Organizations

American Academy of Ophthalmology (National Eyecare Project). PO Box 7424, San Francisco, CA 94120–7424. (800) 222–EYES. http://www.eyenet.org.

American Optometric Association. 243 North Lindbergh Boulevard, St. Louis, MO, 63141. (314) 991–4100. http://www.aoanet.org.

Lighthouse International. 111 East 59th Street, New York, NY 10022. (800) 829–0500. http://www.lighthouse.org.

Prevent Blindness America. 500 East Remington Road, Schaumburg, IL 60173. (800) 331–2020. http://www.prevent-blindness.org.

CEREBRAL ANEURYSM

DEFINITION

A cerebral aneurysm (pronounced an-yuh-RIH-zim) occurs at a weak spot in an artery that supplies blood to the brain. Once weakened, the artery wall bulges outward and fills with blood. This bulge is called an aneurysm. An aneurysm can burst, spilling blood into the brain. When this happens, permanent brain damage, disability, or death may occur.

DESCRIPTION

Arteries are blood vessels that carry blood from the heart to other parts of the body. For a variety of reasons, weak spots sometimes develop in the walls of an artery. When that happens, an aneurysm develops. An aneurysm in the brain is one of the most dangerous types.

The greatest danger of an aneurysm is rupture. A ruptured aneurysm in the brain allows blood to flow into the surrounding area. Blood may also flow into the area that surrounds brain tissue. This event is called a subarachnoid hemorrhage (SAH; pronounced sub-uh-RAK-noid hem-uh-RIJ).

About 1 percent of individuals with an aneurysm are at risk for a hemorrhage. Under age forty, more men tend to experience an SAH. After age forty, more women than men are affected. There are seldom any warning signs of an SAH. Most people who have a hemorrhage never knew they had an aneurysm. Based on autopsies (medical studies of dead bodies), 1 to 5 percent of the total population has had some type of cerebral aneurysm.

WORDS TO KNOW

Angiography: A procedure in which a dye is pumped into a person's blood vessels so that X-ray photographs can show the structure of organs and tissues more clearly.

Atherosclerosis: Hardening of the arteries.

Cerebrospinal fluid: A clear liquid that bathes the brain and spinal column.

Computed tomography (CT) scan: A procedure by which X rays are directed at a patient's body from various angles and the set of photographs thus obtained assembled by a computer program.

Computerized axial tomography (CAT) scan: Another name for a computed tomography (CT) scan.

Congenital disorder: A medical condition that is present at birth.

Lumbar puncture: A procedure in which a long, thin needle is used to withdraw cerebrospinal fluid from a patient's spine.

Subarachnoid hemorrhage (SAH): Loss of blood into the subarachnoid space, the fluid-filled area that surrounds brain tissue.

CAUSES

Most cases of cerebral aneurysm are caused by congenital factors. Congenital means that the person was born with the defect. The person has artery walls that are thinner than normal in some places. It is in these regions that aneurysms develop. Aneurysms may be caused by other factors, as well. These factors include injury to the brain, infection, hardening of the arteries (see atherosclerosis entry), or abnormally rapid growth of brain cells.

SYMPTOMS

Most aneurysms go unnoticed until they rupture. In about 10 to 15 percent of cases, however, there are symptoms. Common warning signs include an enlarged pupil in one eye, a drooping eyelid, or pain above or behind the eye. Other symptoms include a headache in one specific part of the head, difficulty in walking, double vision, or numbness in the face.

Some aneurysms bleed without rupturing. In such cases, symptoms may develop gradually. They include headache, nausea, vomiting, neck pain, blackouts, ringing in the ears, dizziness, or seeing spots.

Aneurysms do not always rupture suddenly. Sometimes, they begin to ooze blood slowly. When this happens, patients may experience certain warning signs. These warning signs include headaches, nausea, vomiting, and dizziness. Unfortunately, these symptoms are easily confused with ordinary tension headaches. An individual may not realize that these are symptoms of a more serious problem.

SYMPTOMS OF A CEREBRAL ANEURYSM INCLUDE A HEADACHE IN ONE SPECIFIC PART OF THE HEAD, DIFFICULTY IN WALKING, DOUBLE VISION, OR NUMBNESS IN THE FACE.

When an aneurysm ruptures, most patients experience a sudden, extremely severe headache. The headache is often described as the worst the patient has ever had. The headache is often accompanied by nausea, vomiting, and loss of consciousness. The patient may also experience a stiff neck, fever, and unusual sensitivity to light. About one-quarter of all patients experience problems that affect the nervous system, including swelling of the brain.

DIAGNOSIS

The symptoms described may prompt a doctor to order a series of tests for a cerebral aneurysm. The most reliable test is a computed tomography

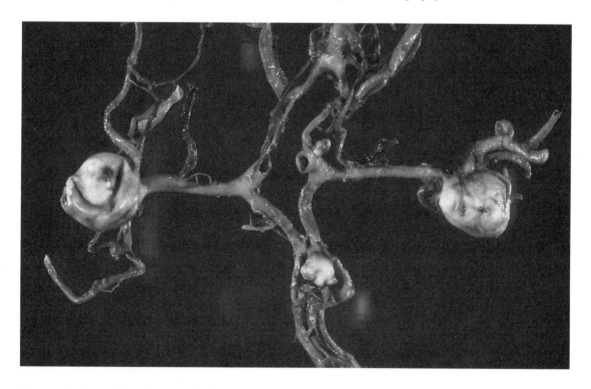

Three pre-burst aneurisms in the cerebral arteries of a human brain. (© Martin Rotker. Reproduced by permission of Phototake NYC.)

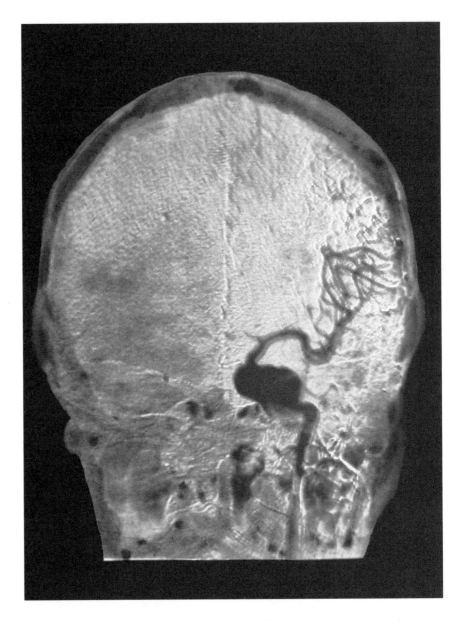

X ray of a human head showing a brain aneurysm. (Reproduced by permission of CNR/National Audubon Society Collection/Photo Researchers, Inc.)

(CT) scan. In a CT scan, X rays are projected through the brain at various angles. These X rays produce photographs of the brain from different directions. A computer program is then used to combine the pictures, which produces a broad, overall view of the brain. CT scans are also sometimes called computerized axial tomography (CAT) scans.

A CT scan is usually able to determine whether or not an aneurysm exists. It is also able to pinpoint the region of the brain in which the rupture has occurred. To get the clearest result, the scan must usually be done within seventy-two hours after rupture.

If questions remain after a CT scan, follow-up tests might be run. One such test is a lumbar puncture, or spinal tap. In a lumbar puncture, a long, thin needle is used to remove cerebrospinal fluid (CF, liquid surrounding the brain and spinal column) from a patient's spine. The fluid is studied for certain characteristic materials formed when blood products are released in the brain.

Another follow-up test is a cerebral angiography (pronounced an-gee-AH-graffee). Cerebral angiography is a procedure in which a dye is injected into the blood. The dye is carried throughout the body, including to the brain. An X ray is then taken of the brain. The dye shows the presence of any abnormal structures in blood vessels.

TREATMENT

If an aneurysm has not ruptured, it may be left untreated. A person with an aneurysm has a 1 percent chance of having a rupture each year. As time goes on, a doctor may eventually decide to remove an aneurysm surgically. But the surgery may be more risky than leaving the aneurysm in place and monitoring any changes that may occur in its shape and size.

Once an aneurysm ruptures, the first step is to save the patient's life. Left untreated, a ruptured aneurysm can cause death in a short period of time. Patients may require both oxygen and fluids to remain stable. Medications may be needed to keep damaged blood vessels from collapsing. A drug known as nimodipine (pronounced ni-MO-dih-peen, trade name Nimotop) is often used for this purpose.

If the patient survives the rupture of an aneurysm, surgery is usually necessary. The purpose of the surgery is to close off the aneurysm and prevent it from further bleeding. In one approach, a clip is placed around the base of the aneurysm. The clip usually solves the problem for a while. However, the aneurysm may break loose again later, close to the point where the clip was placed.

PROGNOSIS

An unruptured aneurysm may not cause any symptoms over an entire lifetime. Surgical procedures are available for dealing with the aneurysm, but the risk from surgery may be at least as great as that from the aneurysm itself. The prognosis for people who experience a ruptured aneurysm is not good. About 15 to 25 percent of those who experience a rupture do not survive the event. An additional 25 to 50 percent survive the immediate episode, but die of complications caused by bleeding in the brain. Of those who do survive, about 15 to 50 percent suffer permanent brain damage or physical disability.

PREVENTION

There are no known methods for preventing the formation of an aneurysm. If an aneurysm is discovered before it ruptures, it may be removed surgically. Some doctors recommend CT scans or angiograms for relatives of patients who have had aneurysms.

FOR MORE INFORMATION

Organizations

The Brain Aneurysm Foundation, Inc. 66 Canal Street, Boston, MA 02114. (617) 723–3870. http://neurosurgery.mgh.harvard.edu/baf.

Web sites

Aneurysm and AVM Support Page. [Online] http://www.westga.edu.~wmaples/aneurysm.html (accessed on October 13, 1999).

CEREBRAL PALSY

DEFINITION

Cerebral palsy (CP) is the name given to a collection of movement disorders. Movement disorders are conditions in which a person's muscles do not respond normally. CP is also known as static encephalopathy (pronounced in-seh-fuh-LAH-puh-thee). It is caused by brain damage that occurs before, during, or just after birth. A person with CP is often also affected by other conditions caused by brain damage.

DESCRIPTION

If a person is affected by CP his or her muscles may become either rigid or very loose. Sometimes an individual may lose control of his or her muscles, resulting in problems with balance and coordination. The condition may affect the legs only, which is called paraplegia (pronounced par-uh-PLEE-jee-uh) or diplegia (pronounced die-PLEE-juh); the arm and leg on one side of the body, which is known as hemiplegia (pronounced hem-i-PLEE-juh); or all four limbs, called quadriplegia (pronounced kwod-ruh-PLEE-jee-uh).

Other problems experienced by someone with CP include visual or hearing problems, mental retardation (see mental retardation entry), learning disabilities (see learning disorders entry), and attention deficit disorder (ADD). Some CP patients experience no problems beyond their movement disorder.

CP affects about 500,000 children and adults in the United States. About 6,000 new cases are diagnosed in newborns and young children each year. CP is not a genetic disorder, and there is currently no way of predicting which children will develop it. CP is not a disease and is not communicable, which means it cannot be passed from one person to another.

CP is a nonprogressive disorder. That is, it does not become better or worse over time. However, some conditions may appear to become worse. For example, when muscles are rigid for a long period, arms and legs may become deformed. In such cases, additional treatments may be necessary.

CAUSES

Cerebral palsy is caused by damage to brain cells that control the movement of muscles. When those cells die, signals can no longer be sent to muscle cells. This loss of muscle control results in the symptoms of CP.

A number of factors can cause brain cell damage. These include lack of oxygen (asphyxia, pronounced az-FIK-see-uh), infection, trauma (shock), malnutrition (poor diet), drugs or other chemicals, or hemorrhage (bursting of blood vessels). In most cases, it is impossible to discover the exact cause for any one person's CP. Premature birth is regarded as one important and common factor. Most researchers now believe that brain cell damage occurs before birth. This damage is also responsible for other conditions that tend to occur along with CP.

Asphyxia may occur as the result of various problems. First, the circulatory system may not develop normally prior to birth. Asphyxia may occur during the birth process, however asphyxia at birth usually indicates that the newborn has other neurological problems. Asphyxia

WORDS TO KNOW

Ataxia: A condition in which balance and coordination are impaired.

Athetonia: A condition marked by slow, twisting, involuntary muscle movements.

Attention-deficit/Hyperactivity Disorder: A behavior disorder marked by inattentiveness, a high level of activity, and impulsive behavior.

Contracture: Shortening of a muscle.

Diplegia: Paralysis of the arm and leg on one side of the body.

Dystonia: Loss of the ability to control detailed muscle movement.

Hemiplegia: Paralysis of one side of the body.

Hypotonia: A condition in which muscles become floppy and lacking in strength.

Quadriplegia: Paralysis of both arms and both legs.

Spastic: A condition in which muscles are rigid, posture may be abnormal, and control of muscles may be impaired.

after birth can be caused by choking, exposure to poisons (such as carbon monoxide), or near drowning.

A child's brain may also be damaged prior to birth by infections acquired by the mother. These infections include rubella (German measles; see rubella entry), toxoplasmosis (a blood infection), cytomegalovirus (a virus that causes herpes; pronounced SIE-tuh-MEG-uh-lo-VIE-rus), and HIV (the virus that causes AIDS; see AIDS entry). Two kinds of brain infection, encephalitis (see encephalitis entry) and meningitis (see meningitis entry), can also cause CP in infants.

Physical trauma (shock) to the pregnant mother or fetus may cause brain damage leading to CP. Trauma can be caused by a car accident, violent shaking, or physical abuse. Malnutrition and drug use by the mother can also cause brain damage.

Erika Moore, who suffers from cerebral palsy, sits next to a playground at the Children's Care Hospital and School in Sioux Falls, South Dakota. The hospital plans to add equipment for children with special needs. (Reproduced by permission of AP/Wide World Photos)

Differences in certain blood factors (Rh factors) between mother and child was once a major cause of one form of CP. Today these differences can be detected by tests and a pregnant woman can be treated to prevent damage to her child.

SYMPTOMS

The symptoms of cerebral palsy are usually not noticeable at birth. Instead, they begin to show up during the first eighteen months of a child's life.

Normal children pass through a series of developmental stages. At each stage, they learn how to perform one or more common tasks. Infants with CP have difficulty performing these tasks. Such difficulties may indicate that an infant has CP. The tasks considered to be milestones in normal development include the following:

- Babbles (6 to 8 months)
- Sits well with support (8 to 10 months)
- Crawls (9 to 12 months)
- Walks alone (12 to 15 months)
- Uses one or two words other than dada and mama (12 to 15 months)
- Eats with fingers; holds bottle (12 to 18 months)
- Turns pages in books; removes shoes and socks (24 to 30 months)
- Walks up and down steps (24 to 36 months)

Because children develop at different rates, using these milestones to diagnose cerebral palsy (or any other disorder) must be used with great caution. The fact that an otherwise healthy child does not reach one of these milestones at the suggested age is not necessarily a sign that the child has CP. He or she may just be developing at a slower rate. In addition, problems with vision or hearing may cause such delays.

Five forms of cerebral palsy are recognized. They are defined according to the kind of muscle damage and the location of that damage:

- **Spastic:** Muscles are rigid (tight), posture may be abnormal, and the ability to do delicate work is impaired.
- **Athetoid:** Muscular movements are slow, twisting, and involuntary (beyond the person's control).
- **Hypotonic:** Muscles are floppy, without firmness.
- **Ataxic:** Balance and coordination are impaired.
- **Dystonic:** Any combination of the above symptoms.

Cerebral palsy is also described according to the parts of the body affected:

- **Hemiplegia:** One arm and one leg on the same side of the body are involved.

- **Diplegia:** Both legs are involved; in addition, one or both arms may also be involved.
- **Quadriplegia:** Both arms and both legs are involved.

A diagnosis of CP usually involves combining terms. For example, someone with spastic diplegia shows symptoms of rigid muscles in both legs. In addition, the terms mild, moderate, and severe are sometimes used to describe the seriousness of the disorder.

Loss of muscle control as a result of CP can cause other problems with bones and muscles. Examples of these problems include scoliosis (curving of the spine; see scoliosis entry), hip dislocation, and contractures. A contracture is a permanent shortening of a muscle. It can cause muscles to become fixed in awkward positions, resulting in clenched fists or equinus (pronounced eh-KWI-nuss). Equinus is a foot deformity that prevents one's heel from touching the ground when walking. Contractures can be painful and can interfere with the normal activities of daily living.

Brain damage that causes cerebral palsy may also cause a variety of other disorders. These include:

- Mental retardation
- Learning disabilities.
- Attention deficit disorder
- Seizure disorder (tendency toward convulsions)
- Visual problems, especially strabismus ("cross-eye")
- Loss of hearing (see hearing loss entry)
- Speech problems

About one-third of children with CP have some moderate-to-severe mental retardation, one-third have mild mental retardation, and one-third have normal to above average intelligence. For some children, disorders related to CP can have an even greater impact on a child's life than the physical handicaps caused by CP.

DIAGNOSIS

Cerebral palsy is usually diagnosed using the described developmental milestones. Using these milestones, most children with CP can be diagnosed by the age of eighteen months. However, differences in the rate of development and the presence of other medical problems must always be taken into account.

Certain tests can also be used to diagnose CP. The Apgar test is used with newborn babies. It measures the newborn's heart rate, cry, color, muscle tone, and motor (muscular) reactions. An Apgar score of less than three (out of a possible ten) is a warning sign that the baby may have cerebral palsy. Babies with abnormal organs or abnormal behaviors may also have CP. A variety of tests, such as an ultrasound test, can be used to diagnose these problems.

As in most medical cases, tests can also be performed to rule out potential problems other than cerebral palsy. X rays can be used to look for abnormal structures in the brain, for example, and blood tests can be used to check for infection.

TREATMENT

Cerebral palsy cannot be cured. However, the physical and other problems it causes can usually be managed through planning and timely care. Treatment plans depend on the type of impairment as well as associated problems the child may have, such as learning disabilities. Many CP patients require the help of physical and occupational therapists only. These professionals help the child learn to deal with loss of muscle control. Other specialists, such as speech-language therapists, special education teachers, nutritionists, and neurosurgeons (nerve specialists) may be needed to help with problems related to CP.

While cerebral palsy does not become worse over time, the needs of a CP child do change and new treatment plans may have to be developed as the child grows older. Most parents do not have the knowledge and skills to provide a CP child with all the care he or she needs. Medical professionals then become essential. Other parents who have CP children are also an important resource. They can provide both practical advice and emotional support for parents of newly-diagnosed CP children. These support groups exist throughout the United States. They can be contacted with the help of the United Cerebral Palsy Association or a local hospital or social service agency.

WHAT IS ULTRASOUND?

Ultrasound is a method by which doctors can study organs and tissues inside the human body. The technique was developed during World War II (1939–45) when scientists used very high pitched sound waves (ultrasound) to search for submarines under the water. The sound waves were sent out from a ship. They traveled through the water and bounced off objects, such as submarines and fish. The reflect sound waves formed characteristic patterns, depending on the objects from which they rebounded. By the 1950s scientists began to realize that ultrasound had many other uses and could be especially helpful in the field of medicine.

A problem doctors face is that they cannot see through the body to find out what organs and tissues look like. They *can* shine X rays through the body, which does produce photographs. However, only teeth, bone, and other hard substances can be seen. Ultrasound is an ideal method for taking pictures of organs and tissues. It is reflected off these objects in much the same way it reflect off submarines, and it does not harm the organs and tissues it strikes. Today, ultrasound is widely used for many medical purposes, such as diagnosing cerebral palsy.

Posture and Mobility

Cerebral palsy affects both posture and one's ability to move about. Physical therapists work with a child to develop good posture, to move affected arms and legs, and to develop normal body movements. Special equipment, such as wheelchairs, crutches, braces, and walkers, may be needed to achieve this goal.

SPASTICITY. Spasticity is a condition in which muscles become tight and stiff. It can cause muscles to shorten, joints to tighten, and posture to change. It can also affect the ability to walk, use a wheelchair, or sit unaided. Spasticity can prevent a person from being able to feed, dress, or care for himself or herself.

Treatments for spasticity depend on its severity. Mild spasticity is treated with regular stretching exercises. Moderate spasticity may require braces or casts to keep a limb in its normal position. More serious cases of spasticity may require more aggressive treatments. For example, spasticity can be treated with muscle-relaxing drugs, such as diazepam (pronounced di-AZE-uh-pam, trade name Valium) or dantrolene (pronounced DAN-tro-leen, trade name Dantrium). Surgery can also be used. Tendons in the affected muscle are cut. The limb is then placed into a cast until the tendons grow back in a normal position.

SCOLIOSIS. Scoliosis, or curvature of the spine, can develop when back muscles become weak or spastic. When that happens, the vertebrae (bones that make up the spinal column) may be pulled out of alignment. Scoliosis causes pain, changes in posture, and possible damage to internal organs. Scoliosis is usually treated with a brace that holds the back in a normal position. Surgery can also be used to join the vertebrae in a normal position.

Ataxia and Coordination

Ataxia (pronounced uh-TAK-see-uh) is a loss of balance control. It impairs a person's ability to move normally. Physical therapy can help a child with CP regain the sense of balance.

Seizures

Seizures (see epilepsy entry) occur in 30 to 50 percent of children with cerebral palsy. The seizures may occur only in one arm or leg, or throughout the body. They can be treated with various drugs, such as carbamazepine (pronounced KAHR-buh-MAZ-uh-peen, trade name Tegretol) or ethosuximide (pronounced ETH-o-SUK-sih-mide, trade name Zarontin). Some children need antiseizure drugs for a limited time only, while others must continue to use them throughout their lives. Careful control of one's diet can also reduce the risk of having seizures.

Strabismus

Strabismus (cross-eye, pronounced struh-BIZ-muss) is treated with eye patches and corrective lenses. If these treatments do not work, injections of botulinum toxin or surgery on eye muscles may help relieve the disorder.

Nutrition

People with cerebral palsy may have trouble eating because they cannot control the tongue and mouth muscles. They may also have difficulty holding eating utensils. As a result, they may not get enough of the foods needed for normal, healthy development. In such cases, the symptoms of CP may actually become worse.

Twenty-month-old Ashley Neisis who suffers from cerebral palsy, with her service dog, BJ. The dog has warned Ashley's parents when she was having trouble breathing. (Reproduced by permission of AP/Wide World Photos)

Nutritionists can help children with CP learn what foods they should eat. Nutritional supplements, such as vitamins and minerals, may also be needed. Speech-language therapists can teach people with CP more effective ways to use their throat and mouth muscles, reducing the risk of aspiration. Aspiration is the inhaling of food and saliva into the airways, causing choking and suffocation. In severe cases, a tube can be inserted through the abdomen and into the stomach to carry food directly into the digestive system.

Other Common Medical Problems

Drooling, dental caries (cavities), and gum disease are more common in people with CP than in the general population. These problems can be prevented to some degree by drugs or with the help of a physical therapist. Constipation is another common problem. It can be relieved with changes in the diet or with enemas or suppositories when needed. Enemas and suppositories help loosen the bowels and make bowel movements easier.

Communication

Poor coordination of tongue and mouth muscles can cause speech problems in people with CP. Problems with speaking can retard a child's mental development. Picture boards can help with speech problems. They allow the CP child to point to objects rather than naming them. A number of mechanical devices are available for school-age children with communication problems. These include typing programs and computer-assisted speech devices. Speech-language therapists can offer valuable advice on the types of equipment available.

Education

Children with mild symptoms of cerebral palsy can often be placed in a regular school classroom. This practice is known as inclusion or mainstreaming. Inclusion has the advantage of making CP children feel less different from other children.

Children with more severe forms of CP may be placed in separate classrooms with teachers trained to work with special education problems. On the federal level, such schools operate under and are financed by the Individuals with Disabilities Education Act (IDEA). Most states have legislation similar to IDEA. Educational specialists can help parents understand the options and opportunities provided for their CP children by these acts.

Behavioral and Mental Health Services

Children with cerebral palsy sometimes develop behavioral or emotional problems. These problems may require special treatments, such as behavioral modification (structured programs for changing behavior) and/or individual and family counseling.

Alternative Treatment

Some alternative treatments that have been effective with some CP individuals include massage therapy, vitamin supplements, herbal medicine, and acupuncture (a Chinese therapy technique where fine needles puncture the body).

PROGNOSIS

Cerebral palsy is a nonprogressive disorder that does not become worse or better over time. However, it does pose different kinds of problems at different stages of life. Treatments that are devised for children with CP usually have to be changed and adjusted as the person grows older. Some form of professional help is usually needed at every stage of the disorder.

Cerebral palsy itself is generally not the cause of death. However, it can shorten a person's life span for other, related reasons. For example, lung infections that can lead to pneumonia (see pneumonia entry) and other diseases are more common among people with CP. Poor nutrition can also contribute to the likelihood of infection. Overall, more than 90 percent of infants with CP survive to adulthood, and the vast majority with mild symptoms live near-normal lifespans.

PREVENTION

The specific cause of cerebral palsy is usually not known, so prevention is difficult or impossible. Difficulties with the birth process itself are no longer thought to be a major risk factor for CP. Instead, problems with normal development before birth seem to be the most common cause of CP. Until these problems are better understood, prevention will be difficult.

Ironically, better health care may actually contribute to an increase in the number of cerebral palsy cases. Doctors have learned to keep premature babies alive more effectively, but these babies are at high risk for the disorder.

The best hope for reducing the risk of cerebral palsy appears to be for pregnant women to follow good health practices. These practices include a healthy diet, avoiding alcohol and tobacco, and prompt treatment for infections.

FOR MORE INFORMATION

Books

Geralis, Elaine, ed. *Children With Cerebral Palsy: A Parents' Guide,* 2nd edition. Bethesda, MD: Woodbine House, 1998.

Kramer, Laura. *Uncommon Voyage: Parenting a Special Needs Child in the World of Alternative Medicine.* Winchester, MA: Faber & Faber, 1996.

Leonard, Jane Faulkner, Margaret E. Myers, Sherri Lynn Cadenhead. *Keys to Parenting a Child With Cerebral Palsy.* Hauppauge, NY: Barron's Educational Series, 1997.

Miller, Freeman, and Steven J. Bachrach. *Cerebral Palsy: A Complete Guide for Caregiving.* Baltimore: Johns Hopkins University Press, 1995.

Periodicals

Exceptional Parent Magazine. 555 Kinderkamack Road, Oradell, NJ 07649–1517. 800–EPARENT; 201–634–6550.

Organizations

National Information Center for Children and Youth with Disabilities. PO Box 1492, Washington, DC 20013–1492. (800) 695–0285.

United Cerebral Palsy Association. 1660 L Street NW, Suite 700, Washington, DC 20036–5602. (800) 872–5827; (202) 776–0406; (202) 973–7197 (TTY). (202) 776–0414 (fax). ucpnatl@ucpa.org. http://www.ucpa.org.

CHICKENPOX

DEFINITION

Chickenpox, also called varicella (pronounced VAR-ih-SEL-uh), is a common and very infectious childhood disease, which sometimes affects adults. Chickenpox produces an itchy rash with blisters that lasts about a week. Fever and other symptoms may also be present. A single attack of chickenpox generally produces lifelong immunity (protection) against the disease, which means once you have chickenpox you usually never have it again.

Chickenpox can almost always be treated at home. The symptoms are unpleasant, but they are rarely dangerous. If complications develop, professional medical attention is essential.

DESCRIPTION

Chickenpox is caused by the varicella-zoster virus (a herpes virus; see herpes infections entry) and affects about four million Americans each year. Of this number, five thousand to nine thousand require hospitalization. About one hundred people die of the disease each year.

A person becomes infectious (able to pass on the virus) a day or two before a rash first appears. He or she remains infectious until the blisters have formed scabs. Scabs form four to seven days after the rash first appears.

During this period, a child with chickenpox is expected to stay home from school so that he or she will not pass the disease to other children.

Chickenpox has always been a common disease among children in the industrialized world. The disease can occur at any age. However, about 80 to 90 percent of all American children under the age of ten have already been infected. Because a single attack of the virus provides immunity, chickenpox occurs in only 5 percent of adults in the United States. If an adult contracts chickenpox he or she is more likely to experience complications than children; more than half of all deaths from chickenpox occur among adults.

CAUSES

Chickenpox is caused by a virus that is transmitted through the air or by direct contact with an infected person. Once the virus enters a person's body, there is an incubation period of ten to twenty-one days. During this period, the virus reproduces and grows in the body, but no symptoms appear.

SYMPTOMS

The first signs of chickenpox are usually a slight fever and a general feeling of illness. Within a few hours or days, small red spots begin to appear on the scalp, neck, or upper half of the body. About twelve to twenty-four hours later, these spots become itchy and develop into fluid-filled bumps. These bumps, called vesicles, go through a series of changes. First they turn into blisters. Then they break open, and scabs begin to form on top of them. This process goes on for a period of two to five days.

Blisters can also form on other parts of the body, including the insides of the mouth, nose, ears, vagina, and rectum. Some people develop only a few blisters. In most cases, however, the number reaches 250 to 500. Toward the end of the disease, scabs begin to fall off. Scarring normally does not occur unless the blisters are scratched and become infected.

The amount of itchiness caused by the blisters can range from barely noticeable to severe. People with chickenpox may also have headaches, stomach pain, and a fever. Full recovery usually takes five to ten days after symp-

WORDS TO KNOW

Acetaminophen: A drug for relieving pain and fever. Tylenol is the most common example.

Acyclovir: An antiviral drug used for combating chickenpox and other herpes viruses.

Reye's syndrome: A rare but often fatal disease that involves the brain, liver, and kidneys.

Shingles: A disease that causes a rash and a very painful nerve inflammation. An attack of chickenpox eventually gives rise to shingles in about 20 percent of the population.

Varicella-zoster immune globulin (VZIG): A substance that can reduce the severity of chickenpox symptoms.

Varicella-zoster virus: The virus that causes chickenpox and shingles.

Varivax: A vaccine for the prevention of chickenpox.

ABOUT 80 TO 90 PERCENT OF ALL AMERICAN CHILDREN HAVE HAD CHICKENPOX BY THE AGE OF TEN.

toms first appear. Again, the most severe cases of the disease are usually found among older children and adults.

Some groups of people are at risk for developing complications in connection with chickenpox. The most common of these complications are bacterial infections of the blisters, pneumonia (see pneumonia entry), dehydration (loss of water from the body), encephalitis (brain fever; see encephalitis entry), and hepatitis (inflammation of the liver; see hepatitis entry). The groups at risk for these complications include:

- **Infants.** Complications occur more often among children less than one year old than among older children. The risk is greatest to newborns, among whom the death rate is greater than for any other age group. Babies are especially at risk when born to women who had chickenpox while they were pregnant. In such cases, the child faces the risk of physical disorders, brain damage, or death.
- **Children with damaged immune systems.** A child's immune system can be damaged by many factors, including genetic disorders or disease. Children in this group have the second highest death rate from chickenpox.
- **Adults and children over the age of 15.** Chickenpox is generally more serious in these age groups than it is among younger children.

DIAGNOSIS

It is usually quite easy to diagnose chickenpox in children. A school nurse or a parent is often able to recognize the disease. A doctor can sometimes diagnose the disease over the telephone. The doctor should also be called if:

- The child's fever goes above 102°F (39°C) or lasts more than four days.
- The child's blisters appear to be infected. Signs of infection include leakage of pus from blisters, or excessive redness, warmth, tenderness, or swelling around the blisters.
- The child seems nervous, confused, unresponsive, or unusually sleepy. A stiff neck or severe headache, poor balance or trouble walking, sensitivity to bright lights, breathing problems or excessive coughing, and chest pain or

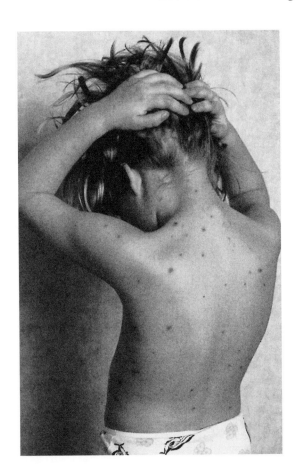

Chickenpox produces an itchy rash with blisters that lasts about a week. (© Jim Selby/Science Photo Library, National Audubon Society Collection. Reproduced by permission of Photo Researchers, Inc.)

vomiting could be signs of more serious illnesses, such as Reye's syndrome (see Reye's syndrome entry) or encephalitis.

TREATMENT

With children, treatment of chickenpox usually takes place in the home and focuses on reducing fever and discomfort. Because chickenpox is caused by a virus, antibiotics are not effective against the disease. Applying wet compresses (folded cloths) can help relieve itching. Cool or lukewarm baths once a day may also help. The addition of baking soda or oatmeal to the bath water makes the bath more soothing. Only mild soaps should be used for the bath. The child should be patted dry, not rubbed, to prevent irritating the blisters. Calamine lotion also helps to reduce itching.

The child's fingernails should be kept short during the disease. That will prevent scratching of the blisters, which can lead to infection. Older children should be warned not to scratch. For babies, light mittens or socks on the hands can help guard against scratching.

Blisters in the mouth can make eating and drinking uncomfortable. Children may find it easier to have cold drinks and soft, bland foods. Genital blisters can be treated with an anesthetic (pain-killing) cream recommended by a doctor or pharmacist. Antibiotics are used if blisters become infected.

Acetaminophen (pronounced uh-see-tuh-MIN-uh-fuhn) and other drugs can be used to treat fever and discomfort. Aspirin should be avoided when treating children. It has been shown to cause Reye's syndrome in children, a serious disease of the nervous system.

Children with weakened immune systems may be given antiviral (virus-killing) drugs, such as acyclovir (pronounced a-SI-klo-veer, trade name Zovirax). The drug has been recommended by some doctors for the relief of chickenpox symptoms in children and adults with normal immune systems, but experts still disagree about the use of acyclovir for this purpose.

Alternative Treatment

Along with cool or lukewarm baths, alternative practitioners recommend the use of various natural products, such as aloe vera, witch hazel, or a combination of rosemary and calendula, for treating itching caused by blisters. Some common homeopathic remedies include windflower, poison ivy, and sulfur.

PROGNOSIS

Most cases of chickenpox last about a week without causing lasting harm. One long-term effect of chickenpox is seen in about 20 percent of the population, however. This effect occurs most often in people over the age of fifty, and is the disease known as shingles. Shingles is caused by the same virus that causes chickenpox. After a chickenpox infection has disappeared, the virus may remain in a person's body. At some time later in life, the virus may once again become active. It produces a new form of infection—shingles.

Shingles is a very painful inflammation of the nerves caused by the chickenpox virus. It is accompanied by a rash that covers the trunk of the body (the part of the body that does not include the arms, legs, or head) and the face for ten days or more. In some cases, the pain caused by shingles can last for months and even years.

In 1998 two new drugs for the treatment of shingles were introduced. They are valacyclovir (trade name Valtrex) and famciclovir (trade name Famvir). Both prevent the virus from reproducing if taken within seventy-two hours after the rash first appears. Certain restrictions apply to the use of both drugs.

PREVENTION

A vaccine for chickenpox called Varivax was approved for use in the United States in 1995. The vaccine consists of live, but weakened, viruses and is effective in preventing chickenpox in 70 to 90 percent of all cases. In the remaining 10 to 30 percent of cases, the severity of a chickenpox infection is lessened by the vaccine. The U.S. Centers for Disease Control and Prevention recommend that all children (with a few exceptions) be given the vaccine between the ages of twelve and eighteen months. It can be combined with their measles-mumps-rubella vaccination. The vaccine is also recommended for older people who may be at risk for the disease. Health care workers and women of childbearing age are examples of such groups.

Children under the age of twelve receive one dose of the vaccine. Those over the age of twelve receive a second dose four to eight weeks after the first dose. The vaccine is useful when given soon after someone has been exposed to chickenpox. It can also prevent the disease if given during the incubation period.

The Varivax vaccine is still not widely used. Some doctors believe that a second dose later in life may be necessary to protect individuals and worry that individuals may not remember to get the second dose once they grow up. Other doctors are concerned that the live virus in the vaccine might cause shingles later in life. Because of such fears, only 20 percent of all two-year-olds had been vaccinated for chickenpox as of 1997. Health professionals are still debating the best way to use Varivax.

A substance known as varicella-zoster immune globulin (VZIG) is also available for the treatment of children with weakened immune systems and others at risk for complications from chickenpox. To be effective, the drug must be given within ninety-six hours after a person has been exposed to the virus. In such cases, it can reduce the severity of chickenpox symptoms.

FOR MORE INFORMATION

Books

The Burton Goldberg Group. *Alternative Medicine: The Definitive Guide.* Puyallup, WA: Future Medicine Publishing, 1993.

Silverstein, Alvin, Virginia Silverstein, and Laura Silverstein Nunn. *Chicken Pox and Shingles.* Hillside, NJ: Enslow Publishers, Inc., 1998.

Weitzman, Elizabeth. *Let's Talk about Having Chicken Pox.* Powerkids Press, 1997.

Periodicals

Kump, Theresa. "Childhood without Chickenpox? Why Parents Are Still Wary of This New Vaccine." *Parents Magazine* (April 1996): pp. 39–40.

Napoli, Maryann. "The Chickenpox Vaccine." *Mothering* (Summer 1996): pp. 56–61.

Organizations

Centers for Disease Control and Prevention. National Immunization Hotline. 1600 Clifton Road, NE, Atlanta, GA 30333. (800) 232–2522 (English). (800) 232–0233 (Spanish). http://www.cdc.gov.

CHRONIC FATIGUE SYNDROME

DEFINITION

Chronic fatigue syndrome (CFS) is a condition that causes extreme tiredness. People with CFS are so tired that they are unable to carry on normal activities for a period of at least six months. They also have other symptoms, such as pain in the joints and muscles, headaches, and sore throat. There is no single known cause for CFS; it appears to result from a number of factors.

DESCRIPTION

Chronic fatigue syndrome is known by many different names. These names include chronic fatigue and immune disorder (CFIDS), myalgic encephalomyelitis (pronounced my-AL-jik en-SEF-uh-lo-MY-uh-LY-tiss), low natural killer cell disease, post-viral syndrome, Epstein-Barr disease, and Yuppie flu. Such names suggest a number of possible causes for CFS. Researchers have not been able to find out which of these causes, or which combination of factors, is responsible for the disease.

Reports of a CFS-like disease date back to 1869. People with the disease were said to have neurasthenia ("nerve weakness," pronounced noor-ess-THEE-nee-uh) or fibromyalgia ("muscle pain," pronounced FI-bro-my-AL-ja). These disorders are now thought to be related to chronic fatigue syndrome.

Another clue to the cause of CFS appeared in the mid-1980s when doctors found antibodies to the Epstein-Barr virus (EBV) in the blood of many people with CFS. Antibodies are produced by the body when it needs to fight off an infection. Some doctors believed that these antibodies meant that chronic fatigue syndrome was caused by the Epstein-Barr virus. It was soon discovered, however, that many people who did not have CFS also had EBV antibodies in their blood. Some scientists now think that EBV may contribute to CFS, but it is not the only factor.

The term Yuppie flu became popular because so many young, middle-class people developed the disease. More detailed studies showed that people of every age, gender, race, and income group can get CFS. The group most at risk for the disease, however, is women aged 25 to 45 years.

Estimating the number of people with CFS is difficult because its symptoms are so similar to those of other diseases. The U.S. Centers for Disease Control and Prevention (CDC) now believe that 4 to 10 out of every 100,000 Americans have CFS. The CFIDS Foundation estimates that about 500,000 adults (0.3 percent of the population) have CFS. These estimates do not include children.

WORDS TO KNOW

Depression: A psychological condition with feelings of sadness, sleep disturbance, fatigue, and inability to concentrate.

Epstein-Barr virus (EBV): A virus that causes mononucleosis and other diseases.

Fibromyalgia: Pain, tenderness, and stiffness in muscles.

Lymph nodes: Small organs of the immune system in the neck, armpits, groin, and other parts of the body.

Myalgia: Muscle pain.

Myalgic encephalomyelitis: An inflammation of the brain and spinal cord.

Natural killer cells: Cells in the immune system that help fight off infections.

Neurasthenia: Nervous exhaustion.

CAUSES

There is no single known cause for chronic fatigue syndrome. Some factors that are thought to be responsible for the disease are:

• Viral infections
• Chemical toxins (poisons)
• Allergies
• Abnormalities in the immune system
• Psychological disorders

Many doctors now believe that CFS is not one illness, but a combination of symptoms caused by several factors. According to one theory, the first step in chronic fatigue syndrome is infection by a virus. About 90 percent of all people have a virus in the herpes family in their bodies. Herpes viruses (see herpes infections entry) cause a number of problems, including cold sores and a painful inflammation of the nerves called shingles (see chickenpox entry).

These viruses are usually dormant (not active) in the body. The viruses can become active again, however, if the body is disturbed in some way. Certain chemicals in the air, for example, can cause the viruses to become active and begin to grow. When that happens, the body's immune system starts to fight off the viral infection. It produces chemicals designed to kill the virus. But these chemicals can cause other effects, too. Those effects are similar to ones observed in people with CFS.

MANY DOCTORS NOW BELIEVE THAT CFS IS NOT ONE ILLNESS, BUT A COMBINATION OF SYMPTOMS CAUSED BY SEVERAL FACTORS.

The role of psychological factors in CFS is very controversial. Some think that people who are depressed are more likely to develop CFS. A person's mental state, they believe, may influence the way his or her body works. For example, depression (see depressive disorders entry) might cause dormant viruses to become active again. Other experts disagree with this analysis. They say a person's mental state is more likely to be caused by the disease, rather than being a cause of the disease.

SYMPTOMS

Some people think that chronic fatigue syndrome means only that a person is very tired, but the disease involves much more than that. A person may become so tired that he or she cannot go to work, attend school, or take part in social activities. CFS can also cause problems with sleeping. A person may wake up being just as tired as before he or she went to sleep.

Some CFS patients try to keep up with their normal daily activities, but they may experience "payback." Payback is a state of being even more exhausted than usual. The person may have to stay in bed for days to recover.

Other symptoms of CFS include:

- Muscle pain (myalgia)
- Joint pain (arthralgia)
- Sore throat
- Headache
- Fever and chills
- Tender lymph nodes
- Problems with concentrating
- Memory loss
- Hypotension (low blood pressure)

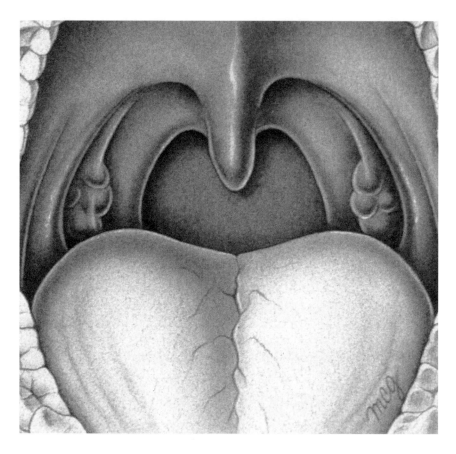

One of the symptoms of CFS is discoloration of the pharyngeal pillar at the sides of the back of the mouth. (© 1994 Margie Caldwell-Gill. Reproduced by permission of Custom Medical Stock Photo.)

DIAGNOSIS

One step in diagnosing CFS is taking a medical history. Doctors ask patients about their symptoms, about other illnesses they have had, and about medications they are taking. They also conduct a physical examination and may order laboratory tests. They try to eliminate causes of the person's symptoms other than CFS. In the United States, many doctors use a standard created by the CDC for defining CFS. According to this standard, patients have chronic fatigue syndrome if they meet both of the following criteria:

- Chronic (continuous and ongoing) fatigue for at least six months. The condition is not caused by activity and is not relieved by rest. It greatly interferes with the person's job, school, social, or personal activities.
- Four or more of the following symptoms: loss of short-term memory or the ability to concentrate; sore throat; tender lymph nodes; muscle pain; pain

in more than one joint without swelling or redness; headaches not previously experienced by the patient; failure of sleep to help the patient feel better; and a feeling of discomfort or tiredness that lasts more than twenty-four hours following exercise. In addition, these symptoms must occur more than once over a six-month period.

TREATMENT

There is no cure for chronic fatigue syndrome, but most symptoms can be treated successfully. The first treatment most doctors recommend is a combination of rest, exercise, and proper diet. The patient is advised to attempt only the most important activities, to avoid over-exerting himself or herself, and to rest whenever necessary. A moderate amount of exercise is important, but too much exercise can make the disease worse. Counseling and stress reduction (learning how to better handle the pressures of everyday life) can also be helpful.

Many medications, nutritional supplements (like vitamins and minerals), and herbal preparations have been used to treat CFS. Doctors and patients should work together to arrange the best plan for each individual.

Drugs

Nonsteroidal anti-inflammatory drugs (NSAIDs), such as ibuprofen (pronounced i-byoo-PRO-fuhn) and naproxen, can be used to relieve pain and reduce fever. Antidepressants can be used to help patients relax and feel less depressed. Antianxiety drugs, such as benzodiazepines (pronounced ben-zo-die-A-zuh-peenz), are prescribed for people with anxiety that has lasted for at least six months.

A number of other drugs are being tested for use with CFS patients. These include fludrocortisone (pronounced FLOO-dro-KOR-tih-zone, trade name Florinef) and beta-adrenergic drugs, such as atenolol (pronounced uh-TEN-uh-lol) and propranolol (pronounced pro-PRAN-uh-lol), to control blood pressure, and gamma globulin (pronounced GA-muh GLAH-byu-lun) and ampligen (pronounced AM-plih-jen), to help fight off infections.

Alternative Treatment

Nutritional supplements such as vitamins A, B_{12}, C, and E, as well as some minerals, are used to treat CFS. These supplements are thought to improve the immune system and improve mental functions. Some CFS patients report improvement after using certain herbal medicines, such as echinacea (pronounced ek-i-NAY-see-uh), garlic, ginseng, ginkgo, evening primrose oil, shiitake mushroom extract, and borage seed oil.

Other therapies that have been tried in the treatment of CFS include meditation, acupuncture (a Chinese therapy treatment involving the puncturing of small needles into the body), and yoga. These therapies sometimes help people to relax and get more rest. They may also help reduce depression and anxiety.

PROGNOSIS

The course of CFS varies widely for different people. Some patients get progressively worse over time. Others improve slowly. Some individuals have periods of illness that alternate with periods of good health. Many people never fully recover from CFS. Most patients, however, find some relief by following a treatment plan that includes adequate rest, nutrition, exercise, and other therapies.

PREVENTION

There are currently no recommended ways of preventing CFS.

FOR MORE INFORMATION

Books

Hoffman, Ronald L. *Tired All the Time.* New York: Poseidon Press, 1993.

Johnson, Hillary. *Osler's Web: Inside the Labyrinth of the Chronic Fatigue Syndrome Epidemic.* New York: Crown Publishers, 1996.

Periodicals

Weiss, Rick. "A Cure for Chronic Fatigue Syndrome?" *The Nurse Practitioner* (July 1997): pp. 30–40.

Organizations

American Association for Chronic Fatigue Syndrome. 7 Van Buren Street, Albany, NY 12206. (518) 435–1765.

The CFIDS Association. Community Health Services. PO Box 220398, Charlotte, NC 28222–0398. (704) 362–2343.

The National CFS Association. 919 Scott Avenue, Kansas City, KS 66105. (913) 321–2278.

The National CFIDS Foundation. 103 Aletha Road, Needham, MA 02192. (781) 449–3535. http://www.cfidsfoundation.org.

Web sites

Centers for Disease Control and Prevention. "The Facts about Chronic Fatigue Syndrome." [Online] http://www.cdc.gov/ncidod/diseases. (accessed on October 15, 1999).

National Institutes of Health, Public Service Resources. "Chronic Fatigue Syndrome." [Online] http://www.niaid.nih.gov/publications. (accessed on October 15, 1999).

COLOR BLINDNESS

DEFINITION

Color blindness is a condition in which people have mild to severe difficulty identifying colors. Color blind people may not be able to recognize various shades of colors and, in some cases, cannot recognize colors at all.

DESCRIPTION

Normal color vision requires the use of special cells in the retina (the innermost lining) of the eye called cones. There are three types of cones—blue, green, and red—which allow an individual to recognize a large spectrum of colors. Cones sometimes do not function normally. When that happens, a person has trouble recognizing colors.

The three basic types of color blindness are as follows:

- **Red/green color blindness.** Red/green color blindness is the most common form of the disorder. It affects about 8 percent of all Caucasian (white) males and 0.5 percent of all Caucasian females. People with this disorder can distinguish red from green if the two colors are next to each other, but they cannot identify red or green by itself. For example, they can pick out red or green from a package of colored pencils, but if handed a red pencil, they could not identify that the pencil was red.
- **Blue color blindness.** Blue color blindness is rare. People with this disorder cannot distinguish blue or yellow. Both colors are seen as white or gray. The disorder occurs with equal frequency in men and women and usually accompanies certain other physical disorders, such as liver disease or diabetes (see diabetes mellitus entry).
- **Total color blindness.** Total color blindness is called achromatopsia (pronounced a-KRO-muh-tope-see-uh). This disorder is the rarest of all forms of color blindness. People with this disorder see everything as white, black, or some shade of gray. The disorder affects about 1 person in 33,000 in the United States. It is

WORDS TO KNOW

Cone cells: Cone cells are special cells in the retina and are responsible for color vision.

Retina: The retina is the innermost lining of the eye, containing light sensitive nerve tissue composed of rod and cone cells.

caused by hereditary factors. Achromatopsia is usually accompanied by other vision problems, such as extreme sensitivity to light.

CAUSES

Most cases of color blindness are inherited, with males being affected far more often than females. Color blindness can also be acquired in other ways. These include:

- Chronic (long-term) illnesses, such as Alzheimer's disease (see Alzheimer's disease entry), diabetes, glaucoma (see glaucoma entry), leukemia (see leukemia entry), liver disease, chronic alcoholism (see alcoholism entry),

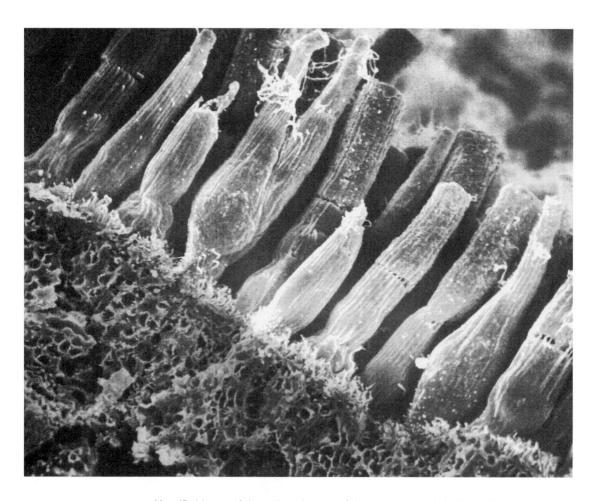

Magnified image of the rods and cones of the human eye. (© Omikron. Reproduced by permission of Photo Researchers, Inc.)

multiple sclerosis (see multiple sclerosis entry), and retinitis pigmentosa, a disease of the retina.

- Traumas, such as those caused by accidents or strokes (see stroke entry).
- Medications, such as antibiotics and drugs used to treat tuberculosis (see tuberculosis entry), high blood pressure, and nervous disorders.
- Industrial toxins (poisons), including carbon monoxide, carbon disulfide, fertilizers, and chemicals that include lead.
- Aging, people are at higher risk after the age of sixty.

SYMPTOMS

The symptom of color blindness is the long-term inability to distinguish colors or to see colors at all.

DIAGNOSIS

A variety of tests can be used to diagnose color blindness. The most common of these tests is the American Optical/Hardy, Rand, and Ritter (AO/H.R.R.) Pseudoisochromatic (pronounced SOO-doe-I-so-kro-MAT-ik) Test. This test includes the use of a plate covered with spots of one color (green or red, for example). In the middle of the plate is a figure, such as a number or letter, made of spots of a different color. A person with normal color vision can see the figure against the background. A color blind person cannot.

A similar test, the Ishihara test, uses eight test plates similar to those used in the AO/H.R.R. test. The person looks for numbers made up of dots of various colors on each plate.

A third test is the Titmus II Vision Tester Color Perception Test. In this test, a person looks into a viewing device at a series of figures on a black background framed by a yellow border. The test can easily be performed in a doctor's office. It is not considered to be a very accurate test, however, and can only test for red/green color blindness.

TREATMENT

There is no cure or treatment for color blindness. Most people with the disorder learn to live with the problem and learn how to adjust to it.

JOHN DALTON AND DALTONISM

The first person to describe color blindness was the English chemist and physicist John Dalton (1766–1844). Dalton is famous because he was the first modern scientist to develop the atomic theory. However, Dalton was interested in many topics besides atoms. For example, he was keenly interested in meteorology (the study of the weather) and kept daily weather records for fifty-seven years. His records, published as *Meteorological Observations and Essays,* are among the most complete in all of scientific history. The first scientific paper Dalton ever wrote was about color blindness. He probably became interested in the subject because he, as well as his brother, was color blind. In honor of his research, the condition of color blindness is still sometimes called *daltonism.*

PROGNOSIS

Hereditary forms of color blindness do not change during a person's lifetime. In cases where color blindness was not inherited, the disorder may gradually become more or less severe over time.

PREVENTION

Hereditary color blindness cannot be prevented. Acquired color blindness can be prevented if all possible causes of the disorder can be avoided.

FOR MORE INFORMATION

Books

D'Alonzo, T. L. *Your Eyes! A Comprehensive Look at the Understanding and Treatment of Vision Problems.* Clifton Heights, PA: Avanti, 1992.

Rosenthal, Odeda, and Robert H. Phillips. *Coping with Color-Blindness.* Garden City Park, NY: Avery Publishing Group, 1997.

Organizations

Achromatopsia Network. c/o Frances Futterman, PO Box 214, Berkeley, CA 94701–0214. http://www.achromat.org.

Prevent Blindness America. 500 East Remington Road, Schaumburg, IL 60173. (847) 843–2020; (800) 331–2020. http://www.preventblindness.org.

COLORECTAL CANCER

DEFINITION

Colorectal (pronounced KO-lo-REK-tul) cancer is cancer of the colon or rectum. The colon is the lowest portion of the large intestine and is the last part of the digestive system through which food passes. The rectum is the final section of the colon, through which solid wastes are eliminated from the body.

DESCRIPTION

Colorectal cancer is one of the most common forms of cancer. It ranks third in frequency behind lung and prostate cancer (see lung cancer and prostate cancer entries) in men in the United States. It is also third in frequency behind lung and breast cancer (see breast cancer entry) in women.

Colorectal cancer accounts for about 10 percent of all new cases of cancer each year in the United States. It is also responsible for about 10 percent of all deaths from cancer.

Cancer can occur anywhere in the colon or the rectum. It usually begins as a benign (noncancerous; pronounced bih-NINE) growth on the lining of the colon or rectum. These benign growths are known as polyps (pronounced PAH-leps). Over time, some polyps may begin to grow at a very rapid rate. When that happens, they become malignant (pronounced muh-LIG-nent). Malignant means capable of causing disease and/or death.

CAUSES

Researchers do not know the cause of colorectal cancer. But they do know that certain risk factors make it more likely that a person will develop the condition. These risk factors include:

- **Family history.** About 10 percent of all cases of colorectal cancer are thought to be hereditary. People whose family members have had the disorder are more likely to contract it themselves.
- **History of colorectal cancer.** Some people contract colorectal cancer more than once. New cancers develop in areas other than those in which the cancer first appeared.
- **Recurrent intestinal polyps.** Most polyps are benign. However, some people tend to get polyps frequently on the lining of their intestines. People with this tendency are at higher risk for colorectal cancer.

WORDS TO KNOW

Barium enema: An X ray is taken of the bowel after the patient has been given an enema containing a white chalky liquid (barium) that outlines the structure of the colon and rectum.

Benign: Not cancerous.

Chemotherapy: Treatment with drugs that destroy cancer cells.

Colonoscopy: A medical procedure in which a doctor looks at the colon through a flexible lighted instrument called a colonoscope.

Colostomy: An opening created surgically that runs from the colon to the outside of the body to provide an alternative route for the evacuation of body wastes.

Digital rectal examination: A medical procedure in which a doctor inserts a lubricated gloved finger into the rectum to look for abnormal structures.

Enema: The injection of liquid into the intestine through the anus.

Fecal occult blood test: A laboratory test designed to find blood in feces.

Polyps: Small, abnormal masses of tissue that can form on the lining of an organ.

Radiation therapy: Treatment that uses high-energy radiation, like X rays, to treat cancer.

Sigmoidoscopy: A medical procedure in which a doctor looks at the rectum and lower colon through a flexible lighted instrument called a sigmoidoscope.

- **Inflammatory bowel disease.** Inflammatory bowel disease refers to a number of different conditions in which the colon becomes irritated and inflamed. Ulcers (open sores; see ulcers entry) often develop on the lining of the bowel. This pattern can increase the risk of colorectal cancer.
- **Age.** The risk of having colorectal cancer increases with age. About 90 percent of all cases are diagnosed in people over the age of fifty.
- **Diet.** Eating foods that are high in fat and/or low in fiber may increase the risk of colorectal cancer.
- **Physical inactivity.** People who tend to be less active are at greater risk for colorectal cancer.

SYMPTOMS

The earliest sign of colorectal cancer may be bleeding. A person may notice that blood is produced during bowel movements. Blood can also be found in the feces. As the disorder develops, a person's pattern of bowel movements may change. The stools may change in size and become more narrow.

SYMPTOMS OF COLORECTAL CANCER INCLUDE GENERAL STOMACH DISCOMFORT, STOMACH CRAMPS, GAS PAINS, AND DIARRHEA OR CONSTIPATION.

Other symptoms of colorectal cancer include general stomach discomfort, stomach cramps, gas pains, and diarrhea or constipation. The patient may feel that the bowel does not empty completely during a movement. Constant tiredness and weight loss for no known reason may also be a symptom.

DIAGNOSIS

Colorectal cancer can be diagnosed by means of a physical examination and a fecal occult blood test. A fecal occult blood test is a test for the presence of blood in stools. The test can be performed very easily by patients themselves. A small sample of stool is placed on a test strip. The test strip is then sent to a laboratory for analysis. The presence of blood in the stool is an indication that colorectal cancer may be present.

Colorectal cancer can also be detected by physical tests. In the simplest test, a doctor inserts a gloved finger up the rectum. The doctor may be able to feel the presence of any abnormal structures in the rectum.

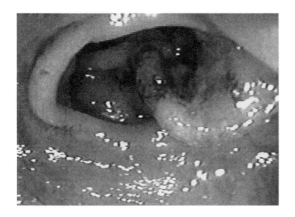
Endoscopic view of colorectal cancer. Tumors can be seen through the opening. (Photograph by S. Benjamin. Reproduced by permission of Custom Medical Stock Photo.)

A more advanced test is sigmoidoscopy (pronounced SIG-moi-DOSS-kuh-pee). A sigmoidoscope (pronounced sig-MOI-doe-skope) is a thin, hollow tube that contains a light on one end. The tube is inserted up the patient's rectum into the lower part of the colon. The doctor is able to examine closely the inner walls of the colon and rectum. The presence of any abnormal structures will be apparent.

An even more advanced test is a colonoscopy (pronounced KO-lon-OSS-kuh-pee). A colonoscope (pronounced ko-LON-o-skope) is similar to a sigmoidoscope, but it contains a longer tube and can be inserted farther into the patient's colon. The colonoscope is connected with a video camera and display that allows the doctor to view the inner walls of the colon.

Another test for colorectal cancer is a barium enema. A barium enema consists of a white chalky liquid inserted into the patient's rectum. The liquid flows upward into the colon and coats the walls of the colon and rectum with a white lining that is opaque (dark) to X rays. An X-ray photograph of the colon and rectum is then taken. The photograph shows the detailed structure of the colon and rectum.

TREATMENT

The preferred method for treating colorectal cancer is surgery. Two forms of surgery are used. In one, a tube similar to a sigmoidoscope is inserted into the rectum. The tube has a light and a small knife. The cancerous region in the colon or rectum can be cut out and removed. This procedure can be used when cancer is still at an early stage.

At more advanced stages, a second surgical method may be used. In this method, an incision (a cut) is made into the wall of the abdomen. The colon is opened up and the cancerous tissue removed. Some healthy tissue surrounding the cancer may also be taken out. In this way, the doctor can be more certain that all of the malignant tissue has been removed. If there is any reason to suspect that the cancer has spread, the lymph nodes near the cancer may also be removed. The colon is then closed.

In some cases, the colon cannot be restored to its original condition. Surgery may be so extensive that the normal passageway by which wastes are eliminated from the body is closed off. In that case, the doctor may find it necessary to create a colostomy (pronounced kuh-LAHS-tuh-mee). A colostomy is an opening from the colon to the outside of the body through the wall in the abdomen. A plastic bag is attached to the opening to collect body wastes that would normally be excreted through the rectum. In some cases, patients have a colostomy for a limited period of time until their own colon heals. In other cases, they may have a colostomy for the rest of their lives.

Radiation and chemotherapy may also be used to treat colorectal cancer. These techniques are used when it is difficult to reach cancerous tissue or to make sure that all cancerous tissue has been removed. One way to provide radiation treatment is with an X-ray-like machine that gives off high-energy radiation. The radiation passes through the body and kills cancer cells. Another way to provide radiation is with pellets implanted into the colon or rectum. These pellets contain radioactive materials that give off radiation similar to X rays.

Chemotherapy consists of certain drugs that are able to kill cancer cells. The drugs may be given orally (by mouth) or by injection.

PROGNOSIS

The key to a promising prognosis for colorectal cancer is early detection. More than 90 percent of patients treated at an early stage of the disease live at least five more years. The problem is that only one-third of colorectal cancer cases are found at an early stage. The longer it takes for cancer to be diagnosed, the more the survival rate drops. Once cancer has begun to spread, the five-year survival rate drops to 64 percent. If it has metastasized (spread, pronounced muh-TASS-tuh-sized) to more distant body parts, the survival rate is only about 7 percent.

PREVENTION

Since the exact cause of colorectal cancer is not known, there is no certain way to avoid the disorder. The main priority, then, is to reduce one's risk factors and to follow a program of regular testing. Experts suggest that both men and women over the age of fifty should have annual tests for colorectal cancer. These tests should include a fecal occult blood test and an annual digital (finger) rectal examination. Sigmoidoscopy should be done every five years and a colonoscopy every five to ten years.

Two important keys in reducing risk factors include proper diet and exercise. Experts recommend a diet high in fruits and vegetables, breads, cereals, rice, pasta, beans, and other grain products. Avoiding high-fat and low-fiber foods is also recommended. A regular program of thirty minutes of physical exercise daily is also suggested.

FOR MORE INFORMATION

Books

Dollinger, Malin. *Everyone's Guide to Cancer Therapy*. Toronto: Somerville House Books, Ltd., 1994.

Morra, Marion E. *Choices*. New York: Avon Books, 1994.

Murphy, Gerald P. *Informed Decisions: The Complete Book of Cancer Diagnosis, Treatment, and Recovery*. Atlanta, GA: American Cancer Society, 1997.

Organizations

American Cancer Society. 1599 Clifton Road NE, Atlanta, GA 30329. (800) 227–2345. http://www.cancer.org.

Cancer Research Institute. 681 Fifth Avenue, New York, NY 10022. (800) 992–2623. http://www.cancerresearch.org.

National Cancer Institute. 31 Center Drive, Bethesda, MD 20892–2580. (800) 4–CANCER. http://www.nci.nih.gov.

United Ostomy Association, Inc. 19772 MacArthur Boulevard, Suite 200, Irvine, CA 92612–2405. (800) 826–0826. http://www.uoa.org.

Web sites

University of Pennsylvania Cancer Center. *Oncolink*.[Online] http://cancer.med.upenn.edu. (accessed on October 13, 1999).

COMMON COLD

DEFINITION

The common cold is a viral infection of the upper respiratory system. The upper respiratory system includes the nose, throat, sinuses, eustachian (pronounced yoo-STA-shuhn) tubes, trachea (pronounced TRAY-kee-uh), larynx, and bronchial tubes. More than two hundred different viruses can cause a cold. A group of viruses known as the rhinoviruses, however, causes about 30 to 50 percent of all colds. Almost all colds clear up in less than two weeks without complications.

DESCRIPTION

Colds are sometimes called rhinovirus or coronavirus (pronounced kuh-RO-nuh-vie-russ) infections. They are the most common infections to affect any part of the body. Experts estimate that the average person has more than fifty colds during a lifetime. Anyone can catch a cold. The disease is most common, however, among chil-

WORDS TO KNOW

Bronchial tubes: The major airways that lead to the lungs.

Coronavirus: A type of virus that can cause the common cold.

Eustachian tube: A thin tube between the middle ear and the pharynx at the back of the mouth.

Rhinovirus: A type of virus that can cause the common cold.

dren. Repeated exposure to the viruses that cause colds helps to prevent against future occurrences of the disease.

An individual who has a cold usually recovers without special treatment. Still, colds are the leading cause of visits to doctors and of time lost from work and school. Americans spend millions of dollars each year for over-the-counter medications designed to treat cold symptoms.

Cold season in the United States begins in early fall and extends through early spring. Some people think, incorrectly, that becoming cold or wet can cause a cold. Only exposure to a cold virus can bring on the disease. Some factors can, however, increase the likelihood of catching a cold. These include:

- Fatigue and overwork
- Emotional stress
- Poor nutrition
- Smoking
- Living or working in crowded conditions

Colds make the upper respiratory system less resistant to bacterial infections. Some of these infections include middle ear infection, bronchitis (see bronchitis entry), pneumonia (see pneumonia entry), sinus infection, and strep throat (see strep throat entry).

CAUSES

Colds are caused by more than two hundred different viruses. The most common groups of viruses are rhinoviruses and coronaviruses. Knowing which virus has caused a cold is not important because treatment does not depend on the type of virus.

People with colds are contagious (can pass on the virus) during the first two to four days of infection. The virus can be **COLDS ARE CAUSED BY MORE THAN** passed in various ways. When an infected per-**TWO HUNDRED DIFFERENT VIRUSES.** son coughs, sneezes, or speaks, for example, fluid droplets containing the virus are discharged. People nearby may breathe in the droplets and may then become infected.

Cold viruses can be passed from person to person through direct contact, such as shaking hands. The viruses can also be spread through non-living objects, such as doorknobs, telephones, and toys. This method of transmission is common in day-care centers. A child with a cold may transfer the cold virus to a toy with which he or she is playing. When another child picks up the same toy, he or she may also pick up the cold virus.

Once acquired, the cold virus attaches itself to the lining of the nasal (nose) passages and sinuses. Infected cells begin to give off a chemical called histamine (pronounced HISS-tuh-meen). Histamine causes swelling, congestion (stuffiness), and increased production of mucus. One to three days after infection, a person begins to feel cold symptoms caused by these changes.

The first of these symptoms include a tickle in the throat, runny nose, and sneezing. Initially, discharge from the nose is clear and thin. Later it changes to a thick, yellow or greenish discharge. Young children often develop a fever of up to 102°F (39°C). Adults are less likely to have a fever with a cold.

Other signs of a cold are coughing, sneezing, nasal congestion, headache, muscle ache, chills, sore throat, hoarseness, watery eyes, tiredness, and lack of appetite. The cough that accompanies a cold is usually intermittent (it comes and goes) and dry.

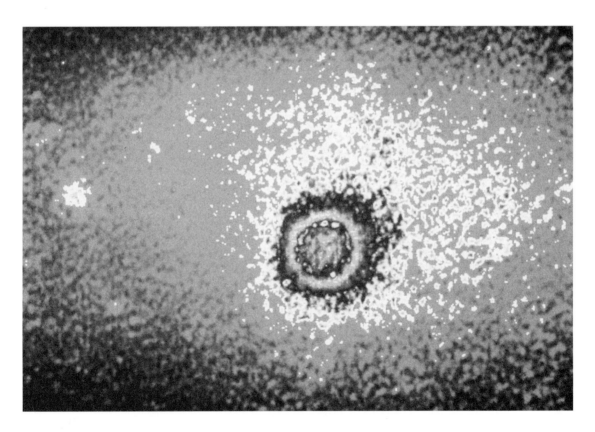

The rhinovirus (magnified 100,000 times) causes between 30 and 50 percent of all colds. (© 1991 CHSP. Reproduced by permission of Custom Medical Stock Photo.)

A runny nose is one of the earliest warning signs of a cold. (Reproduced by permission of Custom Medical Stock Photo)

Most people begin to feel better four or five days after cold symptoms first appear. All symptoms are usually gone within ten days. Sometimes a dry cough can linger for up to three weeks.

Colds make people more open to bacterial infections, such as strep throat, middle ear infection, and sinus infections. Some warning signs of a bacterial infection include chest pain, fever for more than a few days, difficulty breathing, bluish lips or fingernails, skin rash, and swollen glands. A person with these symptoms should see a doctor for possible treatment.

For some people, colds can cause more serious health problems. Anyone with complications of the respiratory (breathing) system, such as emphysema (pronounced em-fi-SEE-muh; see emphysema entry), chronic lung disease, diabetes (see diabetes entry), or with a weakened immune system (as caused by AIDS) should see a doctor if they catch a cold.

DIAGNOSIS

Colds are diagnosed by observing a person's symptoms. There are no laboratory tests to detect the cold virus. However, doctors sometimes do a throat culture or blood test to make sure the patient's symptoms are not caused by some other disease.

Influenza (or the flu; see influenza entry) is sometimes confused with the common cold. But the flu is accompanied by more severe symptoms, including a fever. Allergies (see allergies entry) often cause cold-like symptoms also. But allergy symptoms last much longer than cold symptoms. Exposure to cold air can also sometimes cause cold-like symptoms. However, these symptoms do not indicate the presence of a viral infection.

TREATMENT

There are no medicines that will cure the common cold. Given time, the body's immune system will make antibodies to fight the infection and the cold will get better on its own. Antibiotics have no effect on colds because they do not kill viruses.

A very large number of medications are available for the treatment of cold symptoms. These include antihistamines, decongestants, and pain relievers. Antihistamines block the action of histamine. They relieve sneezing, runny nose, itchy eyes, and congestion. Side effects include a dry mouth and drowsiness. For this reason, antihistamines should not be taken by people who must drive or operate heavy machinery. Some common trade name antihistamines include Chlor-Trimeton, Dimetapp, Tavist, and Actifed. The generic (family) name for these drugs are chlorpheniramine (pronounced KLOR-fen-er-uh-meen) and diphenhydramine (pronounced DIE-fen-HI-druh-meen).

Decongestants reduce blood flow and shrink tissues in the nose and make it easier to breathe. A side effect is nervousness and an inability to sleep. People with heart disease, high blood pressure, or glaucoma (an eye disorder; see glaucoma entry) should not use decongestants. Some common trade name decongestants are Neo-Synepherine, Novafed, and Sudafed. The generic names of common decongestants include phenylephrine (pronounced fen-uhl-EF-reen), phenylpropanolamine (pronounced FEN-uhl-PRO-puh-NOL-uh-meen), pseudoephedrine (pronounced soo-doe-i-FED-run), and, in nasal sprays, naphazoline (pronounced nuh-FAZ-uh-leen), oxymetazoline (pronounced OX-si-muh-TAZ-uh-LEEN), and xylometazoline (pronounced ZIE-luh-met-uh-ZOE-leen).

Many over-the-counter medications are combinations of two or more drugs. They may contain an antihistamine, decongestant, pain reliever, and/or cough suppressant. Some common pain relievers include acetaminophen (pronounced uh-see-tuh-MIN-uh-fuhn, trade names Datril, Tylenol, Panadol) and ibuprofen (pronounced i-byoo-PRO-fuhn, trade names Advil, Nurpin, Motrin, Medipren). The most common cough suppressant is dextromethorphan (pronounced dek-struh-mi-THOR-fan). Medications that include combinations of drugs are Tylenol Cold and Flu, Triaminic, Sudafed Plus, and Tavist D. Aspirin should not be given to children with a cold. It may cause a serious condition known as Reye's syndrome (see Reye's syndrome entry).

Nasal sprays and nose drops can also help to reduce nasal congestion. These products are used to apply a decongestant directly to the nose. It can take effect and act more strongly, therefore, than decongestants in pills or liquids. One problem with nasal sprays and nose drops is that people may become dependent on them. Once an individual stops using the products, he or she may experience withdrawal symptoms. For that reason, nasal sprays and nose drops should not be used for more than a few days.

People react differently to various cold medications, therefore each person needs to find the medication that works best for himself or herself. The effectiveness of medications can also change over time. It should be especially noted that children sometimes react differently from adults to medications. Over-the-counter cold remedies should not be given to infants without first consulting a doctor.

Care should always be taken not to exceed the recommended dosage for any cold medication. People need to remember that cold remedies do not cure a cold or shorten its duration. They can only relieve symptoms. Pharmacists can often advise a cold-sufferer about the best medications to try.

Cold symptoms can also be relieved by some simple self-care steps. These include:

• Drinking plenty of fluids, but avoiding acidic juices (such as grapefruit juice) that may irritate the throat
• Gargling with warm salt water for a sore throat
• Not smoking
• Getting plenty of rest
• Using a cool-mist room humidifier to ease congestion and sore throat

- Rubbing a lubricant such as Vaseline under the nose to prevent irritation from frequent nose-blowing
- Removing mucus from the nose of infants who are too young to blow their noses. Infant nasal aspirators are available for this purpose

Alternative Treatment

The goal of many alternative treatments for colds is to strengthen a person's immune system. Alternative practitioners point out that everyone is exposed to cold viruses, but only some people get sick. Those people, they argue, are more likely to have weak immune systems. Practitioners recommend strengthening the immune system by eating a healthy diet low in sugars and high in fresh fruits and vegetables, practicing meditation to reduce stress, and getting regular, moderate exercise.

Some practitioners do not believe in treating the symptoms of a cold. They say the infection should be allowed to run its course naturally. Others suggest a variety of treatments, such as:

- Inhaling a steaming mixture of lemon oil, thyme oil, eucalyptus (pronounced yoo-kuh-LIP-tus), and tea tree oil
- Gargling with a mixture of water, salt and turmeric powder or other astringent (drying-out agent), such as alum, sumac, sage, and bayberry to ease a sore throat
- Taking one of a variety of herbs, such as echinacea. (ek-i-NAY-see-uh), goldenseal, yarrow, eyebright, garlic, or onion to relieve symptoms
- Taking one of a variety of Chinese herbal medicines, such as loquat syrup (for coughs and sinus congestion), or Chinese ephedra (for runny nose)
- Using zinc throat drops along with high doses of vitamin C

PROGNOSIS

Given time, the body's natural immune system will cure a cold. Most colds last a week to ten days. People usually start feeling better within four or five days. Colds sometimes lead to bacterial infections, including strep throat, bronchitis, pneumonia, sinus infection, or a middle ear infection. These conditions can be treated with antibiotics.

PREVENTION

Colds cannot be prevented because the viruses that cause them are very common and highly infectious. However, their spread can be reduced by some simple steps:

- Washing hands well and frequently, especially after touching the nose or before handling food.

- Covering the mouth and nose when sneezing.
- Disposing of used tissues properly.
- Avoiding close contact with anyone who has a cold during the first two to four days after infection.
- Not sharing food, eating utensils, or cups with anyone.
- Avoiding crowded places where cold germs can spread.
- Eating a healthy diet and getting adequate sleep.

FOR MORE INFORMATION

Books

Brody, Jane E. *Jane Brody's Cold and Flu Fighter.* New York: W. W. Norton & Company, 1995.

Burton Goldberg Group. "Colds and Flu," in *Alternative Medicine: The Definitive Guide,* edited by James Strohecker. Puyallup, WA: Future Medicine Publishing, 1994.

Inlander, Charles B., and Cynthia K. Moran. *77 Ways to Beat Colds and Flu.* New York: Walker and Company, 1994.

Silverstein, Alvin, Virginia B. Silverstein, and Laura Silverstein Nunn. *Common Colds.* New York: Franklin Watts, Inc., 1999.

Silverstein, Alvin, et al. *Common Cold and Flu.* Springfield, NJ: Enslow Publishers, 1996.

CONCUSSION

DEFINITION

Concussion is a change in mental status caused by trauma (shock). It is accompanied by confusion, loss of memory, and, sometimes, loss of consciousness.

DESCRIPTION

A concussion occurs when the head hits or is hit by an object. A concussion can also occur when the brain is pushed against the skull with a strong force. In such cases, parts of the brain that control mental function may be damaged. The injured person may become disoriented (confused) and may briefly lose consciousness.

The U.S. Centers for Disease Control and Prevention (CDC) estimates that about three hundred thousand people experience mild to moderate concussions each year as a result of sports injuries. Most of these people are men between the ages of sixteen and twenty-five.

A concussion usually gets better without any long-term effect. On rare occasions, it is followed by a more serious injury called second-impact syndrome. Second-impact syndrome occurs when the head receives a second blow before the original concussion totally healed. Brain swelling may increase, resulting in a fatal condition. Since 1984, more than twenty people have died from second-impact syndrome.

CAUSES

Motor vehicle accidents and sports injuries are the major causes of concussion. In motor vehicle accidents, concussion can occur without an actual blow to the head. Instead, concussion occurs when the vehicle starts or stops suddenly. In such a case, the brain is pushed strongly against the skull. Contact sports, especially football, hockey, and boxing, are leading causes of concussion. Other significant causes are falls, collisions, or injuries due to bicycling, horseback riding, skiing, and soccer.

RESEARCH SHOWS THAT ABOUT 1 IN 5 HIGH SCHOOL FOOTBALL PLAYERS SUFFER A CONCUSSION OR MORE SERIOUS BRAIN INJURY AT SOME POINT DURING THEIR HIGH SCHOOL FOOTBALL CAREERS.

The risk of concussion from football is extremely high, especially at the high school level. Research shows that about 1 in 5 high school football players suffer concussion or more serious brain injury at some point during their high school football career. The comparable rate at the college level is 1 in 20.

Concussion and lasting brain damage is also very common among boxers. After all, the goal of this sport is to knock out an opponent, that is, to give him or her a concussion. For this reason, the American Academy of Neurology (a group of doctors who specialize in problems of the nervous system) has called for a ban on boxing.

Repeated concussions over many months or years can eventually cause more serious brain injury. For example, boxers can develop a form of permanent brain damage called "punch drunk" syndrome or dementia pugilistica (pronounced dih-MEN-sha pyoo-juh-LIS-tuh-kuh). Perhaps the best known example is the great boxer Muhammad Ali. Ali eventually developed Parkinson's disease (see Parkinson' disease entry), believed to be caused by head injuries sustained while he was active as a boxer.

WORDS TO KNOW

Amnesia: Loss of memory sometimes caused by a brain injury, such as concussion.

Parkinson's disease: A disorder of the nervous system that includes shaking, muscular weakness, stiffness, and problems with walking.

Young children are likely to suffer concussions from falls or bumps on the playground or at home. Child abuse is another common cause of concussion.

SYMPTOMS

Symptoms of concussion include:

- Headache
- Disorientation (confusion) as to time, date, or place
- Dizziness
- Vacant stare or confused expression
- Speech that is difficult to understand
- Lack of coordination or weakness
- Amnesia (loss of memory) about events just preceding the blow
- Nausea or vomiting
- Double vision
- Ringing in the ears

These symptoms may last from several minutes to several hours. More severe or longer-lasting symptoms may indicate more severe brain injury. If a person loses consciousness, it will be for several minutes at the most. If unconsciousness last for a longer period, a more serious form of brain injury may have occurred.

Doctors use a three-point system to determine the seriousness of a concussion. This system helps them to choose the appropriate treatment.

- **Grade 1:** No loss of consciousness, brief confusion, and other symptoms that clear up within 15 minutes.
- **Grade 2:** No loss of consciousness, brief confusion, and other symptoms that clear up in more than 15 minutes.
- **Grade 3:** Loss of consciousness for any period of time.

Days or weeks after the original concussion, certain symptoms may reoccur. These symptoms are called post-concussion syndrome. They include:

- Headache
- Loss of ability to concentrate and pay attention
- Anxiety
- Depression
- Sleep disturbance
- Inability to tolerate light and noise.

DIAGNOSIS

Anyone who receives a concussion must be watched very carefully after the accident. It is important to notice how long unconsciousness lasts and how

Professional basketball player Reggie Miller is helped from the court after sustaining a concussion during a game. (Reproduced by permission of AP/Wide World Photos)

serious the symptoms seem to be. These signs are indications of how serious the brain injury was, and are important in deciding how to treat the patient.

A medical professional can decide how serious a concussion is with some simple tests. He or she may examine the pupils of the patient's eyes, test the patient's coordination and sense of feeling, and observe his or her memory, orientation, and concentration. Patients with mild concussions do not require hospitalization or further tests. Those with more serious injuries may need some form of brain test, such as a computer-aided tomographic (CAT) scan.

TREATMENT

The symptoms of concussion usually clear up quickly and without lasting effects. Medical specialists decide how soon a person can return to sports activities based on the severity of his or her injury. All treatment plans are designed to prevent a second blow to the head during recovery. A second blow may cause very serious long-term brain damage.

A Grade 1 concussion is usually treated with rest and continued observation only. The person can return to sports activities the same day if a medical professional approves and all symptoms are gone. If a second concussion occurs on the same day, the person should not be allowed to continue contact sports until he or she is free of symptoms for one week.

A person with a Grade 2 concussion must discontinue sports activities for the day. He or she must be observed by a medical professional and be observed throughout the day until all symptoms have disappeared. If symptoms become worse or continue beyond a week, further brain tests, such as a CAT scan, may be necessary. The person cannot return to contact sports until one week after symptoms have disappeared and a medical professional has given permission.

A person with a Grade 3 concussion should be seen immediately by a medical professional. If symptoms are severe, brain tests and hospitalization may be necessary. Prolonged unconsciousness and worsening symptoms require immediate examination by a neurologist.

A neurologist is a doctor who specializes in problems of the nervous system. The patient should be carefully observed after discharge from medical care. If symptoms reappear or become worse, further neurological tests may be necessary.

A person with a Grade 3 concussion should avoid contact sports for at least a month after all symptoms have disappeared. If brain tests indicate that brain swelling or bleeding has occurred, the athlete should give up contact sports for the season and, if symptoms are bad enough, indefinitely.

PROGNOSIS

There are usually no long-term effects of concussion. However, symptoms of post-concussion syndrome may last for weeks or months. The risk of a second concussion in contact sports is even higher than the risk for a first concussion. For that reason, a person who has received a concussion needs to avoid contact sports until the first concussion has entirely cleared up.

PREVENTION

Many cases of concussion can be prevented by using certain types of protective equipment. These include seat belts and air bags in cars, and helmets in contact sports. Helmets should also be worn when bicycling, skiing, or horseback riding. Soft material, such as sand or matting, should be placed under playground equipment.

Young people should think about the value of high-contact sports, such as boxing, football, and hockey, compared to their risk for head injuries. They may decide to take part in sports activities that are fun to participate in, but less risky to one's health.

FOR MORE INFORMATION

Books

Gronwall, D. M. A., Philip Wrightson, and Peter Waddell. *Head Injury—The Facts: A Guide for Families and Care-Givers.* New York: Oxford University Press, 1998.

Stoler, Diane Roberts. *Coping With Mild Traumatic Brain Injury.* Garden City Park, NY: Avery Publishing Group, 1998.

Organizations

American Academy of Neurology. 1080 Montreal Avenue St. Paul, MN 55116–2325. (800) 879–1960.

CONJUNCTIVITIS

DEFINITION

Conjunctivitis (pronounced kuhn-junk-tuh-VIE-tis) is an inflammation (redness) of the conjunctiva. The conjunctiva is the membrane that lines the white part of the eye and the underside of the eyelid. Conjunctivitis can be caused by infection, an allergic reaction, or a physical agent, such as infrared or ultraviolet light. Conjunctivitis is often referred to as pink eye because the infection causes the eye to become very bloodshot.

DESCRIPTION

Conjunctivitis is an inflammation of the conjunctiva. The condition is very common since the conjunctiva is exposed to many substances that can cause infection or an allergic reaction. Conjunctivitis can be either acute or chronic. An acute condition is one that flares up suddenly

WORDS TO KNOW

Herpes virus: A group of viruses that cause many different infections in the human body, including cold sores and infections of the genital area.

and lasts a fairly short time. A chronic condition is one that lasts for a long time, usually many years.

Conjunctivitis can affect one or both eyes. If caused by an infection, it can usually be transmitted to other people quite easily. The disease is very common among children in day care or schools. In such settings, children come into close contact with each other and conjunctivitis spreads quickly throughout the group. The disease is also known by the name of pink eye or red eye. These names come from the physical appearance of the eye as a result of conjunctivitis.

CAUSES

Conjunctivitis can be caused by a bacterial or viral infection; by certain environmental factors, such as smoke, dust, or pollen; or by other factors. Viruses cause many kinds of infections, such as the common cold (see common cold entry), acute respiratory infections, or diseases such as measles (see measles entry). These infections can spread easily to the eye. If they infect the conjunctiva, conjunctivitis results.

SYMPTOMS

Symptoms of conjunctivitis can range from mild to serious. They can affect one eye or both. Some common symptoms include redness of the eye, swelling of the eyelid, and a discharge from the eye. The discharge is watery and either yellow or green in color. Some kinds of viruses cause more serious reactions. They may cause the eye to feel scratchy and have a pus-like discharge. These infections also can cause swelling and tenderness of the lymph nodes behind the ear.

Bacterial infections of the conjunctiva also cause redness of the eye and swelling of the eyelids. They may produce a pus-like discharge that turns crusty during the night. Some forms of bacteria that cause sexually transmitted diseases (see sexually transmitted diseases entry), such as gonorrhea, can also cause conjunctivitis. Infections of this kind may result in intolerance to light and tenderness in the lymph nodes behind the ear. These symptoms may last up to three months.

Some environmental conditions that cause conjunctivitis include wind, smoke, dust, pollen,

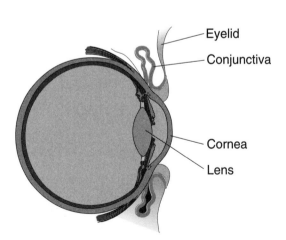

Eyelid

Conjunctiva

Cornea

Lens

Conjunctivitis is an inflammation of the conjunctiva, the membrane that lines the white part of the eye and the underside of the eyelid. (Reproduced by permission of Electronic Illustrators Group)

and grass. As with infections, these factors can cause redness in the eye, swelling of the eyelid, and discharge from one or both eyes. Chemicals in contact lens solutions can sometimes produce similar reactions. Less common causes of conjunctivitis include exposure to sun lamps and problems with the tear ducts, the structures that produce tears for the eyes.

DIAGNOSIS

Diagnosis of conjunctivitis is usually based on a medical history and physical examination. A doctor will ask when the symptoms began, how long the condition has been going on, the symptoms experienced, and if the patient has had any recent infections or diseases. Contact with anyone who has had conjunctivitis is also important information.

Diagnosis is usually relatively simple because symptoms are obvious. In rare cases, smears may be taken. A smear is obtained by collecting discharge from the eye on a cotton swab. The discharge can then be kept in a warm place until any bacteria that are present begin to grow. The bacteria can then be studied under a microscope.

CONJUNCTIVITIS IS OFTEN REFERRED TO AS PINK EYE.

TREATMENT

The treatment of conjunctivitis depends on the cause of the condition. In all cases, symptoms are usually relieved by the use of a warm compress placed directly on the eye. A compress is a moist pad. The treatment is repeated several times a day.

There are relatively few direct treatments for viral infections. If a herpes infection is suspected, medical advice should be sought. A herpes infection is one caused by a herpes virus (see herpes infections entry). The herpes virus causes a variety of infections, including cold sores and infections of the genital area. Sometimes antibiotics are used to prevent secondary infections. A warm compress is advised to relieve discomfort. The viral infection usually clears up after a few days.

Bacterial conjunctivitis can be treated with antibiotics. Ointments (lotions) or eye drops containing the antibiotic can be placed directly into the eye. The treatment is usually used once a day for one or two weeks. Improvement is usually seen in the first three days. If there is no

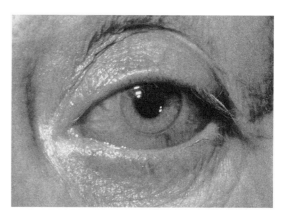

Common symptoms of conjunctivitis include redness of the eye, swelling of the eyelid, and a discharge from the eye. (Photograph by SPL. Reproduced by permission of Custom Medical Stock Photo.)

change, a different drug may be needed, or another cause for the infection should be considered.

Cases of conjunctivitis related to sexually transmitted diseases require special types of care. In some cases, injections of antibiotics may be necessary. Sexual partners should also be notified and treated.

Cases of conjunctivitis caused by environmental factors are treated by removing the agent responsible for the problem. For example, a person who is allergic to dust or pollen should try not to be exposed to these substances. Symptoms can be treated with a cool compress applied directly to the eye. Drugs such as diphenhydramine hydrochloride (pronounced DIE-fen-HI-druh-meen HI-dro-KLOR-ide, trade name Benadryl) can also provide relief when administered as eye drops.

Alternative Treatment

Conjunctivitis caused by a sexually transmitted disease should be treated by a medical doctor. With other forms of conjunctivitis, some types of alternative treatments may be helpful. Some practitioners suggest strengthening of the immune system with herbs such as St. John's wort. Some symptoms of conjunctivitis may be relieved by the use of herbs, such as windflower, eyebright, and *Belladonna*. These herbs can be prepared in the form of eye drops or eye washes. Preparations should be kept sterile. If no improvement is seen, medical advice should be sought.

A simple home remedy for the relief of the symptoms of conjunctivitis is a boric acid eyewash. A warm compress applied to the eyes for five to ten minutes three times a day can also be helpful. Allergic conjunctivitis should be treated with a cool compress.

PROGNOSIS

If treated properly, conjunctivitis usually disappears within a week or two. In cases caused by environmental agents, it gets better only when those agents can be removed or avoided. Cases in which symptoms do not disappear after seventy-two hours, in which there is severe eye pain or changes in vision, or in which a herpes infection is suspected, should be treated by a medical doctor. Untreated cases of conjunctivitis can result in more serious eye problems, such as diminished vision or loss of eyesight.

PREVENTION

Many cases of conjunctivitis can be prevented by some simple hygienic practices. These include the following:

• Frequent hand washing with antiseptic soap, followed by hand drying with paper towels (to prevent spreading the infection).

- Avoidance of substances in the environment known to cause conjunctivitis, such as dust and pollen.
- Use of protective eye wear and screens in areas where unusual light conditions are used (such as in tanning salons).
- Use of a clean tissue to remove discharge from the eyes.
- Careful attention to instructions for the use of antibiotics in the treatment of conjunctivitis, making sure that all of the prescribed medication is used up.
- Avoiding contact with people who already have the disease.

FOR MORE INFORMATION

Books

Salmans, Sandra. *Your Eyes: Questions You Have . . . Answers You Need.* Allentown: People's Medical Society, 1996.

Organizations

American Academy of Ophthalmology (National Eyecare Project). PO Box 7424, San Francisco, CA 94120–7424. (800) 222–EYES. http://www.eyenet.org.

American Optometric Association. 243 North Lindbergh Boulevard, St. Louis, MO, 63141. (314) 991–4100. http://www.aoanet.org.

CREUTZFELDT-JAKOB DISEASE

DEFINITION

Creutzfeldt-Jakob disease (CJD; pronounced KROITS-felt-YAH-kop) is a highly infectious disease that affects the nervous system. It is related to a condition known as "mad cow disease."

DESCRIPTION

Before 1995 CJD was little known outside the medical profession. In fact, many doctors knew little about it and few of them had ever seen a case. In 1995 that situation changed, when a new form of the disease was discovered. That form is called "mad cow disease." It seemed that people could contract a new form of CJD by eating beef from cows that had "mad cow disease."

WORDS TO KNOW

Encephalopathy: A brain disorder characterized by loss of memory and other mental problems.

Iatrogenic: Caused by a medical procedure.

Prion: A form of protein that can cause an infectious disease.

Before long, CJD was one of the most talked about diseases in the world. In spite of that fact, relatively few people actually died from the new form of CJD.

Creutzfeldt-Jakob disease was first described in the 1920s. It affects the nervous system and progresses very rapidly. The major sign is dementia (pronounced dih-MEN-sha), or madness. Death usually occurs less than eight months after symptoms first appear.

CREUTZFELDT-JAKOB DISEASE IS VERY RARE.

The disease is very rare. No more than one person in a million is affected by it worldwide. In the United States, CJD is thought to affect about 250 people each year. It occurs in adults of all ages, but is rare in young adults.

Creutzfeldt-Jakob disease belongs to a group of diseases known as spongiform encephalopathies (pronounced SPUN-jih-form in-se-fuh-LAH-puh-theez). This term refers to the appearance of the brain of a person who develops one of these diseases. Holes develop in the brain that then fill up with liquids, giving it a sponge-like appearance.

Cases of CJD have been grouped into three types: familial, iatrogenic (pronounced eye-a-truh-JE-nik), and sporadic.

- Familial CJD accounts for 5 to 15 percent of all cases. It is an inherited disorder that often does not show up until a person is an adult.
- Iatrogenic CJD occurs as the result of a medical procedure, such as a blood transfusion or organ donation. In these procedures, the patient receives blood or tissue from another person, the donor. In some cases, the donor may carry the agent that causes CJD. That agent can be passed on to the patient during the medical procedure. This source of CJD is relatively uncommon.
- Sporadic CJD is the name given to any case of the disease where the cause is not known. It represents about 85 percent of all cases of CJD.

"Mad Cow Disease" in Animals

Spongiform encephalopathies also occur in animals. The disease that affects sheep is known as scrapie, and was discovered more than two hundred years ago. Other forms of spongiform encephalopathies infect elk, mule deer, domestic cats, mink, zoo animals, and cows. The form that affects cows is known as bovine (for cow) spongiform encephalopathy (BSE).

BSE was first recognized in Great Britain in 1986. Cows infected with the disease behaved in very peculiar ways: they dashed around and acted as if they had gone crazy, hence the name "mad cow disease."

Researchers soon discovered how "mad cow disease" is spread. At one time, the wastes produced in slaughterhouses were used to make animal feed.

These British cattle are headed for slaughter. Tens of thousands of cows were sent to slaughter in Britain in an effort to prevent "Mad Cow Disease" from spreading a new form of Creutzfeldt-Jakob disease to humans. (Reproduced by permission of AP/Wide World Photos)

That is, the feed given to domestic cows usually contained wastes obtained from the slaughter of other cows. Some of the slaughtered cows were infected with BSE, but they may not have shown any signs of the disease. Like kuru (see box: Kuru Among Cannibals), BSE has a very long incubation period.

By 1988 the British government realized that BSE was a serious problem. Cows had been eating contaminated feed for many years and animal feed companies continued to produce contaminated feed without realizing the dangers involved. The British government made the decision to slaughter all cows believed to be infected with BSE. There were two problems with this decision. First, most cows infected with BSE acted normally. The only way to know that they were infected was to kill them and analyze their brains. Second, BSE had already spread widely through British cattle. By one estimate, 25,000 cows in Great Britain had been infected with the disease by 1992. That number accounted for 1 percent of the total British herd. By 1997 that number had increased to 170,000 cows.

The Jump to Humans

The similarities between BSE and kuru are obvious. Both diseases are transmitted when a person or a cow eats the meat of another member of its species. Early on, medical researchers began to wonder if BSE could mutate (change) in some way so that it would infect humans as well as cows. That is, could it jump the species barrier between cows and humans.

In 1995 this question was answered. Reports began to appear of CJD-like symptoms in a few people in Great Britain. These people were all relatively young adults whose brain-wave tests were similar to those of patients with CJD. The people were diagnosed with a form of Creutzfeldt-Jakob disease called new-variant Creutzfeldt-Jakob, or nvCJD. Patients with this disease lived an average of twelve months, rather than eight. As of 1998, twenty-three patients had been diagnosed with nvCJD.

KURU AMONG CANNIBALS

A disease that belongs to the spongiform encephalopathies family is kuru. At one time, kuru was very common among the Fore tribe in Papua, New Guinea. The disease was spread in a very unusual way. Members of the Fore tribe were cannibals. As part of their culture, they ate the organs (including the brain) of their dead relatives. They believed this custom was a way of honoring the dead. Thus, the disease spread from infected individuals after their death.

Kuru fascinated medical researchers, who discovered that the incubation period for the disease is incredibly long. The incubation period is the time it takes for symptoms to appear after a person has been infected. In the case of kuru, the incubation period is between four to thirty years or more, which means an individual infected with the disease may not show any symptoms for a very long time. This discovery earned Carleton Gadjusek the Nobel Prize in 1976 and introduced researchers to

CAUSES

The search for the agent that causes the spongiform encephalopathies is one of the great medical stories of the twentieth century. At first, researchers suspected that the disease was caused by some kind of virus. But they had no success in locating a virus that could cause infections of this kind.

One theory proposed as early as 1981 was regarded as a "crackpot" idea by many scientists. This theory was developed by the American biologist Stanley Prusiner. Prusiner suggested that spongiform encephalopathies might be caused

A sign in a British McDonald's restaurant advertises that it does not use British beef. (Reproduced by AP/Wide World Photos)

by certain kinds of protein molecules. Proteins are chemicals that perform many essential functions in the body. Prusiner suggested the name prion for the infectious forms of proteins.

Many researchers did not take Prusiner's idea seriously because no form of protein had ever been found to cause any infectious disease. After more than fifteen years of research, however, Prusiner's theory was confirmed. Unusual types of protein were finally discovered in the brains of animals with various kinds of spongiform encephalopathies. Scientists now believe that kuru, BSE, nvCJD, and related diseases are caused by the transmission of prions from an infected person to a healthy person. In the vast majority of cases (sporadic CJD), no one knows how this transmission occurs.

SYMPTOMS

About 1 in 4 people with CJD shows relatively mild symptoms of the disease at first. These symptoms include a generalized weakness, changes in sleep pattern, weight loss, or loss of appetite or sexual drive. Vision problems are also common.

Eventually, the most common symptom of CJD appears. This is dementia, or loss of mental function. Dementia is marked by:

• Memory loss
• Decreased ability to do abstract thinking and planning
• Problems with language and comprehension (understanding)
• Poor judgment
• Disorientation (confusion)
• Decreased ability to pay attention and increased restlessness
• Personality changes
• Hallucinations

Physical symptoms may also appear. These symptoms include muscle spasms, jerking movements, problems with balance and coordination, and muscle stiffness.

DIAGNOSIS

Creutzfeldt-Jakob disease is usually diagnosed by means of an electroencephalogram (EEG; pronounced ih-LEK-tro-in-SEH-fuh-luh-gram). An EEG is a procedure in which wires are attached to the brain. These wires detect electrical activity taking place in the brain. Certain distinctive patterns in the EEG are an indication of CJD.

CJD can be confirmed in an autopsy. An autopsy is a medical examination carried out on a dead body to determine what caused death. The autopsy can reveal the presence of abnormal proteins in the person's brain.

TREATMENT

There is no cure for CJD. There is also no treatment that will slow the progress of the disease. Drug therapy can be used to help some of the psychiatric symptoms of the condition. The fundamental problem, however, is the speed with which the disease develops. In most cases, there is relatively little time to try any form of treatment that can provide patients with much relief from their symptoms.

PROGNOSIS

Creutzfeldt-Jakob disease is always fatal. The typical survival time is eight months after symptoms first appear. About 5 percent of patients live longer than two years. The usual survival time for patients with nvCJD is twelve months after onset (beginning).

PREVENTION

Since the causes of sporadic CJD are not known, there is no known way to prevent the disease. Cases of iatrogenic CJD can be prevented by screening donor tissue for possible infection. Standard sterile procedures can also provide some protection against possible transmission of the disease during surgery. Since CJD is a genetic disorder, there is no way to prevent the condition. However, couples who wish to have children may want to be tested for the presence of a defective CJD gene.

Methods for preventing the spread of nvCJD are under considerable debate. In Great Britain, the government ordered the slaughter of tens of thousands of cows in the hopes of wiping out the disease by killing all animals that carried the prions that caused it. But the cost to the livestock industry was enormous. And, in most cases, no one really knew which cows were infected and which were not.

Other nations have tried to protect themselves from infected British cows. They have passed laws preventing the shipment of beef from Great Britain. So far, these laws appear to have been relatively effective. BSE and nvCJD have not yet broken out in other parts of the world.

FOR MORE INFORMATION

Books

Rampton, S., and J. C. Stauber. *Mad Cow U.S.A.: Could the Nightmare Happen Here?* Monroe, ME: Common Courage Press, 1997.

Ratzan, S. C., ed. *Mad Cow Crisis: Health and the Public Good.* New York: New York University Press, 1998.

Periodicals

Prusiner, S. B. "The Prion Diseases." *Scientific American* (January 1995): pp. 48–57.

Organizations

Creutzfeldt-Jakob Disease Foundation. PO Box 611625, North Miami, FL 33261–1625. http://www.cjdfoundation.org.

Web sites

The UK Creutzfeldt-Jakob Disease Surveillance Unit. [Online] http://www.cjd.ed.ac.uk (accessed on October 18, 1999).

CROHN'S DISEASE

DEFINITION

Crohn's disease (pronounced krohnz) is a type of inflammatory bowel disease. It results in swelling of the intestinal tract. It may also restrict the function of the intestinal tract.

DESCRIPTION

The term inflammatory bowel diseases (IBD) refers to a large group of disorders that affect the gastrointestinal (digestive) system. The gastrointestinal (GI) system includes the stomach, small intestine, and large intestine. For reasons that are still not understood, portions of the GI system sometimes become inflamed. Researchers think that the body's immune system may sometimes cause this inflammation. It attacks the lining of the GI system the way it normally attacks invading foreign bodies.

Two of the most important of these disorders are Crohn's disease and ulcerative colitis (see ulcerative colitis entry). These disorders differ from each other in two primary ways:

• The inflammation caused by Crohn's disease may occur in patches separated from each other on the GI lining. Ulcerative colitis produces one large area of inflammation.
• The inflammation of Crohn's disease can penetrate deep into the wall of the intestine. Ulcerative colitis affects only the lining of the intestine.

Crohn's disease can affect people of all ages and both sexes. It occurs most commonly in individuals between the ages of fifteen and thirty-five. About 2 to 4 out of 10,000 people develop the condition. Crohn's disease occurs more commonly among whites, especially people of Jewish ancestry. Crohn's disease is a chronic (ongoing) disorder. Its symptoms may improve, but a person is never completely cured.

CAUSES

The cause of Crohn's disease is unknown. Some researchers believe that it may be triggered by an infection. But no infectious agent, such as a bacterium or virus, has ever been discovered. There is some evidence that the disease may be an autoimmune disorder (see autoimmune disorder entry). An autoimmune disorder is a condition in which the body's immune system becomes confused. It begins to attack body tissue just as it would attack invading organisms, such as bacteria or viruses. However, no proof for this theory has yet been obtained.

SYMPTOMS

The first symptoms of Crohn's disease include diarrhea, fever, abdominal pain, inability to eat, weight loss, and fatigue. The abdominal pain is somewhat like that experienced by an individual with appendicitis (see appendicitis entry). An ongoing symptom of Crohn's disease may be malnutrition. Inflammation caused by the disorder interferes with the absorption of nutrients in foods and a patient may slowly become more and more malnourished.

Crohn's disease also can lead to a number of complications. These complications include:

- Obstructions. An obstruction is a blockage of the intestine. Partially digested food is not able to pass through the intestine. It may back up, causing constipation, vomiting, and intense pain.
- Abscesses. An abscess is a pocket of infection within tissue. Abscesses in the intestine may cause fever and severe abdominal pain.
- Fistulas. A fistula is an abnormal tube-like passage in tissue. Fistulas may allow fluids to drain out of the intestine into another part of the body. When they do so, bacteria that live in the intestine may cause infections in other areas of the body.
- Gallstones and kidney stones
- Kidney damage
- Arthritis (see arthritis entry)
- Inflammation of the vertebrae, the bones of the spine

WORDS TO KNOW

Abscess: A pocket of infection within tissue.

Arthritis: Inflammation of a joint.

Barium enema: A procedure in which a white liquid is injected into a patient's rectum in order to coat the lining of the colon so that X-ray photographs of the colon can be taken.

Colonoscope: An instrument consisting of a long, flexible tube with a light attached to the end, used for examining the lining of the colon.

Fistula: An abnormal tube-like passage in tissue.

Gastrointestinal system: The digestive system consisting of the stomach and intestines.

Immune system: A network of organs, tissues, cells, and chemicals designed to protect the body against foreign invaders such as bacteria and viruses.

Inflammation: Redness, swelling, and loss of function caused by the body's attempt to fight off an infection.

Inflammatory bowel disease: A large group of disorders that affect the gastrointestinal system.

Obstruction: A blockage.

- Ulcers of the mouth and skin
- Painful, red bumps on the skin
- Inflammation of the eyes, liver, and gallbladder

DIAGNOSIS

An individual may be suspected to have Crohn's if he or she begins to experience the described symptoms. Blood tests may provide some additional information by showing the presence of infection or malnutrition. Stool samples may be needed to rule out other GI disorders, such as ulcerative colitis, that have symptoms similar to those of Crohn's disease.

The most reliable method for diagnosing Crohn's disease is with a colonoscopy (pronounced KO-lon-OSS-kuh-pee). A colonoscope (pronounced ko-LON-o-skope) consists of a long, flexible tube with a light attached to the end. The tube is inserted into the patient's rectum. It is then threaded upward into the colon. With the colonoscope, a doctor is able to examine the walls of the colon. The presence of inflammation suggests a diagnosis of Crohn's disease.

The colonoscope may also have a small, sharp knife attached at the end. With the knife, a doctor can remove a tiny sample of tissue, which can then be examined under a microscope. Certain distinctive characteristics of cells indicate the presence of Crohn's disease.

A barium enema is sometimes used to confirm a diagnosis of Crohn's disease. A barium enema consists of a white liquid that is injected into the patient's rectum. The liquid moves upward into the colon and coats the lining of the colon. X-ray photographs of the colon are then taken. The white lining produces a clear X-ray photograph that shows the presence of any abnormal structures in the GI tract.

CROHN'S NAMESAKE

Scientists have known about Crohn's disease for more than two hundred years. The first description of the condition was probably written by the Italian physician Giovanni Battista Morgagni (1682–1771). But the real pioneer of research on this disease was the American physician, Burrill B. Crohn (1884–1983). Crohn was born in New York City and earned his medical degree from Columbia University College of Physicians and Surgeons. He spent most of his professional career at Mount Sinai Hospital in New York. Crohn first described the condition that now bears his name in 1932.

How did Crohn first become interested in digestive problems? When asked this question, he gave an interesting answer. According to Crohn, his father had long suffered from very bad cases of indigestion, so he decided to become a doctor in order to learn what would bring his father relief. Crohn was obviously a very good son and a very good physician!

TREATMENT

Treatment for Crohn's disease focuses on four major objectives:

- Reduction of inflammation of the intestine
- Dealing with the patient's nutritional problems

- Relieving the uncomfortable symptoms of abdominal pain and diarrhea
- Treating possible complications, such as obstructions, abscesses, and fistulas

Inflammation is usually treated with a drug called sulfasalazine (pronounced SULL-fuh-SAL-uh-zeen). Sulfasalazine consists of two parts. One part is an antibiotic and the other part an anti-inflammatory agent. For patients who do not respond to sulfasalazine, steroids may be used. Steroids are very effective in reducing inflammation. However, they have some undesirable side effects.

CROHN'S DISEASE IS A CHRONIC, LIFELONG ILLNESS.

Nutritional supplements are used to treat malnutrition. The supplements are chosen because they are easily absorbed through the intestinal wall. Patients may also need to learn which foods they cannot digest (such as milk or spicy foods) and avoid eating those foods. In severe cases, a patient may need to be fed intravenously. Intravenous feeding involves the insertion of a tube into a vein. Nutrients are then given to the patient through the tube.

A number of medications are available to reduce pain and cramping. High-fiber medications may also be helpful.

Complications such as obstructions, abscesses, and fistulas are sometimes treated with antibiotics. The antibiotics kill the bacteria that produce these complications. If antibiotics are unsuccessful, surgery may be necessary. The purpose of surgery is to remove an obstruction or abscess or to repair a fistula. In the most severe cases, a portion of the intestine may have to be removed.

PROGNOSIS

Crohn's disease is a chronic, lifelong illness. The severity of the condition differs for various patients. Some patients go through periods when they have no symptoms. Symptoms then flare up again at a later time.

The complications of Crohn's disease can lead to serious health problems. The risk for these complications increases over time. More than 60 percent of all patients with the disorder

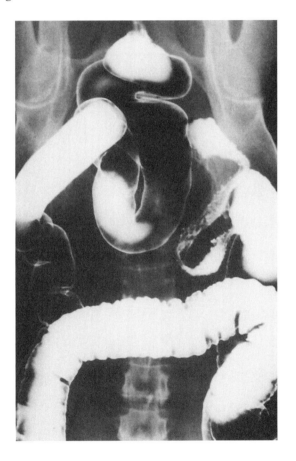

A barium X ray showing the colon of a patient with Crohn's disease where the large and small intestines join at the bottom left. (Photo by CNRI/Science Photo Library. Reproduced by permission of Custom Medical Stock Photo)

require surgery at one time or another. More than half require more than one operation. About 5 to 10 percent of all Crohn's patients die of the disorder. In most cases, death is caused by widespread infection.

FOR MORE INFORMATION

Books

Long, James W. *The Essential Guide to Chronic Illness.* New York: Harper Perennial, 1997.

Saibil, Fred. *Crohn's Disease and Ulcerative Colitis.* Buffalo, NY: Firefly Books, 1997.

Thompson, W. Grant. *The Angry Gut: Coping With Colitis and Crohn's Disease.* New York: Plenum Press, 1993.

Organizations

Crohn's & Colitis Foundation of America, Inc. 386 Park Avenue South, 17th Floor, New York, NY 10016–8804. (800) 932–2423.

CYSTIC FIBROSIS

DEFINITION

Cystic fibrosis (CF) is a hereditary disease that affects the lungs, digestive system, sweat glands, and male reproductive organs.

DESCRIPTION

Cystic fibrosis affects the body's ability to move salts and water in and out of cells. This defect causes the lungs and pancreas to secrete (release) thick mucus. The mucus blocks various passageways in the body, preventing them from functioning normally.

CF affects about thirty thousand children and young adults in the United States. About three thousand babies are born with the condition each year in this country. The disorder primarily affects people of white, northern European ancestry. Nonwhite populations have a much lower rate of cystic fibrosis.

There is no cure for CF. However, symptoms of the disease can be treated. Proper care and treatment can greatly improve the lifestyle of a person with the condition. For example, prompt attention to digestive and respiratory (breathing) problems has extended the lives of many patients. At one time, children with CF usually died by the age of two years. Today, many people with CF live beyond the age of thirty.

CAUSES

Cystic fibrosis is a genetic disorder. Genes are the chemical units in every cell that tell cells what functions they should perform and what substances they should manufacture in order to operate normally. Genes can be damaged in a variety of ways. For example, certain chemicals contained in the foods we eat can damage a gene. When that happens, the gene is no longer able to give correct instructions to a cell and the cell does not have the information it needs to produce all the substances it requires to stay healthy. When this happens, a medical problem develops in some part of the body.

Genes are passed down from one generation to the next. A person whose body contains a damaged gene may pass that gene to his or her children. The children may develop the same genetic disorder that the parent had.

Cystic fibrosis is caused by a defect in the gene known as the CFTR gene. The abbreviation CFTR stands for cystic fibrosis transmembrane conductance regulator. The CFTR gene carries instructions for the production of mucus in cells. Mucus is a mixture of water, salts, sugars, and proteins. Its job is to cleanse, lubricate, and protect passageways in the body.

Cells that contain a defective CFTR gene have lost the ability to make mucus properly. The mucus they produce has too little water in it and is thick and syrupy. This mucus does not improve the functioning of passageways in the body. Instead, it causes them to become clogged. Substances that are supposed to pass through passageways, such as air and blood, are unable to flow normally and the symptoms of CF begin to appear.

SYMPTOMS

The most severe symptoms of CF occur in two body systems: the gastrointestinal (digestive)

WORDS TO KNOW

CFTR: An abbreviation for cystic fibrosis transmembrane conductance regulator, a chemical that controls the amount of water in mucus.

Genes: Chemical units that carry the information that tells cells what functions to perform.

Genetic disorder: A medical condition caused when a person has one or more defective genes.

Meconium ileus: A condition that appears in newborn babies with cystic fibrosis, in which the baby's first bowel movement is abnormally dark, thick, and sticky.

Mucolytic: Any type of medication that breaks up mucus and makes it flow more easily.

Mucus: A mixture of water, salts, sugars, and proteins, which has the job of cleansing, lubricating, and protecting passageways in the body.

Pancreas: An organ near the stomach that secretes enzymes needed to digest food.

Screening: Using a test or group of tests to look for some specific medical disorder.

system and the respiratory tract. CF also affects the sweat glands and the male reproductive organs.

Gastrointestinal System

One of the first symptoms of CF in young babies is meconium ileus (pronounced muh-KO-nee-um ILL-ee-us). Meconium ileus is characterized by a thick, sticky, dark stool. The stool has these features because the mucus it contains is thicker than normal. Meconium ileus is also marked by abdominal swelling and vomiting. The presence of meconium ileus is a strong indication of cystic fibrosis.

A defective CFTR gene also causes damage to the pancreas. The pancreas provides enzymes needed in the digestion of food. Enzymes are chemicals present in all cells that make possible hundreds of different chemical reactions. If these enzymes are not present, necessary chemical reactions may not occur. In the case of CF, the pancreas makes a very thick type of mucus. The mucus blocks openings in the pancreas and enzymes produced by the pancreas cannot get out of the organ. Food passes through the stomach without being digested.

Failure to digest food can produce a number of symptoms. The feces may become bulky, oily, and foul-smelling. The patient may constantly be hungry because food that is eaten is not digested. The patient may not grow to normal size without the nutrients provided by food. Over time, other symptoms that may develop include malnutrition, anemia (see anemias entry), bloating, and loss of appetite.

Respiratory Tract

The most life-threatening symptoms of CF occur in the lungs. The job of the lungs is to take oxygen from the air and deliver it to blood. Blood then takes oxygen to the cells of the body, where it is used to make energy.

The mucus that lines the lungs has a number of functions. One function is to prevent infection of the lungs. The mucus captures bacteria, viruses, fungi, and other agents that might cause disease. It then passes these materials back out of the lungs and into the throat. From there, they can be coughed up or swallowed.

In patients with CF, the mucus in the lungs becomes much thicker. Disease-causing agents are still captured, but they cannot be passed back into the throat very easily. Instead, the thick mu-

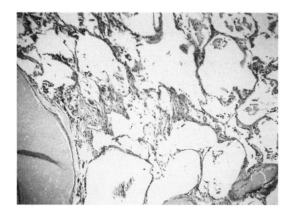

Cystic fibrosis lung tissue with thick mucus seen through a microscope. (Reproduced by permission of Custom Medical Stock Photo)

cus holds bacteria, viruses, and other organisms in the lining of the lungs. The longer these organisms remain there, the greater the chance they will cause an infection of the lungs.

The presence of organisms in the lungs causes the immune system to become active. The immune system is a network of organs, tissues, cells, and chemicals designed to protect the body against infection by foreign agents. The immune system sends specialized cells to fight the disease-causing organisms trapped in the patient's lungs. These cells cause the lungs to become inflamed and swollen. The inflammation and swelling may close down passageways in the lungs, making it difficult for air to pass in and out of the lungs.

The thick mucus that lines the lungs also makes it more difficult for air to pass through the lungs. Patients may find themselves gasping for breath in order to get enough air. They may also begin to develop the symptoms of emphysema (see emphysema entry).

Sweat Glands

A defective CFTR gene can also affect the formation of sweat. A person with cystic fibrosis has sweat that is much saltier than normal. This problem is usually not serious except during heavy exercise or hot weather. In such cases, patients with CF usually eat more salty foods to make up for the salt lost in their sweat.

Male Reproductive System

Abnormally thick mucus can block the vas deferens in males. The vas deferens are tubes through which sperm passes. If these tubes are blocked, males are not able to produce sperm and are, therefore, infertile (incapable of producing children).

DIAGNOSIS

A number of factors may suggest that a child be tested for cystic fibrosis. The presence of any of the described symptoms may lead to such tests. These symptoms include gastrointestinal or respiratory problems that do not disappear, and the presence of salty sweat. A baby born with meconium ileus will be tested before leaving the hospital. Some hospitals now require routine CF screening for newborn babies.

The easiest and most accurate test for CF is a sweat test. A sample of an individual's sweat is collected. The sample is then tested for salt content. If the salt content is 1.5 to 2 times greater than normal, the individual probably has CF.

Genetic testing can also be used to diagnose CF. A small blood or tissue sample is taken from the patient. The sample can then be analyzed to determine whether the individual's CFTR gene is normal or defective. The presence of a defective gene means that the person has cystic fibrosis.

Screening of newborn babies is done with a test known as the IRT test. This test measures the amount of a particular chemical in the blood known as immunoreactive trypsinogen (pronounced trip-SIN-uh-juhn). Babies with CF have a high level of this chemical.

TREATMENT

There is no cure for cystic fibrosis, but there are many types of treatment that can help patients live longer and more comfortable lives. Early diagnosis is an important element of treatment. With proper management, many people with CF engage in the full range of normal activities.

Nutrition

People with CF often do not receive full benefit from the foods they eat. They may need a high calorie diet with vitamin supplements. In addition, pancreatic enzyme pills are often recommended. The pills provide enzymes to the patient's digestive system that would normally come from a healthy pancreas.

Some people cannot absorb enough nutrients from foods even with special diets and enzyme pills. For these people, tube feeding is an option. A tube is inserted through the nose or through a hole made in the abdominal wall. Food can be supplied through the tube at any time of the day or night, allowing constant intake of high-quality nutrients. The feeding tube may be removed during the day, allowing the patient to eat meals normally.

Respiratory Health

The key to survival for many patients with CF is careful monitoring of the respiratory system. Lung function tests are done frequently. These tests measure the amount of air the person's lungs are able to take in. Sputum (spit) tests are done to find out what kinds of bacteria are present in the lung and how many there are. Chest X rays monitor any changes in the size and shape of the lungs.

An important element of good respiratory health is exercise. Exercise keeps the lungs healthy, active, and free of bacteria.

Clearing mucus from the lungs also helps protect against infection. Physical therapists have developed a number of techniques to help CF patients prevent mucus from collecting in the lungs. For example, a patient may lie on his or her stomach on a tilted surface with the head downward. An assistant then thumps on the patient's rib cage to help loosen mucus.

Drugs also can help maintain healthy lungs. For example, bronchodilators (pronounced brong-ko-die-LATE-urs) are substances that cause small air passages in the lungs to expand, allowing air to flow more freely. A group of drugs known as mucolytics (pronounced myu-kuh-LIH-tiks) also may be used. Mucolytics help loosen mucus and allow it to be expelled from the lungs more easily.

The use of antibiotics also may be necessary. Some doctors have their patients take antibiotics continuously to protect against lung infections. Other doctors use antibiotics only when an infection has actually developed.

In extreme cases, patients with CF may need oxygen therapy. Oxygen therapy is a procedure in which patients breathe air that is rich in oxygen. The higher oxygen content makes it easier for the body to get the oxygen it needs without working too hard.

Lung transplantation is a treatment of last resort. However, this form of treatment has its own set of problems. The drugs used during and after a

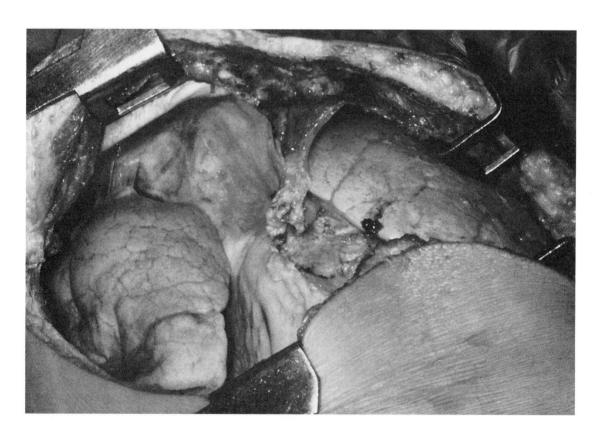

Lung transplantation for cystic fibrosis is a treatment of last resort. (© 1992 Michael English, M.D. Reproduced by permission of Custom Medical Stock Photo.)

transplant operation cause severe problems of their own. One such problem is the weakening of the immune system.

On a long-term basis, the best hope for treating CF may be genetic therapy. Genetic therapy is a procedure by which correct copies of the CFTR gene are injected into a patient. The hope is that the correct genes will take over the task that the defective CFTR genes are unable to perform. Although much research is being done in this area, gene therapy is still in the experimental phase.

Alternative Treatment

Alternative practitioners recommend many of the same treatments used in traditional medicine. For example, they suggest the use of mucolytics to thin mucus and pancreatic enzymes to aid in digestion.

Efforts are also made to improve the patient's overall health and immune system. A variety of herbs is available to achieve these goals. In addition, hydrotherapy (water therapy) techniques may be helpful in relaxing the body and helping the patient breathe better.

PROGNOSIS

The key to a good prognosis for cystic fibrosis is early detection and treatment. The effectiveness and variety of treatment methods greatly increased during the 1980s and 1990s. About half of all patients living with CF during this time could expect to live past the age of thirty. Researchers predict that a person born in the late 1990s with the disorder can expect to live to the age of forty.

EXPERIMENTING WITH GENE THERAPY

It may be possible to cure cystic fibrosis with gene therapy. The problem is to find ways to get good copies of the CFTR gene into a patient's body. Scientists are now working on techniques for accomplishing this goal.

One approach is to make good copies of the CFTR gene in the laboratory. These copies are then combined with viruses. Viruses are very good at infecting cells. This property is usually not beneficial for humans because it is the reason people become ill with viral diseases.

The combination of CFTR gene and virus is made into a nasal spray. Some fat droplets are also added to the spray. The fat serves as a carrier that takes the virus and gene to cells in the patient's body. If all works well, the virus enters cells in the patient's body, bringing the good copy of the CFTR gene with it. The gene begins to function properly, and the patient is cured.

Trials of the new nasal spray have been going on since the mid-1990s. The first step in the trials is to make sure that the spray does not harm people. The second step is to find out if the spray really works. That is, does it actually deliver good genes to the patient's body?

PREVENTION

Since CF is a genetic disorder, there is no way to prevent the condition. However, couples who wish to have children may want to be tested for the presence of a defective CFTR gene. If that gene is present, it may be passed to any future children, placing those children at risk for cystic fibrosis.

FOR MORE INFORMATION

Books

Harris, Ann, and Maurice Super. *Cystic Fibrosis: The Facts.* New York: Oxford University Press, 1995.

Hopkins, Karen. *Understanding Cystic Fibrosis.* Jackson: University Press of Mississippi, 1998.

Orenstein, David. *Cystic Fibrosis: A Guide for Patients and Family.* Philadelphia: Lippincott-Raven, 1997.

Silverstein, Alvin, Robert Silverstein, and Virginia B. Silverstein. *Cystic Fibrosis.* New York: Franklin Watts, 1994.

Organizations

Cystic Fibrosis Foundation. 6931 Arlington Road, Bethesda, MD 20814. (301) 951–4422. http://www.cff.org.

CYSTITIS

DEFINITION

Cystitis (pronounced sis-TIE-tess) is inflammation of the bladder. The condition is often associated with inflammation of other structures adjoining the bladder. For example, cystitis is often accompanied by urethritis (pronounced yur-ih-THRI-tess). Urethritis is inflammation of the urethra. The urethra is the tube through which the bladder empties to the exterior of the body. Cystitis and urethritis together are sometimes called lower urinary tract infections (UTI).

DESCRIPTION

In children under the age of twelve months, cystitis is about four times more common among boys than girls. Among adults, this pattern is very different. The condition is fifty times as common among women as among men. After the age of fifty, the pattern changes again. The rate of cystitis among men increases because of a greater number of prostate problems among men. The prostate is a gland surrounding the male urethra in front of the bladder.

The nature of cystitis varies considerably in men and women. The reason for this variation is the difference between the urinary tract in males and females.

BEFORE THE AGE OF FIFTY CYSTITIS IS FIFTY TIMES AS COMMON AMONG WOMEN AS AMONG MEN.

Cystitis is a common female problem. About one-quarter of all adult women are thought to have had at least one episode of cystitis. Between 2 and 5 percent of women's visits to doctors are for UTI symptoms. About 90 percent of these cases are uncomplicated. Many women, however, experience repeated bouts of cystitis.

UTIs are uncommon in younger and middle-aged men. They become more common as men grow older. Older men are more likely to develop bacterial infections of the kidney or prostate gland. These infections may spread and cause cystitis.

Cystitis in children is usually a congenital problem. A congenital problem is one that is present at birth. For example, some children are unable to empty their bladders completely. Urine may remain in or flows backward into the bladder. This condition may lead to cystitis.

WORDS TO KNOW

Ascending infection: An infection that begins at the outer edge of a body opening and works its way upward.

Catheterization: A medical procedure in which a long, thin tube (a catheter) is inserted into some part of the human body.

Circumcision: The procedure in which the foreskin is removed from the penis.

Congenital problem: A problem that is present at birth.

Diaphragm: A thin rubber cap inserted into the vagina as a method of birth control.

Lower urinary tract infection (UTI): Inflammation of the bladder or urinary tract.

Urethra: The tube through which the bladder empties to the exterior of the body.

CAUSES

The causes of cystitis are somewhat different in women than in men. Most bladder infections in women are so-called ascending (going upward) infections. Ascending infections are caused when disease agents travel upward through the urethra from outside the body. The female urethra is relatively short, about 1 to 2 inches in length. Microorganisms that cause disease can travel this distance very easily. The organism that most commonly causes cystitis in women is *Escherichia coli* (or *E. coli*; pronounced ESH-ur-ick-ee-uh KO-lie). It is responsible for about 80 percent of all cases of the disease.

Other organisms that can cause cystitis include *Staphylococcus saprophyticus* (pronounced STAFF-uh-lo-kock-us SAP-ro-FIT-ick-us), and members of the *Klebsiella* (pronounced KLEBsee-ell-uh), *Enterobacter* (pronounced EN-terr-o-BACK-tur), and *Proteus* (pronounced PRO-tee-us) families of bacteria.

A number of other factors increase a woman's risk for cystitis. These factors include:

- Sexual intercourse. The more sexual partners a woman has, the greater her risk for cystitis.
- Use of a diaphragm for birth control
- An unusually short urethra
- Diabetes (see diabetes entry)
- Poor personal hygiene. Bacteria from vaginal discharges or feces can easily enter the female urethra. The opening to the urethra in women is very close to the vagina and the anus.
- History of previous UTIs. About 80 percent of women who have one case of cystitis will develop another case within two years.

Males

Cystitis in men usually occurs as a complication of kidney or prostate gland infection. The most common cause of cystitis in men, as in women, is the bacterium *Escherichia coli*. Factors that increase men's risk for cystitis include:

- **Lack of circumcision.** Circumcision is the procedure in which the foreskin is removed from a man's penis. If the foreskin has not been removed, bacteria can grow beneath it. The bacteria can then travel up the urethra to the bladder.
- **Urinary catheterization.** Urinary catheterization is a medical procedure in which a long, thin tube (a catheter) is inserted into the urethra. It is pushed up into the bladder. Some men require this procedure if they are unable to urinate normally. The presence of the catheter provides a pathway by which bacteria can travel up into the bladder and cause infection.

SYMPTOMS

The symptoms of cystitis are similar in women and men. The most common symptoms involve changes in urination patterns. Patients

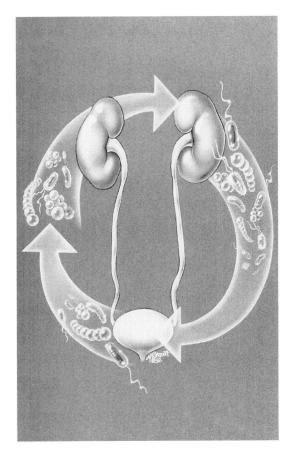

This illustration depicts the cycle of recurring urinary tract infection. The lower tract (urethra and bladder) is relatively resistant to infection. The kidneys are more vulnerable. (Reproduced by permission of Custom Medical Stock Photo)

may feel pain during urination, may feel a sudden and strong desire to urinate, or may have to urinate more frequently. About half of all patients experience fever, pain in the lower back, nausea and vomiting, or chills.

DIAGNOSIS

The first step in diagnosing cystitis is often a physical examination. A doctor examines the patient's abdomen and lower back. Swelling of the kidneys or bladder can often be felt.

The next step in diagnosis is collection of a urine sample. Normal human urine is sterile. It does not contain bacteria, blood, pus, or other abnormal substances. The presence of any of these substances in urine suggests the presence of an infection.

The patient is asked to urinate into a collecting bottle. The urine can then be tested immediately with a dip stick. A dip stick is a strip of paper that contains one or more testing chemicals. The chemicals change colors if certain abnormal substances are present in the urine. The urine may also be examined using a microscope.

If questions remain about a diagnosis, more advanced tests can also be used. For example, a dye may be injected into the urinary tract and X-ray photographs taken. The dye helps the shape of the urinary tract stand out more clearly. Any abnormal structures present can be seen on the X-ray photograph.

TREATMENT

Since cystitis is a bacterial infection, it can be treated with antibiotics. Some drugs that are commonly used include penicillin, ampicillin (pronounced AMP-ih-SIL-in), amoxicillin (pronounced uh-MOK-sih-SIL-in), sulfisoxazole (pronounced SUL-fuh-SOK-suh-zole), trimethoprim (pronounced tri-METH-o-prim), cephalosporin (pronounced seff-a-lo-SPORE-in), or fluoroquinolone (pronounced FLOOR-o-KWIN-o-lone). Women usually respond to antibiotic treatment in less than three days. Men usually require a longer period of treatment, ranging from seven to ten days.

Alternative Treatment

Some forms of alternative treatment involve changes in one's diet. Practitioners often recommend eliminating all sugar from the diet and drinking lots of water. Some herbal remedies that are suggested include garlic, goldenseal, and bearberry. These herbs are thought to kill bacteria. Acupuncture (the Chinese therapy of inserting fine needles into the skin) and homeopathic medicine may also be effective in treating cystitis.

PROGNOSIS

The prognosis for recovery from uncomplicated cystitis is very good. With proper treatment, the infection usually clears up quickly. In many cases, the condition may reoccur. However, it can be treated in essentially the same way each time it appears. More complicated infections in men may be difficult to treat if antibiotics are not able to clear up the problem.

PREVENTION

Women can reduce their risk for cystitis by becoming aware of risk factors and adjusting their lifestyles accordingly. For example, improving one's personal hygiene is an easy step to help prevent a lower urinary tract infection. In some cases, patients are advised to take an antibiotic tablet following sexual intercourse. Other preventative measures include drinking large amounts of fluid and urinating frequently, especially after intercourse.

The primary method of preventing cystitis in men is to obtain prompt treatment for prostate infections.

FOR MORE INFORMATION

Books

Chalker, Rebecca. *Overcoming Bladder Disorders: Compassionate, Authoritative Medical and Self-Help Solutions for Incontinence, Cystitis, Interstitial Cystitis, Prostatitis.* New York: HarperCollins, 1991.

Gillespie, Larrian, and Sandra Blakeslee. *You Don't Have to Live With Cystitis,* revised and updated edition. New York: Avon Books, 1996.

Simone, Catherine M. *To Wake In Tears: Understanding Interstitial Cystitis.* Cleveland, OH: IC Hope, 1998.

Where to Learn More

BOOKS

Abel, Ernest L. *America's 25 Top Killers.* Hillside, NJ: Enslow, 1991.

American Heart Association. *Living Well, Staying Well.* New York: American Heart Association and American Cancer Association, 1996.

Atkinson, David R., and Debbie Atkinson. *Hope Springs Eternal: Surviving a Chronic Disease.* Virginia Beach, VA: Are Press, 1999.

Bellenir, Karen, and Peter D. Dresser, eds. *Contagious and Non-contagious Infectious Diseases Sourcebook.* Detroit: Omnigraphics, Inc., 1996.

The Burton Goldberg Group. *Alternative Medicine: The Definitive Guide.* Puyallup, WA: Future Medicine Publishing, 1993.

Ciesielski, Paula F. *Major Chronic Diseases.* Guilford, CT: The Dushkin Publishing Group, 1992.

Daly, Stephen, ed. *Everything You Need to Know about Medical Treatments.* Springhouse, PA: Springhouse Corp., 1996.

Darling, David. *The Health Revolution: Surgery and Medicine in the Twenty-first Century.* Parsippany, NJ: Dillon Press, 1996.

Graham, Ian. *Fighting Disease.* Austin, TX: Raintree Steck-Vaughn, 1995.

Horn, Robert, III. *How Will They Know If I'm Dead? Transcending Disability and Terminal Illness.* Boca Raton, FL: Saint Lucie Press, 1996.

Hyde, Margaret O., and Elizabeth H. Forsyth, M.D. *The Disease Book: A Kid's Guide.* New York: Walker and Company, 1997.

Isler, Charlotte, R.N., and Alwyn T. Cohall, M.D. *The Watts Teen Health Dictionary.* New York: Franklin Watts, 1996.

The Johns Hopkins Medical Handbook: The 100 Major Medical Disorders of People over the Age of 50. *New York: Rebus, Inc., 1995.*

Long, James W. *The Essential Guide to Chronic Illness.* New York: Harper Perennial, 1997.

Roman, Peter. *Can You Get Warts from Touching Toads? Ask Dr. Pete.* New York: Julian Messner, 1986.

Shaw, Michael, ed. *Everything You Need to Know about Diseases.* Springhouse, PA: Springhouse Corp., 1996.

Stoffman, Phyllis. *The Family Guide to Preventing and Treating 100 Infectious Illnesses.* New York: John Wiley & Sons, 1995.

Weil, A. *Natural Health, Natural Medicine: A Comprehensive Manual for Wellness and Self-Care.* Boston: Houghton Mifflin, 1995.

WEB SITES

Centers for Disease Control and Prevention. http://www.cdc.gov

The Children's Health Center. http://www.mediconsult.com/mc/mcsite.nsf/conditionnav/kids~sectionintroduction

Healthfinder®. http://www.healthfinder.gov

InteliHealth: Home to Johns Hopkins Health Information. http://www.intelihealth.com

Mayo Clinic Health Oasis. http://mayohealth.org

National Institutes of Health. http://www.nih.gov

NOAH: New York Online Access to Health. http://www.noah.cuny.edu

WHO/OMS: World Health Organization. http://www.who.int

U.S. National Library of Medicine: Health Information. http://nlm.nih.gov/hinfo.html

ORGANIZATIONS

Centers for Disease Control and Prevention. 1600 Clifton Rd., NE, Atlanta, GA 30333. (404)639–3311. http://www.cdc.gov

National Institutes of Health (NIH). Bethesda, MD 20892. (301)496–1776. http:www.nih.gov

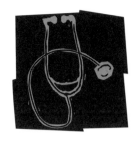

Index

Italic type indictes volume numbers; **boldface** type indicates entries and their page numbers; (ill.) indicates illustrations.